Mindful Coaching

How mindfulness can transform coaching practice

Liz Hall

KoganPage

LONDON PHILADELPHIA NEW DELHI

First published in Great Britain and the United States in 2013 by Kogan Page Limited

120 Pentonville Road	1518 Walnut Street, Suite 1100	4737/23 Ansari Road
London N1 9JN	Philadelphia PA 19102	Daryaganj
United Kingdom	USA	New Delhi 110002
www.koganpage.com		India

© Liz Hall, 2013

The right of Liz Hall to be identified as the author of this work has been asserted by her in accordance with the Copyright, Designs and Patents Act 1988.

ISBN   978 0 7494 6566 7
E-ISBN   978 0 7494 6567 4

British Library Cataloguing-in-Publication Data

A CIP record for this book is available from the British Library.

Library of Congress Cataloging-in-Publication Data

CIP data is available.
Library of Congress Control Number: 2012046241

Typeset by Graphicraft Limited, Hong Kong
Printed and bound in India by Replika Press Pvt Ltd

Dedication

I dedicate this book to my late beloved father David, who inspired me with his love of words, his gentleness and his wonder at what lies within and beyond these lives of ours; to my wonderfully supportive husband, Ray, and to our beautiful children Molly, Emma and Dylan who've been so understanding of the times when yet again I've said those words, 'Not now, I'm working.'
With love and gratitude, always.

PRAISE FOR
MINDFUL COACHING

There's a lot of buzz around mindfulness at the moment. Liz Hall makes a great job of explaining what it is and why it's so fascinating. Especially, she makes a compelling case for the benefits of mindfulness practice in the coaching context – both for coaches and their clients. She explains why mindfulness is something to be *practised*, not just thought about. This book could change your coaching practice very much for the better. More importantly, it could actually change your life.

Michael Chaskalson, mindfulness trainer and coach, author of
The Mindful Workplace

Reading Liz Hall's *Mindful Coaching* will fill you with the awe of the French soldier who first brushed sand from the Rosetta Stone and knew something significant had just occurred. Liz has integrated three fields; coaching, health and resilience, and mindfulness to reveal a technique for helping others (and ourselves) pursue dreams and shared visions. These are the practices that will also transform teams, organizations and communities. Read this book slowly to fully grasp its significance!

Professor Richard Boyatzis, Case Western Reserve University, Adjunct Professor of Human Resources, ESADE, co-author (with Dan Goleman and Annie McKee) of the international best-seller, *Primal Leadership*, and co-author with (Annie McKee) of the recent *Resonant Leadership*

CONTENTS

ACKNOWLEDGEMENTS

I am deeply grateful to so many people for their help and support in writing this book. I'm grateful to Matt and Martina from Kogan Page for believing in me. Thanks too to those of you who have looked through the manuscript or part of it and made helpful suggestions including: Ray Freeman, Ros Soulsby, Stephen Palmer, John Whitmore, Eunice Aquilina and Shanida Nataraja, and to those of you who offered to do so. Thanks to those of you who have given up your time to be interviewed including Mark Williams, Richard Boyatzis, Dorothy Larios, Mark Leonard, Michael Chaskalson, Aboodi Shabi, John Leary Joyce, Edwina Love-Lawrence, Alister Scott, Neil Scotton, Neela Bettridge, Julie Hay, John Whitmore, Jeremy Hunter, Graham Lee and Linda Woolston. Thanks to all my clients. Thanks to all of you who took part in my *Mindfulness in Coaching* survey including Kate McGuire, Diane Newell, Murray Thomas, Sanjeev Roy, Holly McKinley, Annalise Roache, Emma Donaldson-Fielder, Carolyn Mumby, Henrik Leslye, Jean de Bruyne, David Megginson, Ingrid Bengston, Angela Hill, Sally Dellow, David Clutterbock, Frank Del Fiugo, Michael Forlenza, Elke Vaikla and Derek Watson. And deep thanks to my many mindfulness teachers including Thich Nhat Hanh and the other monastics from Plum Village, the Dalai Lama, Jon Kabat-Zinn, Robina Courtin, Geshe Lamsang, Geshe Tashi Tsering, Angelines de la Torre, Mark Williams, Michael Chaskalson, K and others at the Brighton Buddhist Centre. I bow to you all in gratitude.

FOREWORD

Gregory Bateson, as early as 1969, was writing about the coming ecological crisis, which he said was at root a crisis in human being's epistemology; that is, how we think and know. He taught that if we could not fundamentally shift our consciousness, we did not have a 'snowball in hell's chance' of surviving the next century.

More recently Tim Smit, the founder of the Eden project, in his talk to the Institute of Directors in London, opened his speech with the exciting line: 'The next thirty years will be one of the most exciting times to be alive in the whole of human history, for in that time we will either discover whether "homo" is truly "sapiens" or if we will join the fossil records.' What a choice!

The journalist and author Thomas Friedman wrote:

> What if the crisis of 2008 represents something much more fundamental than a deep recession? What if it is telling us that the whole growth model we created over the last 50 years is simply unsustainable economically and ecologically, and that 2008 was when we hit the wall – when Mother Nature and the market both said: 'No more'.
>
> (*New York Times*, 7th March 2009)

What the world desperately needs is for Humans to discover how to be truly sapiens and to evolve our individual and collective consciousness, and it is time that all coaches recognized that they are part of this great work.

Richard Barratt (2010) who previously spent many years working for the World Bank, has written about how we need to embrace a new leadership paradigm, that moves:

1 from I to We;
2 from what's in it for me, to what's best for the common good (and how can I best contribute);
3 from the aiming to be the best in the world, to focussing on being the best for the world.

He encourages us constantly to recognize that all organizations are embedded in a wider socio-economic system, which itself is embedded in the wider ecological system of the 'more than human world'; a world that supplies all the resources that make our human enterprises possible, but resources that are being drastically overused and depleted.

In 2012 I wrote about how coaching was also at a cross-roads, and for it to continue to grow, it needed to extend its focus beyond the immediate client in the room, to seeing that client as a partner, who shares with the coach the joint endeavour of discovering how to step up to what the world of tomorrow is requiring from them. The benefits of the coaching are, then, not just measured in terms of personal development, but of team and organizational learning, increased shared value for all the organization's stakeholders and creating a greater contribution to repaying part of our indebtedness to the wider environment.

Such work requires both greater depth of engagement from the coach as well as the calm, receptive centre that can listen with compassion, not just to the individual client but to the many levels of systems that comprise their world. To do such work requires great discipline, and in recent years we as coaches have been greatly helped by both the discoveries of the neurosciences and the growing availability of mindfulness practice and training. What we have lacked until now is a book that brings these strands together in a clear and accessible way for coaches, showing all the links and benefits.

Liz Hall, has emerged from behind her role as a very talented editor of *Coaching at Work* to offer us a fuller version of her own story and her own important contribution to the great work. She writes with great clarity and conviction of the role that mindfulness can play in both supporting and deepening our work as coaches, as well as providing a range of methods and practices we can make available for our clients.

Liz recently reminded me that when she interviewed me many years ago for a feature article in *Coaching at Work*, I told her the story of how I had adapted meditation practices for my over-busy life as coach, consultant, teacher and businessman.

Thich Nhat Hanh, the famous Vietnamese Buddhist teacher and writer, had described how he has had to adapt his spiritual practices for the frenetic life of the modern day Westerner. One practice I had learnt from a talk he gave at a crowded Westminster Central Hall was to use the mantra: 'This is home: I have arrived'. You say the first half on the in breath and the second half on the out breath. Now you can practice this whilst climbing the stairs at home, saying it once on every stair; but real practice comes when you do it going up an escalator in the London Underground, or when stuck in a traffic jam on the M6 motorway, or in a busy shopping complex. This too is home, these people crowded round you are part of your wider family.

I am usually so much in a rush to leave this part of creation, to get back to what I call 'home', that I miss the 'gates of heaven' that are open to me right in the middle of busyness.

More recently I have adapted this mindfulness practice, as I realized that in rushing through crowded airports and railway stations I fell into the state of seeing other human beings as barriers to me getting to where I needed to go, and thus arriving at meetings treating all strangers as obstacles to progress! Not a great way to start a meeting. So on the escalator, instead of rushing down past people, for just the few moments it takes to complete the ride, I stand and gaze at each of the people coming in the opposite direction. To each I internally say, this is my brother, this is my sister, (and depending on age) this is my mother, my father, this is my child. Suddenly my consciousness shifts and my perspective changes from a world of barriers and obstacles to one of family and connection.

But it is important, whether we are embarking on learning about mindfulness or coming to this book as a seasoned practitioner, to always ask, 'who is our mindfulness practice in service of?' If it is our self and we are making being mindful another acquisition, or trying to find the fastest escalator up Maslow's pyramid to self-actualization, we are deluding ourselves and adding to the rampant individualism that is helping to degrade our planet. Expanding our little being must ultimately be about our opening into the greater connection with Being, which Gregory Bateson and all the great non-dual spiritual teachers remind us, is the ultimate home, which we can re-enter, right here and right now.

Thank you Liz, for so beautifully not only summarising 70 research reports and 80 books on Mindfulness, but mixing these with your own research, stories and loving compassion. May your book open new windows for all of us, and, like the great poet Mevlana Jallaludin Rumi, constantly remind us that in the plenitude of this great universe we often have chosen to fall asleep in a small dark prison.

Peter Hawkins
Professor of Leadership, Henley Business School;
Emeritus Chairman, Bath Consultancy Group; Honorary President of
The Association of Professional Executive Coaching and Supervision
and author of many books on Leadership, Coaching and Supervision.

Barrett, R (2010) *The New Leadership Paradigm: Leading self, leading others, leading an organization, leading in society*, The Values Centre
Bateson, G (1985) *Steps to an Ecology of Mind*, Ballantine Books, New York
Hawkins, P (2012) *Creating a Coaching Culture*, Open University Press/ McGraw Hill

WHAT YOU WILL FIND IN THIS BOOK

As well as exploring what mindfulness is, where it comes from and what some of the existing research has to say about it, this book seeks to offer pointers for how coaches can practically apply mindfulness within coaching and mentoring – for the coaching process in general, for themselves, and for their clients directly, with a range of issues including stress management and dealing with complexity and change.

In addition to drawing on the expertise, research and experiences of mindfulness practitioners, academics, psychologists and neuroscientists, I draw on the knowledge and wisdom of coaching practitioners already working wonders in the 'mindful coaching' arena, and their clients. I also share my own experiences and those of my clients, and hopefully my growing passion for this topic. I include plenty of case studies and some practices to help you and your clients gain direct experience of mindfulness. I share my own model for using mindfulness in your practice and look at how mindfulness can be and is already integrated with other approaches, including leadership models.

I look at mindfulness in relation to the bigger picture, including ethics, sharing my vision for the future. I believe a world in which we all have mindfulness strategies at our fingertips, practise regular meditation and work mindfully, would be a much better one. And as one participant in a workshop I ran on mindful coaching pointed out, it's fun. Ultimately, I hope that this book will help spread some happiness and ease some suffering.

In gratitude, and with love, Liz.

Introduction

I have a powerful memory of my first encounter with the concept of applying mindfulness to everyday life. I was a working single mother, juggling the childcare of my baby daughter with the demands of freelance journalism. I wrote on topics such as work–life balance and stress management – an irony not lost on me as I struggled through each day, all previous antidotes to stress, which included yoga and meditation, leisurely sessions in the pub and jet-setting off to far-flung places, seemingly out of reach for years to come. I recall one day in particular. I was racing back from the childminder through dense Brighton traffic, late for a telephone call with someone I needed to interview. Molly was throwing a tantrum, my nerves were jangling and I had to dig deep not to scream at my poor child to shut up.

When a friend popped round later, I burst into tears. It was a turning point: this friend suggested I try out an approach she'd just come across. Instead of rushing through tasks to get from A to B as quickly as possible, she suggested I gently focus on what I was doing at that moment, trying to enjoy all the little details and nuances without judgement, without thinking about what I had to do next. Judy had started using this approach when she worked as a counsellor and whilst doing housework. When she made the bed, for example, instead of trying to do it as quickly as possible so she could do something else, she enjoyed the feel of the cotton against her hands, the way the sunlight revealed dust motes dancing in the air, the neatness of the bedspread once she had pulled it straight. If she noticed feelings of frustration, she tried not to get too engaged in these thoughts, just to notice them as part of the process. A penny dropped for me. I got that this was something totally different to anything I'd come across before. This was about doing the same things but in a different way. It was about a different way of being. It was of course about being mindful.

I started to consciously bring my attention to what I was doing from time to time, such as when I was reading my daughter a bedtime story, or even when I was driving. I might not have known exactly what to do but I heard myself laugh more often. More children, more work, more life came along but I maintained an interest in adopting a different approach to whatever I was doing, when I remembered. And I began to make time for meditation again, and yoga. By the time I started coaching, I had years of meditation and mindfulness practice under my belt but I kept this to myself. I felt reluctant to discuss this practice in a professional setting. Despite the work of

Jon Kabat-Zinn and many others, I felt that the multitude still viewed mindfulness/meditation as the preserve of saffron-clad shaven Buddhist monks seeking nirvana amid wafts of incense. Personally, such an association didn't put me off one iota – I have studied mindfulness in a Buddhist context – but I felt my professional reputation could be at stake if I started discussing how sitting on a cushion and watching my breath or contemplating interconnectedness was helping my life and work. I remained a closet meditator for years.

However, it began to dawn on me that coaching and mindfulness would make natural bedfellows. Both are to do with helping people tap into and grow existing inner resources. Both help improve self-awareness and awareness of others. Both help boost resilience and can help bust and prevent stress. The list goes on. Anyhow, I began to feel I was keeping a great treasure all to myself. When I studied approaches such as cognitive behavioural coaching, transpersonal coaching and somatics, I could see where mindfulness came in. The pieces of the jigsaw puzzle were coming together and creating a picture I couldn't ignore. As I began to come out of the mindfulness closet, I met others doing the same.

Nowadays, of course, mindfulness has gone mainstream. It has been incorporated into many healthcare programmes in countries including the United Kingdom and the United States. Kabat-Zinn deserves much of the credit for mindfulness's acceptance through his Mindfulness-Based Stress Reduction (MBSR) programmes. His inkling that medicine and healthcare would prove to be the most fertile ground for introducing meditation and mindfulness was well founded. The MBSR programme has spread far and wide to hospitals, clinics and laboratories all over the world and is being researched clinically and experimented with in ways which would have been inconceivable 30 years ago. It has helped us to build an impressive evidence base, a vocabulary which allows us to discuss what it means to be human, and has helped us to widen access to the transformative and healing potential of mindfulness.

Meanwhile, in the United Kingdom, Mark Williams, professor of clinical psychology at the University of Oxford, has developed Mindfulness-Based Cognitive Therapy (MBCT) to treat depression, and MBCT is now recommended in the United Kingdom's National Institute for Health and Clinical Excellence's clinical guidelines as a front-line psychological intervention for depression sufferers.

In many other settings, mindfulness is taking root too: education, the legal profession, politics and even the armed forces. The Mindfulness in Schools Project in the United Kingdom, for example, is fast gathering momentum, with coaches beginning to get involved as well as teachers. A range of benefits are being reported for students. In politics, Ohio-based Democratic congressman Tim Ryan has become one of mindfulness's most prominent champions, having experienced benefits personally through ongoing practice. And military service members who practise meditation at home have been found to increase their working memories and to exhibit lower levels of negative emotions and higher levels of positive emotions (Jha *et al* 2010).

Of course, we are now seeing mindfulness being applied more widely within the workplace. Growing numbers of organizations including Google, General Mills, PricewaterhouseCoopers, Deutsche Bank, Procter & Gamble, Transport for London, AstraZeneca, Apple, Credit Suisse, KPMG, Innocent, Reuters and GlaxoSmithKline have rolled out mindfulness training programmes for employees, enjoying a host of business benefits. We're seeing the term 'mindful leadership' bandied about by the likes of Richard Boyatzis while others such as Michael Chaskalson, who trains coaches in mindfulness in the United Kingdom, are looking at exactly how to develop mindful leaders. Mindfulness is being incorporated into many leadership development programmes in a number of guises, and numerous courses and institutions dedicated to 'mindful leadership' have sprung up.

Why are we seeing this growth in interest in mindfulness? I think it is partly because of the challenges, complexity and ambiguity of these times we live in. Most of us live in a society that presents us with hordes of choices and information at every turn. Having choices is good, of course, and one of the wonderful things about coaching is that it allows people to see their choices more clearly. But we can get overloaded and overwhelmed with data. We're often expected to be contactable 24/7, we're bombarded constantly with new pieces of information and the pace of change in our modern world is faster than ever before.

At the same time as having to process so much more, many of us feel we're expected to do more than ever before. Many of us crave time to just be, to slow down. Coaches are well accustomed to clients saying that one of the most important things they get from coaching is time out to reflect and stand still. However, many of us have long lost the knack and we're also facing more and more clients crying out for help in getting some space and work–life balance back into their lives.

Not only do we seek an antidote to all the doing we are required or think we are required to do, we're looking for more effective strategies to help us cope with, make meaning from and grow through these difficult times. We're seeing all sorts of crises play out – including economic and environmental crises. Many of us recognize the need to respond as opposed to reacting in a knee-jerk fashion. We can see the need to think medium and long term, not just short term; to think clearly, creatively, responsibly and in a joined-up fashion. The evidence that we are all interconnected lies right in front of our eyes – we can see that in many of the crises while science now supports this view. Yet many of us realize we have lost a sense of that interconnectedness, we feel separate from one another and isolated.

At the same time, mental health problems are on the rise. In 2011, stress topped the league of causes of long-term sickness absence (CIPD 2011). Even as far back as 2001, statistics suggested that one in four people in the United Kingdom will experience some kind of mental health problem during the course of a year, according to the Office for National Statistics (2011), while again in 2001, 450 million people were said to have a mental health problem (World Health Organization 2001). Many clients come to coaching because they simply cannot cope.

Mindfulness in coaching speaks to and helps us meet challenges such as these and it is becoming increasingly obvious that it is no airy-fairy approach. Neither is it a new kid on the block – it has been around for more than 2,500 years, since at least the time of Prince Siddhartha from modern-day Nepal who later became known as the Buddha. It now has a solid evidence base behind it, having been the subject of thousands of studies, many of them looking at the impact of MBSR. Some look at mindfulness in the workplace and within coaching. We will look at some of these studies and benefits in more detail later on but here are some of the many benefits that have been reported:

- enhanced focus and attention;
- improved decision-making ability;
- increased self-awareness and awareness of others;
- higher levels of resilience and emotional intelligence;
- strengthened cognitive effectiveness;
- improved performance;
- heightened ability to manage and prevent stress;
- increased wellbeing;
- greater creativity.

Having experienced and witnessed benefits personally and in others close-hand, I'm delighted to see the interest in mindfulness has spread to coaching. In recent years, both through my work as a coach and as editor of *Coaching at Work* magazine, I have noticed this interest in applying mindfulness within coaching really gathering pace. Sessions on mindfulness at conferences – my own and others' – are frequently packed out. People are hungry to know more about mindfulness and in particular to explore how they can work with it in their coaching practice. Some already have a mindfulness practice and, just as I did, are struggling to join the dots between this and their coaching work. Others don't really know what mindfulness is and want to know more. Others are already passionate about the impact of mindfulness within their practice – even if they call it by another name – and want to link up with others finding the same.

There are many wonderful books out there on mindfulness and meditation as well as thousands of academic papers. I would thoroughly recommend anyone interested in mindfulness and meditation to seek out these sources, some of which I include in the References and Further Reading sections in this book. However, the message I keep hearing is that there is still a lack of material on mindfulness in coaching and related helping professions. My intention in writing this book is to start to fill this gap, to build on and draw on existing material to explore how mindfulness can support – transform even – coaching and mentoring practice, to share questions that have come up for me during this ongoing journey, even if or perhaps particularly where I don't have answers to these questions.

I confess I'm not a huge fan of the word 'mindfulness' as I think it's misleading, implying we're just talking about the mind or brain. I prefer the term 'present-moment awareness', perhaps. However, I have chosen to stay with the word 'mindfulness' throughout this book, as it is so commonly used.

This book is aimed not just at those who are professional coaches and mentors. It is aimed too at all those who use coaching and mentoring skills within their roles at work – perhaps as managers or teachers mentoring other staff. It is aimed at life/personal coaches, sports coaches, wellbeing coaches – anyone who is embracing a coaching or mentoring style. And it will also support anyone who is interested in using a coaching style in some of their conversations. I sometimes use a coaching style with my children, for example. The core skills of coaching which include listening and helping the other person explore for themselves can be used in many of our interactions. And mindfulness can inform, enhance and often transform all of those interactions.

PART ONE
Overview

In this section, we explore mindfulness, its history and documented benefits, with a look at some of the science behind this before moving on in the next section to how we can use it in coaching.

Definitions, origins and relevance to coaching

01

We're in the midst of a mindfulness revolution. I just Googled 'mindful' and got more than 27,000,000 results – by the time you read this, the number will undoubtedly have risen significantly. The drivers behind this movement include the growing repository of scientific research on mindfulness, some of which we will look at in the next chapter. Another driver, which we touched on in the Introduction, is that mindfulness seems to be ideally suited to our times – to all times, I would argue.

Also fuelling the growth in interest in mindfulness is its secularization. I have mixed feelings about this. On the one hand, I see that taking the Buddhism out of mindfulness or at least not mentioning it explicitly in mindfulness teachings such as those included in MBCT and MBSR programmes has made it accessible to a much wider group of people. Increasing reach and access to what I believe to be a profound and wonderfully helpful approach is fantastic and I wholeheartedly believe that anyone of any or no religious persuasion can tap into its wonders as we will see. On the other hand, I do sometimes feel that in some cases, the bid to be wholly secular and to avoid any teachings which mention the S word (spirituality), the B word (Buddhism) or the R word (religion) at all costs can hamper true open enquiry about our meaning and purpose. It can mean missing out on the essence of some powerful teachings which can help us be happier, more fulfilled, more compassionate and more whole beings. Exploring concepts such as impermanence, non-duality and non-self, which crop up in many mindfulness teachings, will not be for everyone and it's possible to reap far-reaching benefits simply from watching our breath for 10 minutes each day, for example, but it's good to know they are out there.

As interest in mindfulness grows, inevitably many are jumping on the bandwagon. We're seeing increasing numbers of people adding the adjective 'mindful' to whatever it is they are doing, in the hope they will attract more business. Mindfulness is becoming a best-selling brand. This in itself may be fine; the problem is there is still widespread ignorance and confusion about what mindfulness really is. Many think mindfulness is about becoming passive or that meditation is about clearing your mind totally. It is neither. If we are going to be working with mindfulness in our coaching, we need to be clear about what it actually means.

Defining mindfulness

Around the same time I encountered mindfulness, or re-encountered it as something to be woven into everyday life, one of my daughters encountered bubbles for the first time. I have a photograph – and a clear memory – of her totally captivated and delighted by these iridescent delicate spheres that danced about and landed on her little hands, only to disappear as she attempted to catch them. She didn't know what they were or what they were called. She was completely caught up in the moment within her direct experience of bubble-ness, no labels, no judgement, just bubbles. Molly's bubble encounter was one akin to mindfulness.

We perhaps have memories of when we were younger and were totally engrossed in something, having just discovered it for the first time. Perhaps more recently too, we've had times when we've been totally caught up in what we're doing. Sometimes we're lucky enough to have something in our lives which we love so much that we often find ourselves lost – or found – in the activity. Accomplished sportspeople report getting 'in flow', a state where everything else just seems to fall away and is very much like mindfulness.

As we mature, we become able to be aware of what we're doing as we're doing it, which we don't have when we're really young – this capacity is part of mindfulness, and it can be developed, as we'll see. However, as we grow older, we also seem to lose our ability to naturally drop into in-the-moment absorption, which is what we're seeking in mindfulness. Again, we can work on this.

For **Linda Woolston**, an executive coach with UK-based coaching provider The Alliance, painting enables her to move into a state of mindfulness. Linda, who has been practising mindfulness for the last decade and uses mindfulness with many of her clients, only discovered painting three years ago. When she plays the piano, much though she loves it, she will sometimes stop to go and send an e-mail. When she paints, however, it's a different scenario. 'For me, being mindful is doing certain things where I have complete focus. When I'm painting, I don't think of anything else.' For one of her clients, it's photography that has this effect; for another, it's crocheting which this client started when she heard about Linda's painting.

Linda does not practise meditation as such but she often prepares for sessions using mindfulness and she does go for mindful walks. Sometimes she 'sits mindfully' in Richmond Park in London. 'When I do, it's such a pleasure, it's absolute bliss. It comes down to noticing more, noticing the rustle of the leaves, the ferns, mindfully aware and appreciating the tiniest things.'

This quality of paying attention in the present moment, without judgement, as Woolston does when she is painting, is very much what mindfulness is about, as we can see in Jon Kabat-Zinn's definition (Kabat-Zinn 1994). Probably the most oft-quoted definition of mindfulness, he defines it thus:

> paying attention in a particular way: on purpose, in the present moment, and non-judgmentally.

One of the difficulties with defining mindfulness is that you only really know what it is once you've experienced or re-experienced it.

As **Neil Scotton**, leadership coach and former president of the UK International Coach Federation, says: 'It's hard to describe, it's more a felt experience. I know when I'm not being mindful. For example, when I am keen to say something or there's lots of self chatter or the client has said something and I've snagged at that point, or when I have an agenda.'

He continues: 'I had a disastrous coaching session when I didn't know what the client wanted. We were both getting frustrated and I was not being mindful that here was a person with lots going on. What is mindfulness? I feel a sense of wanting to say something simple, just being there with the other person, deeply connected to our body. I am constantly reminded of the importance of the body when we are connected to something deep within us that is deeply meaningful and deeply communicates with the other person. Paradoxically mindfulness is a misleading word. It's not a calculating logical experience, it's stepping beyond that. It's something quite natural and we can train ourselves to be aware of it... we've grown mechanistic and everything is very brain-focused.'

Often when people talk about 'being mindful', they aren't talking about meditation, or any particular mindfulness practices such as the ones we explore later. What they often mean is 'being more attentive to what is around them', 'paying more attention to detail', 'being more aware of', perhaps 'being more careful' and so on. A leader might urge employees to 'be more mindful of customer needs', for example, or a manager might say, 'We need to be more mindful of costs.' Others mean mindfulness as a specific approach, backed up by practices including meditation.

Oxford Dictionaries Online offers two definitions for 'mindfulness':

> The quality or state of being conscious or aware of something.

> A mental state achieved by focusing one's awareness on the present moment, while calmly acknowledging and accepting one's feelings, thoughts and bodily sensations, used as a therapeutic technique.

In this book, we will concern ourselves primarily with the first interpretation, although both are relevant to coaching.

Present moment, happy moment

The element of present moment referred to above is very important in mindfulness. The historical Buddha has been quoted as saying, 'Do not dwell in the past, do not dream of the future, concentrate the mind on the present moment.' Vietnamese monk, writer and renowned mindfulness expert Thich Nhat Hanh describes mindfulness as a way of 'keeping one's consciousness alive to the present reality'. Nhat Hanh, or Thay as he is called, teaches that through mindfulness, we can learn to live in the present moment and that doing so is the only way to truly develop peace, both in one's self and in the world.

If you tune into what you're thinking at any one time, you'll notice that lots of these thoughts are about what you've done in the past and what you're planning to do in the future. While we're trying to write a presentation, we might find ourselves suddenly remembering something apparently insignificant that happened 10 years ago or we might find ourselves planning what we're going to have for dinner, or what we're going to do at the weekend, for example. Sometimes – often, in fact – these thoughts seem pretty random. When we become more adept at meditating we can be shocked by the number of seemingly unconnected thoughts that float to the surface. And by the supposedly insignificant events we have locked away. It is all in there! When we're not meditating, if we think about it, we realize we're totally distracted from what we want to be doing by all the thoughts bubbling up. How many times have we driven somewhere and realized once we have arrived that we've been driving on autopilot? Hopefully this only happens on a journey we're familiar with, although many car crashes are caused by our minds being elsewhere.

This 'monkey mind' which jumps from one thought to another, as it is often called in Buddhist literature, certainly takes us away from the present moment (which we'll explore later). It also takes us away from happiness, suggests research published in the United States (Killingsworth and Gilbert 2010). This research found that people's minds tend to wander regardless of the activity (sexual activity being the exception, apparently, although the researchers were male!), and that they're less happy when their mind is wandering. The human mind is a wandering mind and a wandering mind is an unhappy mind – the ability to think about what is not happening in the moment comes at an emotional cost, concludes the research.

Conversely, developing our ability to reside in the present moment is one associated with mindfulness in much of the literature and in many philosophical and spiritual traditions with enhanced happiness and well-being, which we'll explore in more detail later on.

Mind-body-heart-full-ness

For those who haven't encountered mindfulness before, the idea of deliberately paying attention in the moment may suggest a somewhat sparse and clinical approach. However, mindfulness is anything but sparse and clinical. It is a rich, warm, life-enhancing, often difficult and painful but immensely rewarding practice.

Mindfulness is indeed a way of training and transforming the mind. However, it is not just about the mind but the body and heart too. I like to think of it more as 'mind-body-heart-full-ness'. It is about integration. It is a way of being, one which helps us develop empathy, compassion, clarity and wisdom. Kabat-Zinn (1991) himself talks about the heart in mindfulness and many of the practices he recommends include the body and emotions:

> [Mindfulness] is simply a practical way to be more in touch with the fullness of your being through a systematic process of self-observation, self-inquiry, and mindful action. There is nothing cold, analytical, or unfeeling about it. The overall tenor of mindfulness practice is gentle, appreciative, and nurturing. Another way to think of it would be 'heartfulness'.

We are not our thoughts

One of my favourite books, also a favourite with many others across the world, is Viktor E Frankl's *Man's Search for Meaning* (1959). Frankl, a survivor of four Nazi concentration camps, wrote, 'Everything can be taken from a man but one thing: the last of the human freedoms – to choose one's attitude in any given set of circumstances, to choose one's way' (Frankl 1959). Mindfulness incorporates this ability to recognize that we are not our thoughts and that we can choose how we respond. These two strands are recognized in the mindfulness definition from the United Kingdom's Mental Health Foundation's *Be Mindful* report (2010):

> [Mindfulness] is an integrative, mind–body-based approach that helps people change the way they think and feel about their experiences, especially stressful experiences.

It says mindfulness 'involves paying attention to our thoughts and feelings so we become more aware of them, less enmeshed in them, and better able to manage them'.

As we explore in more detail later, mindfulness helps us grow and flex what we might call our response muscle. Part of this 'muscle building' and 'muscle flexing' is down to the 'without judgement' piece of mindfulness. It's about developing or tapping into what we can call 'the Observer mind' or 'Witness', a state of mind which just observes 'what is'. With this definition, we begin to get a sense of how mindfulness might be useful in coaching. One of the things coaching sets out to do is to help people change how they think and feel about their experiences, thus giving them more choice about how they respond, and this is what mindfulness does too.

Mindfulness helps us become friends with our minds, so we become more aware of our triggers, our thoughts, emotions and bodily sensations, putting us into a better position to choose how we respond – rather than react – to the world around us. Some go as far as to say – and I agree with this – that how we think and act shapes how the world responds to us. Through techniques such as the Body scan (see Chapter 4), mindfulness helps us become more aware of what is going on around us and in us. It helps us get more in touch with how things really are: for example, realizing that we are not our thoughts. We have a tendency to get very caught up in our thoughts, identifying closely with them. Mindfulness helps us develop the ability to inhabit a state of mind that doesn't judge, that just observes what is. It might notice that our thoughts pass quickly by, often with no real pattern in how they emerge, popping up unsolicited, floating by like clouds passing through the sky. By developing mindfulness, we can learn not to engage with these passing thoughts unless we choose to, catching ourselves when we are first triggered by something or someone. We can notice what happens in us and to us and gradually develop greater access to choice in how we respond. We might notice how illogical our thoughts are at times or that we are over-identifying with them, for example.

> To allow ourselves to be truly in touch with where we already are, no matter where that is, we have got to pause in our experience long enough to let the present moment sink in; long enough to actually feel the present moment, to see it in its fullness, to hold it in awareness and thereby come to know and understand it better. Only then can we accept the truth of this moment of our life, learn from it, and move on.
>
> Kabat-Zinn, J (1991)

Kabat-Zinn talks of how not knowing we are even in a dream – or nightmare – is what the Buddhists call 'ignorance' or mindlessness. Mindfulness is not necessarily about knowing, it is about being in touch with not knowing.

Meditation

Meditation is incorporated in mindfulness, although there are plenty of people who practise mindfulness who do not meditate. It is still possible to reap benefits without meditating but meditation can have a profound impact.

There are different approaches to meditation – some practices including those such as the Body scan (see Chapter 4) or Awareness of breath (see Chapter 5) are very much about paying attention, focusing and letting go. But there are other meditative practices, including visualization, that may not be considered to be mindfulness per se by some. However, visualizations including the Loving-kindness meditation (see Chapter 7) are part of a strong tradition within mindfulness, and are included in the work of Kabat-Zinn and many others. I work with these in my coaching practice, as do others, so I have opted to include these in this book.

You may still be wondering what on earth mindfulness is. As I said earlier, you really have to experience it to get it. Whether or not this is the case, I would like to invite you to 'dine' with me. All you need is a raisin, 10 minutes or less, and to be willing, curious and open. You might like to read the text first, before then trying the practice.

Practice: The Raisin meditation

You might like to wash your hands first. Then take a raisin and gently place it in the palm of your hand. Try to approach it as if it were the first time you had encountered such a thing, as if you were a young child or an alien with no preconceptions about 'raisin-ness'. Engage all your senses, suspending judgement and concept forming as much as possible.

Look at it sitting there. What do you notice?

What does it look like?

What about its surface, the bumps and shallows?

What colours do you see?

How big/small is it in relation to your palm?

Holding it up to the light, does it look different?

What does it feel like?

What textures does it have?

If you press it, does the texture change?

If you bring it up to your ear and squeeze it, what, if anything, can you hear?

What does it smell like?

Play around with your raisin as if you had all the time and all the naked curiosity in the world. Then, when you are ready, pop it into your mouth.

What does it feel like in your mouth, when you run your tongue over it, when you push it around your mouth?

What happens when you gently begin to bite it?

What are your sensations?

What does it taste like?

You might also like to contemplate the nature of raisin-ness: where does it come from? What is it now? What does it become? Obviously such an exploration draws on existing knowledge an alien or young child may not have, but you should still maintain that sense of curiosity and openness.

When you're ready, draw the practice to a close.

This exercise is one which I and many others have used to help people get a sense of what mindfulness is. I never mind repeating the exercise myself as it's always a unique experience. One thing I pretty much invariably find is that I start to feel calmer and more peaceful. Just from experiencing one little raisin. You can, of course, do this using other food – in the burgeoning Mindfulness in Schools Project in the United Kingdom, chocolate is the substance of choice, which, as you can imagine, goes down better with secondary school pupils than raisins. However, raisins lend themselves to this exercise beautifully, and they don't melt. They are rather incredible little things once you get to know them mindfully!

What was your experience?

Mindful journalling

I invite you to keep your own journal specifically on mindfulness experiences, practices and learnings or to start attending to these in your existing journal. You might like to start by capturing any reflections that emerged from the practice above, any preconceptions, any aversion, any resistance, any surprises and so on. If you've done this practice before, what was your response? Did you groan inwardly, skip this bit in a bid to get on and speed ahead, or did you take it as another opportunity to experience something in the moment?

A brief orientation to coaching

Many of you will be familiar with coaching and have your own definitions of it. However, some of you may be new to it so I'm including a brief orientation to coaching for those of you coming at it for the first time as well as offering a sense to all of you of where I'm coming from.

Sir John Whitmore, author of *Coaching for Performance*, and one of the people who popularized the GROW model (Goal; Reality; Options; Wrap-up or Will), used widely in coaching, defines coaching as:

unlocking a person's potential to improve their performance,

while Myles Downey, founder of the School of Coaching, defines it as:

the art of facilitating the performance, learning and development of another.

When asked what coaching is, I usually say something like this:

Coaching is a conversation or series of conversations with the aim of helping people learn, grow and fulfil their potential.

I might add, with variations according to my audience or readership:

Coaching enables people to tap into their own wisdom to help them achieve their goals, improve their performance, gain clarity, become more self-aware and aware of others, and to develop self-responsibility. It is a developmental dialogue typically involving the coach asking the client skilful questions.

However, it's not all about words, of course. Silence plays an important part in coaching, such as when the coach actively and intuitively listens, intently present for the client, while powerful thinking and awareness take place. Sometimes coaches will weave exercises and practices into the session or as homework, such as creative visualization and, as we will explore, mindfulness practices. Much powerful transformational work takes place when not a word is being uttered, although the words will have played their part.

Coaching is typically non-directive, collaborative and co-creative. The coach is not an expert on the client – rather they're an equal, a partner who can work alongside the client, co-creating and helping the client tap into their own potential. There may be times when the coach does have expertise to share and they would be doing a disservice to the client not to offer this expertise, or the coaching may be at the skills end rather than the transformational end of the spectrum. However, on the whole, coaching is not about imparting skills and knowledge – this is one of the key differences between coaching and mentoring. While mentoring draws on many of the same competencies as coaching – active listening, for example – it differs in that the mentor is expected to share their expertise with their mentee where appropriate.

Coaching tends to be future-focused, but by no means always. Many coaches look at the past too, such as considering how the client has acted in the past or how they have related with others, even looking at relationships with significant others. Coaching deals with the present too, particularly coaching informed by gestalt, mindfulness or somatics. Looking at what is happening right now gives valuable data for the client and coach to work with.

Coaching can be delivered one-to-one or in a group setting, perhaps with a number of team coaches working with a team. It can be delivered face-to-face or on the telephone.

What's mindfulness got to do with it?

Looking at the definitions at the beginning of the previous section, we can start to see how mindfulness and coaching might make natural companions. Mindfulness too helps people learn, develop and fulfil their potential. It helps them tap into their inner wisdom, gain clarity, become more self-aware and aware of others, and develop self-responsibility.

FIGURE 1.1   Qualities that mindfulness and coaching have in common

Observer's mind	Empathy
Beginner's mind	Compassion
Curiosity	Holistic: working with the body,
Contemplation	heart and mind
Reflection	Person is whole
Awareness of self	Spaciousness
Awareness of others	Opening
Awareness of the world at large	Co-creation
Non-judgement	Creativity
Patience	Intuition
Presence	Clarity
Trust	Focus
Respect	Wisdom
Integrity	Self-actualization

With both coaching and mindfulness, there is a strong sense of the person being whole and of the process helping someone tap into their own wisdom. What matters is how the client or mindfulness practitioner experiences and makes sense of what is happening, for themselves and in relation to others.

Coaching is about helping people to have more choice and mindfulness is a way for them to achieve this. There are many ways in which mindfulness can underpin our coaching practice, be that as full-blown professional coaches, as professionals using coaching within our work with others such as managers, or as human beings using a coaching style with fellow human beings, whoever they may be. Developing mindfulness helps us be more present with, attuned to and resonant with others; it helps us become more self-aware and aware of others. We hone our ability to observe ourselves in action as we coach, and open up to more choices about how we work with our clients and how we respond. As Silsbee (2010b) says:

> Mindfulness... is a rigorous attention to observing ourselves in action, such that we become fluid, intuitive, aware, and exquisitely responsive to what is being brought forward in the conversation.

Mindfulness helps us be more compassionate to ourselves and others, it helps us make better decisions, and it helps us look after ourselves. It helps us behave more ethically and think more systemically. It helps us embrace change and work with complexity and ambiguity. Essentially I see mindfulness and coaching as natural companions in many ways, which we will continue to explore. However, there are some potential areas of difference and tension between mindfulness and coaching (see Table 1.1) including the foci on non-striving, being and the present moment in mindfulness, for example.

TABLE 1.1   Some areas of potential difference/tension

Mindfulness	Coaching
Attending to the present moment	Future-focused
Non-striving/letting go	Striving
Non-goal oriented	Goal-focused
Being	Doing
Accepting what is	Trying to change what is
Non-attachment	Attachment eg to goal
Lots of silence	Lots of words
Solitary (not always)	Involves two or more people (apart from self-coaching)
Sense of one-ness	Often focuses on individual's agenda (but should consider system)

We will look at these too as they can cause resistance and confusion when we first start to explore mindfulness in relation to coaching, and to our lives in general.

Non-striving is one of seven attitudes that Kabat-Zinn (1991) recommends as vital as a foundation to mindfulness practice. It is the only one of the seven attitudes that I feel demands debate when applied to coaching. However, the other six can be wholeheartedly applied to coaching as well as mindfulness. They are:

- non-judging;
- patience;
- beginner's mind;
- trust;
- acceptance;
- letting go.

These are all attitudes that serve us well in coaching too. We will explore all of these later.

FIGURE 1.2   Aims/outcomes that mindfulness and coaching have in common

'Time out'

Training the mind

Transforming the mind

Fostering learning

Fostering growth

Helping people fulfil their potential

Self-responsibility

Awareness of self, others and world at large

Attuned communication

Opening

Empathy

Clarity

Tapping into innate wisdom

Paying more attention/heightened attentiveness to what and who are around

Self-regulation, management and flexibility of responses

Fear modulation

Getting in touch with non-knowing

Opening up possibilities and choices

Problem solving

Creativity

Presence

Attunement

Self-actualization

A brief history of mindfulness

02

As I said earlier, mindfulness, for all its current popularity, is no new kid on the block. Mindfulness, including meditation, has roots in Buddhist teachings. The historical Buddha (which means 'the awakened one') lived 2,500 years ago in modern-day Nepal. The story goes that Prince Gautama had been mollycoddled in comfort, shielded by his father from the ills of the world. He escaped the palace grounds one day, coming across sickness, old age and death. Having witnessed such suffering, he vowed to find an antidote. Using only his mind, body and experiences, he made discoveries many modern-day physicists, scientists, psychologists would be proud of. He gained insights into the nature of being, leading him to share a framework based on mindfulness to help ordinary people rid themselves of the 'disease' of suffering caused by the three 'poisons' of greed, hatred (or aversion) and ignorance or delusion (or unawareness). The premise is that as humans, none of us escape suffering, no matter how hard we try, no matter how beautiful or rich we are or become. This can sound pretty depressing. However, the Buddha claimed to have discovered the antidote he was seeking and mindfulness was a core ingredient. The Buddha gave two teachings on mindfulness – the Anapanasati Sutra and the Satipathana Sutra. Since then, although there are many Buddhist schools and much variation in approaches, mindfulness has lain at the heart of all Buddhist teachings, at the core of the 'dharma' (a Sanskrit word with many meanings but often translated as 'the teachings' or 'the path'). In all the Buddhist traditions, mindfulness is part of a wider framework which includes the development of wisdom, compassion and ethics, and of a value of non-harming which has echoes in the Hippocratic Oath within Western medicine.

Not just Buddhist

However, I think it's vital to flag up that mindfulness is not inherently Buddhist. Mindfulness has many other names – including awakening, presence, present-moment awareness and remembrance – and variations in approach, but the concept of developing and enhancing the ability to be here in the moment consciously and to attain a higher state of awareness is a common theme across many spiritual traditions, including Christianity, Taoism and Sufism. Many other traditions have incorporated meditation and focused on how to develop mindfulness, including Chinese Taoist philosopher Chuang Tsu (399–295 BC), the late Indian spiritual teacher Krisnamurti and latterly, Ekhart Tolle, author of *The Power of Now*. One of the Christian tradition's most famous meditators was 16th-century Carmelite nun and Spanish mystic Saint Teresa of Avila, who saw meditation as a way to achieve union with God. Christian meditation was marginalized between the 18th and 20th centuries but is very much alive today, thanks to efforts from people including the late John Main, who opened the first Christian meditation centre in Ealing Abbey in London in 1975. Interest in Zen Buddhism spread among Westerners throughout the 20th century, fuelled by the migration of Zen teachers to the West and the influence of writers such as Roman Catholic Trappist monk Thomas Merton, author of books including *Spiritual Direction and Meditation*.

Of course, as we've seen, mindfulness – often including meditation – is now becoming widely applied in many secular settings. This is not surprising. Being mindful is a universal human skill. The qualities of attentiveness and awareness have been associated with the word for almost 700 years – 'mindful' is an English term dating from the mid-14th century, thus predating its use in English in a Buddhist context by centuries. 'Mindful' as an English term dates from the mid-14th century (*Online Etymology Dictionary*). The term was first recorded in 1340 (*Wikipedia*). The word has also had associations with intention, purpose and memory. What we now think of as mindfulness in a Buddhist context was first translated in the late 19th century from the ancient Pali word *sati* (mindfulness, self-collectedness, powers of reference, retention, alertness) and the Sanskrit equivalent *smrti* (remembrance, reminiscence, thinking of or upon, calling to mind, memory).

Secularization

Mindfulness-Based Stress Reduction (MBSR) began in 1979 in the basement of the University of Massachusetts Medical Center in the United States. Drawing on his studies of Zen, Vipassana (an ancient sitting meditation technique) and yoga, Kabat-Zinn offered a range of practices for the cultivation of mindfulness. The formal practices offered in MBSR include yoga and Tai Chi-based mindful movement; the Body scan, and sitting meditation (awareness of the breath and systematic widening of the field of awareness to include all four foundations of mindfulness: awareness of the body, feeling tone, mental states and mental contents). As we can see, the intention of MBSR is much greater than simple stress reduction. Over the eight-week period of the course, and beyond, participants are invited to see all of their life as fertile ground for cultivating mindfulness, including work and relationships.

Academics and clinicians have since begun to explore the power of marrying mindfulness with the more traditional approach of cognitive behavioural therapy (CBT). Oxford University now offers a Mindfulness-Based Cognitive Therapy (MBCT) graduate programme, developed by Mark Williams, professor of clinical psychology, while at Bangor University in Wales, the Centre for Mindfulness Research and Practice offers a number of mindfulness courses, including a master's. MBSR and MBCT have spawned many other applications of mindfulness including in parenting, education, leadership, schools and so on. Norway, Sweden, Holland, France, Ireland, Germany, South Africa, Switzerland and Italy are among many countries that have institutes and national associations of mindfulness teachers and training.

In the following chapter, we look at some of the research on mindfulness.

References

Sati definition, www.accesstoinsight.org/glossary.html

Smrti definition, Monier Monier-Williams's *Sanskrit–English Dictionary*

The impact of mindfulness

03

In this chapter, we take a look at some of the research into the impact of mindfulness, and at some of the benefits highlighted by this research and by some of the plentiful anecdotal evidence.

Mindfulness is becoming a very popular topic to investigate. These days, more than 30 or 40 research papers are published each month on the topic and we are reaching a tipping point: the sheer volume of research is pointing to mindfulness being indisputably effective. Even though there is still only a small amount of coaching-specific research, there is much we can learn from studies from other fields. One of those is neuroscience, which is where we will start.

When neuroscientist Professor Richard Davidson and his team published their findings on meditation (which we look at in this chapter), in the *Proceedings of the National Academy of Sciences* (Lutz *et al*) in November 2004, they caused quite a stir. And there were even protests by some neuroscientists fearing a detraction from more 'serious' findings when the Dalai Lama was invited to speak at the Society for Neuroscience's annual conference in 2006. We've certainly moved on since then. However, it's worth noting that research on mindfulness, particularly in neuroscientific terms, is still in its infancy. Much of the research in neuroscience is based on the use of fMRI scans and our ability to interpret these is pretty limited. Professor Paul Brown, speaking at the Association for Coaching's annual conference, Edinburgh, 22 June 2012, pointed out that these scans are 'amazing but... very crude information'. He said: 'It's a bit like a helicopter hovering five feet above Edinburgh and seeing a crowd gathering in the square; you don't know why or what they're there for. They're amazing pictures but we've no idea what they mean.' So we should approach some of the research findings with caution.

We can change our spots and learn new tricks

My late mother was fond of spouting sayings at me – I catch myself doing the same with my children too – in an attempt to drum home the received wisdom of the time. She would say, 'A leopard can't change its spots' to stress that we're stuck with our basic natures – or 'You can't teach an old dog new tricks' to highlight the supposed impossibility of adults learning new behaviours, for example. The science of the time appeared to back up much of this thinking – that our brains were hard-wired once we hit adulthood.

Thankfully, we now know differently, due in part to neuroscientific studies. We know everyone, including the elderly, can 'rewire' their brains and form new neural connections. This discovery has huge and very exciting implications for coaching, speaking to one of its *raisons d'être*: helping people change. And evidence appears to be piling up to suggest that mindfulness is the perfect companion as a highly effective method of doing this rewiring.

Neither are we solely a product of environment and genetics. One study, (Weiss, Bates and Luciano, 2008) carried out in 2008 at the University of Edinburgh and the Queensland Institute for Medical Research, Australia suggested that although genetics may account for 50 per cent of the difference between people's happiness levels, and circumstances for 10 per cent, the other 40 per cent is down to what we do and how we think. Meanwhile, the concept of neuroplasticity – the brain's ability to reorganize itself by developing new neural connections – is one of the most exciting discoveries in neuroscience in recent years. Professor Davidson (2011), laboratory director at the Laboratory for Affective Neuroscience, University of Wisconsin-Madison, described neuroplasticity as 'the greatest insight for modern neuroscience in the last decade'. 'The brain is an organ which is designed to change in response to experience and training,' he said.

One good and well-known example of how what we do can change our brain is that of taxi drivers in London. Having to remember and negotiate vast numbers of city streets leads to the development of an enlarged hippocampus in the brains of London cabbies. The hippocampus is a brain region associated with visual-spatial memories (Maguire *et al* 2000).

And there is plenty of research suggesting that meditating and practising mindfulness shape our brains. In June 2002, Davidson's associate Antoine Luz placed 128 electrodes on the brain of Buddhist monk Matthieu Ricard, author of *Happiness*. As Ricard meditated on loving-kindness and compassion, his brain showed powerful gamma activity. Gamma waves are the fastest brainwaves and are apparently a sign of high states of focus and concentration. At the same time, oscillations were synchronized across different parts of the cortex.

'Perceptual binding is when many different elements get bound together in an integrated experience... oscillations and profound synchrony perfectly temporally synchronized across different parts of the brain,' explains Professor Davidson (2011).

These findings were apparently surprising – gamma activity is usually weak and not easily visible and synchronization tends to be associated with patients under anaesthesia. Dr Shanida Nataraja explains: 'Gamma waves are associated with large groups of brain cells all firing at the same time... The synchronicity in the activity of the brain cells may account for the heightened level of consciousness and mental acuity whilst in a meditative state.'

Davidson and Luz brought in more monks and a control group of non-meditating students but still the initial findings bore up. The monks produced gamma waves 30 times stronger than the students' and larger areas of the meditators' brains were active, particularly in the left prefrontal cortex, the part of the brain responsible for positive affect (emotions). Like Ricard, the other monks had also been asked to meditate on compassion and here they were with remarkable brainwaves. With the right training and through mindfulness, compassion can be developed, rather like a muscle. We will look at compassion and emotional intelligence later on in the book (Chapters 7 and 17 respectively).

Brainwaves

Brainwaves are electrical impulses and they are usually measured in terms of their frequency (this determines what type of brainwave we're talking about) and speed of undulation (measured in hertz – cycles per second).

- *Beta waves (14–38 hertz)*: these predominate in most of our waking day and we need them for logical thinking, problem solving and managing normal daily activities. But Beta waves can go into overdrive and we can feel stressed and panicky.

- *Alpha waves (8–14 hertz)*: these predominate when we are particularly focused on one thought, for example, and are somewhat detached from everything else, such as when we are daydreaming. Too many can mean we feel spaced out.

- *Theta waves (4–8 hertz)*: these are 'subconscious' brainwaves and are prevalent during moments of deep insight and creativity.

- *Delta waves (0–4 hertz)*: these are the waves of our 'unconscious' mind, which we experience when we are deeply asleep; they are associated with empathy and intuition.

- *Gamma*: the fastest waves, associated with large groups of cells simultaneously firing, and with intense focus and concentration.

Our 'state of consciousness' consists of some combination of brainwaves. At different times, some combinations are more appropriate than others and ideally, we should be able to choose the best combination. We need to combine all four simultaneously for creative problem solving, for example, in what Anna Wise describes as 'the awakened mind'.

Shanida Nataraja (2008); Anna Wise (1997)

Whole-brain integration

'Whole-brain integration' is the key to meditation's success, according to neuroscientist Dr Shanida Nataraja. She was raised in London in a family which embraced meditation but she was apparently still surprised to find that meditation plays such a role in optimizing brain function and health, from cognitive abilities to cardiovascular wellbeing.

Dr Nataraja studied meditation for her PhD in neurophysiology, and post-doctoral research at the neuroscience department of Johns Hopkins School of Medicine, Baltimore, presenting her findings in her book *The Blissful Brain: Neuroscience and Proof of the Power of Meditation*. Dr Nataraja believes that Westerners use the left halves of their brain too much and their right brain hemispheres too little. 'In the Western world, most individuals navigate through their everyday life in a fashion dominated by left-brained thinking.'

As part of her research, Dr Nataraja used galvanic skin response meters (which detect emotional changes through the skin) and electroencephalograms (or EEGs, which measure electrical activity produced by the brain). She found that entering a meditative state can bring a shift into right-brain mode, with increased alpha brainwave activity. An increase in alpha brainwaves is a sign that we're more relaxed – we're activating the parasympathetic nervous system, as opposed to the adrenaline-releasing sympathetic system. More parasympathetic activity means less stress, which is better for our hearts – we will look at this in more detail later.

She says that both sides of the brain offer different modes of thinking and perceiving. The left hemisphere is associated with analytical, rational and logical processing while the right hemisphere is associated with abstract thought, non-verbal awareness, visual-spatial perception and the expression and modulation of emotions.

Flexibility is key here: 'true insights stem from being able to tap into the potential of both sides of the brain'. She says that the way to tackle our 'left-brained world' is not for us all to become 'right-brained'. It's about 'empowering ourselves with the tools to switch between left-brain and right-brain thinking at will. Meditation triggers a switch to right-brained activity, as attention is a right-brained phenomenon, but the chain of processes shown in the illustration [reproduced here as Figure 3.1] eventually spread to the left brain too. Thus the whole brain is working more synchronously.'

She highlights research by Maxwell Cade (1979) on the 'awakened mind' state, the level of consciousness reached through long-term and regular meditation. 'It involves balanced activity on both sides of the brain. First we let go of our thoughts, but as the process deepens, the thoughts return, but they are driven by left- and right-brained processes,' says Nataraja.

In *The Blissful Brain* (2008) Dr Nataraja outlines the sequence of brain processes that apparently occur when we meditate.

The chain of events in our brains when we meditate

What we're doing/experiencing

We set our intention to quieten our mind, clear our thoughts, focus on a single object such as the breath and so on, attempting to filter out certain information.

What's happening in our brain?

Activity increases in the attention association area while activity decreases in the frontal cortex regions surrounding the attention association area. This is the result of focused attention and reflects a filtering out of all information that is not deemed important.

What we're doing/experiencing

We're drawing our attention to the 'present-now experience'.

What's happening?

As attention is predominantly a right-brained function, there is a shift from 'intellectualized' left-brain thinking to right-brained activity. This helps explain why our experience is a 'direct experience', one which is intuitively felt and cannot be described or analysed as this is not something our right brain can do.

What we're doing/experiencing

We become less aware of sensory information coming from our external environment. We are less aware of where we are in relation to time and space. We might feel 'floaty' and not sure where our limbs begin and end. We find it hard to describe what we're experiencing.

What's happening?

There is decreased activity in the right parietal lobe, reflecting this dissolution of the self/non-self boundary. As well as the impact on activity in the right orientation association area (leading to a loss of sense of space and/or time), there is impact on activity in the right verbal-conceptual area, leading to an inability to convey the experience efficiently through language.

It is thought that this chain of events activates two key structures in the limbic system. There are extensive connections between the parietal lobe's orientation association area and the hippocampus, which in turn stimulates the amygdala. These two structures are responsible for us assigning emotional significance to our experiences. The activation of the hippocampus conveys emotional significance of the experience and imprints the emotionally charged experience in our long-term memory.

The activation of the amygdala confers emotional significance to the lack of sensory information. Through these actions on the hypothalamus, the amygdala modifies the activity of the autonomic nervous system.

What we're doing/experiencing

We experience a 'blissful, peaceful state'.

What's happening?

There is maximal activation of the parasympathetic (relaxation) nervous system.

What we're doing/experiencing

We enjoy a mentally clear and alert state. We notice our breathing has slowed down.

What's happening?

As the different neural, hormonal and other triggers swing in, there is a maximal activation of the sympathetic (arousal) nervous system. Physiological effects, such as changes to breathing rate, heart rate or blood pressure are the result of the amygdala's effect on midbrain structures that control these functions.

What we're doing/experiencing

We feel a sense of unity and wholeness and a dissolving of the self/non-self boundary.

What's happening?

Both the left and right orientation and verbal-conceptual association areas are switched off. The lack of activity in the right orientation association area gives rise to our sense of unity and wholeness, whereas the lack of activity in the left orientation association area results in the dissolving of the self/non-self boundary.

Figure 3.1 shows the chain of processes during meditation.

FIGURE 3.1   Overall chain of brain processes during meditation

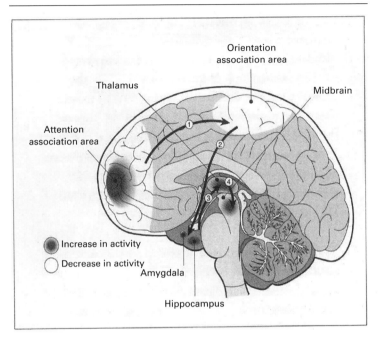

SOURCE: Nataraja (2008) *The Blissful Brain*, reproduced with permission

Figure 3.2 offers a round-up of what the neuroscientists say happens in our brains and bodies when we meditate regularly.

FIGURE 3.2

How mindfulness changes the brain

Regular meditation:

- increases grey matter concentration in brain regions involved in learning and memory processes, emotion regulation, self-referential processing and perspective taking (Hölzel, Carmody, Vangel *et al* 2011).
  These include the insula (Hölzel *et al* 2008; Lazar, S *et al* 2005), the hippocampus (Hölzel *et al* 2008; Luders *et al* 2009; Maguire *et al* 2000) and the prefrontal cortex (Lazar *et al* 2005; Luders *et al* 2009);
- reduces cortical thinning due to ageing in prefrontal regions strengthened by meditation (Lazar *et al* 2005);
- improves attention (Carter *et al* 2005; Tang *et al* 2007);
- enhances compassion (Lutz, Brefczynski-Lewis *et al* 2008);
- improves psychological function of empathy (Lazar *et al* 2005);
- increases activity in left-frontal regions associated with lifting mood (Davidson 2004);
- increases power and reach of fast, gamma-range brainwaves in long-term meditators (Lutz *et al* 2004), showing increased numbers of neurons firing together.

How mindfulness impacts the body

- Decreases cortisol (Tang *et al* 2007) – we will look at why this is a good thing when we look at stress later on.
- Helps activate the parasympathetic nervous system through practices such as mindfulness of the body, deep exhalations and meditation, calming the autonomic nervous system.
- Boosts the immune system (Davidson *et al* 2003; Tang *et al* 2007).
- Improves medical conditions including type II diabetes, cardiovascular disease, asthma, premenstrual syndrome and chronic pain (Walsh and Shapiro 2006).
- Improves psychological conditions such as anxiety, insomnia, phobias and eating disorders (Walsh and Shapiro 2006).

Benefits of mindfulness

Now let's take a look at what the research and anecdotal evidence tell us about the benefits mindfulness can offer.

As you mature as a coach, mindfulness really helps you serve your client. Benefits for my clients and myself include clearer decision making, awareness of impact, control over reactions, and having more options in your reactions.
Neela Bettridge, executive coach and founder of
corporate sustainability consultancy Article13

There is great benefit in just stilling... curiously there seems to be a deeper profound change that any degree of frantic insistent thinking is not getting towards. There's something about working as a whole being.
Neil Scotton, leadership coach and co-founder of the One Leadership Project

I guess from my point of view, mindfulness is central to the whole endeavour. People are seeking coaching to change something and in order to do that, they need to raise their level of attention and that attention can raise awareness of how one is thinking and feeling and only then can they make changes – change at the deepest levels.
Jeremy Paul Hunter, lecturer, Peter F. Drucker and
Masatoshi Ito Graduate School of Management

One of the main reasons coaches practise mindfulness for themselves is to help them live more in the moment – 74 per cent of coaches responding to an online survey I carried out reported this to be the case. Second came becoming more self-aware (73 per cent), followed by managing/preventing stress (67 per cent) and by helping them be more present for their client (65 per cent). I share more from this research in Chapter 20.

In another piece of research, feeling calmer was one of the main reported benefits of mindfulness. Preliminary findings by Emma Dolman from the United Kingdom's Ministry of Defence and Dave Bond, a member of Ashridge leadership faculty, suggest a significantly upwards shift in general levels of satisfaction for individuals who commit to a period of mindfulness. The study explored the value of meditation practice for leaders. Some 90 per cent of participants practising mindfulness noted benefits from having participated in the mindfulness activities – 61 per cent noted a 'feeling of calm'; 30 per cent listed 'enjoyed leaving everything and having time to themselves'; 22 per cent of the items listed related to improved sleep, and 22 per cent of participants also cited 'having a different perspective'. By comparison, only 52 per cent of the non-meditating group noted beneficial value from their self-chosen non-meditation activities (Dolman and Bond 2011).

Better coaching outcomes

One study from the psychotherapeutic arena suggests that practising mindfulness could increase the likelihood of better outcomes from coaching. Patients of psychotherapists who receive mindfulness training enjoyed a reduction in symptoms and better treatment results, according to the study from Germany. (As Michael Chaskalson points out in *The Mindful Workplace*, it seems reasonable that this could be the case for coaching too.) The study (Grepmair *et al* 2007) tracked a group of 124 patients over a nine-week period receiving treatment from psychotherapists in training. During this time, half of the 18 trainee psychotherapists practised Zen meditation, the other half did not. Patients whose therapists had completed mindfulness training enjoyed better results and showed higher reduction than the control group in symptoms including anxiety, anger/hostility, obsessiveness and insecurity in social contact. The researchers concluded that promoting mindfulness in psychotherapists in training could positively influence the therapeutic course and treatment results experienced by their patients.

Quick results

When it comes to mindfulness, a little does go a long way, according to some studies. In one study, people who took part in an eight-week MBSR programme showed increased activity in brain regions including those associated with learning and memory processes, emotion regulation and perspective taking. The study (Hölzel *et al* 2011) took magnetic resonance images from 16 people new to meditation, before and after participating in the programme, comparing them with a control group. The MBSR programme participants were found to have increases in grey matter concentration areas of the brain associated with learning and memory processes, emotion regulation, self-referential processing and perspective taking (the left hippocampus, posterior cingulate cortex, temporo-parietal junction, and the cerebellum). If mindfulness does indeed help us learn, remember, regulate our emotions and take perspectives, this is very interesting for those of us who coach, and for our clients.

In studies carried out to assess the impact of mindfulness on schoolchildren, a range of benefits have been reported after just eight weeks too. Increased confidence, ability to cope with change, a more positive outlook, improved sleeping patterns and lessening of pre-examination nerves were among the benefits reported first-hand by pupils from schools including Tonbridge School, St Paul's Girls' School in London and King Alfred's College in Oxford, all in the United Kingdom, according to a report in *Coaching at Work* (Freeman 2011). The pupils championed the eight-week '.b' mindfulness course developed by the Mindfulness in Schools Project, which is being rolled out in some secondary schools in the UK and overseas. There are also moves to offer a programme in primary schools too.

In other countries including the United States, studies are suggesting a range of benefits rapidly gained by pupils practising mindfulness. The Association for Mindfulness in Education, a group of organizations and individuals working together to provide support for mindfulness training as a component of K-12 education, believes mindfulness training develops skills such as attention and concentration, emotional and cognitive awareness and understanding, bodily awareness and coordination, and interpersonal awareness and skills (Hall 2009).

Anecdotally, from people I coach or fellow participants on an eight-week MBCT programme, I hear novices reporting all sorts of benefits very quickly. Take 'Ana', who was having problems with her teenage daughter, which in turn was making her more irritable at work. She had snapped a few times at colleagues, which was highly unusual for her and not exactly serving her well as she was hoping to be considered for promotion. In week three of her introducing mindfulness practices such as the Three-minute breathing space (Chapter 9) into her daily life, instead of yelling back at her adolescent daughter when she 'acted out', Ana found she was able to just pause, take a few deep breaths and not respond aggressively. By week five, she reported that she was getting on very well with her daughter. The communication channels were open once again and there was a much more pleasant atmosphere in the house, impacting on Ana's other children and husband. She stopped snapping at colleagues. Her male boss even remarked on this – saying something about her hormones perhaps having settled down, which only recently would have definitely elicited a snappy response from Ana!

Unsurprisingly, however, although benefits can be enjoyed quickly, there are more significant benefits and changes associated with long-term practice, as suggested by studies of long-term mindfulness practitioners (Lutz *et al* 2004). As always, it pays to put in the time.

We will continue to explore benefits associated with mindfulness as we go on. In the meantime, Figure 3.3 lists the benefits documented in all the various pieces of research I have looked at – well over 75 research papers and 80 books on mindfulness or which touch on mindfulness and associated topics. And Sheila's story gives a flavour of how mindfulness can help us enjoy the first benefit listed – living more in the moment.

FIGURE 3.3   Some of the benefits documented in research

Living more in the moment

Greater work–life balance

Enhanced resilience

Making more sense of the world in a world of ever-increasing choices and crises such as those in the economy and the environment

Gaining more clarity and focus in challenging times

Increased ability to respond more effectively to complex or difficult situations

Increased ability to see situations more clearly

Improved concentration

Better problem solving

Better decision making

Improved ability to orient attention

Increased working memory

Better planning and organization

More able to think long term as well as short-to-medium term

Enhanced creativity

Improved relationships and communication

Enhanced emotional intelligence, including improved empathy, increased emotional regulation and increased social skills

More able to prevent and deal with conflict, with fewer conduct and anger management problems, for example

Greater 'presence'

Greater self-awareness and awareness of others

Enhanced ability to recognize, slow down or stop automatic and habitual reactions

More authentic leadership

More intuitive

Better able to manage and prevent stress

Increased wellbeing generally

Increased sense of calmness

More relaxed

More self-acceptance

Increased quality of sleep

Lower rates of health-related absenteeism

Lower levels of psychological distress

Higher levels of work satisfaction

Increased self-esteem

Decreased negative affect/emotions

Decreased anxiety

Decreased depression

CASE STUDY   Making every minute count

For Sheila, a Moscow-based lawyer, mindfulness is helping her make the most of her time. She was introduced to mindfulness through her coach, Sally-Anne Airey. Here's her story:

> I trained as a lawyer at a time when every six-minute unit of my working day had to be accounted for. Productivity was measured by my ability to maximize the number of these units I effectively 'worked', recorded and then charged to a client.
>
> Having worked as a lawyer for nearly 20 years and now also juggling life as a wife and mum, I find that I spend much of both my work and personal life making every minute count. And whilst I'm reasonably organized and productive when it comes to to-do lists, I'm not so good at finding time for myself or at relaxing and enjoying just sitting with friends.
>
> Mindfulness and the breathing and visualizing techniques that I understand form a part of this suggest to me a way of finding time for myself and of refocusing priorities a little.
>
> Armed with this expectation, I'd originally started trying some of these techniques but with very little success. My efforts seemed to lead me to an increased sense of physical tension and emotional frustration ('Why can't this work for me?!').
>
> I'm glad I tried again. One size invariably doesn't fit all and it was Sally-Anne's flexible coaching approach with the use of different words and perspectives which helped me to discover the beginnings of an understanding about present-moment awareness.
>
> Funnily enough, I've experimented perhaps more regularly with my children so far than on myself. The benefits of being able to push a pause button are even more clearly seen in children, I suspect – quickening the process of my younger son coming out of a tantrum, helping the older one having trouble settling to sleep at night, even just pausing from the overexcited running, jumping and silliness that come with the anticipation of a special outing.
>
> In a personal context, my challenge has been coming up with effective triggers to remind me to stop, even if for just long enough to bring myself back to the present moment. I can see that it will take practice to grasp both regularly effective triggers and a sense of the present moment for longer periods of time. However, even these initial, very short, interludes have provided a tangible sense of regeneration.
>
> I've experimented with the trigger 'being stuck at a red traffic light' – I love the fact that such a dreaded time waster now gives me a gift instead. I'm also working on trying to remember to attempt present-moment awareness when I feel anger rising at something my children are doing. Of course a little more challenging... but surely worth the reward if I can get there?!
>
> And although my initial explorations into mindfulness have been rather rudimentary, I have experienced some rewards in return. I've felt that sense of calm and clearer thought that comes with taking a little rest. I've also most certainly enjoyed the readjusting of perspective that comes with checking from overview. Most certainly practice is required before any sustained sense of mindfulness can be obtained but these initial rewards have been worth the investment – the 'minutes still count', just for something else these days!

In the next part, we start to look at how we can work with mindfulness around common core underpinnings of the coaching process.

PART TWO
Fundamental principles

In this section, we look at how mindfulness can inform the coaching process generally. We will look at developing presence, attunement and resonance; curiosity and non-judgement; and compassion. We will also explore areas of potential tension between mindfulness and coaching and mindfulness including foci on being versus doing, and present-moment versus the future.

Presence

04

> *If I were to wish for anything, I should not wish for wealth and power, but for the passionate sense of the potential... Pleasure disappoints, possibility never. And what wine is so foaming, what so fragrant, what so intoxicating, as possibility!*
>
> **SØREN KIERKEGAARD, EXISTENȚIAL PHILOSOPHER**

Much is written in the coaching literature about presence – we could say it is the cornerstone of all good coaching. In this chapter, we explore what presence actually is, its importance in coaching and how mindfulness can help us develop it.

As Siegel (2010a) says, 'The way in which we are grounded in ourselves, open to others, and participate fully in the life of the mind are important aspects of our presence at the heart of relationships that help others grow.' Presence is the magic ingredient in coaching. We usually know when we're not being or haven't been present. I know from experience that when I haven't had time to ground myself and become mindful, it takes a while for me to 'land'. I experience disconnect from my client. I'm not truly there for them. If it's a new client, this could be detrimental to our fledgling relationship and it could take longer to reach a place of trust. If it's a chemistry meeting, it could mean the coaching not even going ahead.

Sometimes, we might suddenly catch ourselves in the middle of a session, realizing our mind has wandered ('I wonder if we'll get onto her issue around saying no to people') or thinking about what to ask next, or worrying that the session isn't going very well. We might be congratulating ourselves on how well the session is going. We might catch ourselves thinking about something totally unconnected to the coaching session. These are all examples of us not being present.

What about being present? Again, I think we all know when we are pulling this off. For me, it's as if everything else falls away. I park my ego to some degree, at least. It's all about the client's agenda, and any desires to try out any new tricks I've recently picked up or any concerns about my perform-ance are all put to one side. I'm in flow. I feel very engaged and alert. I feel a pull towards the client and a connection between us. It's just the client and myself, and as Peter Hawkins, founder of the Bath Consultancy Group, would say, 'the space in between'. Nothing else matters for now. I am listen-ing intently, with my mind, body, heart and soul or spiritual essence of some sort. I am fully available for my client, fully centred and grounded and open to what may emerge. It feels brilliant. And it is at times like these that coach-ing works best. Sadly, being fully present for every single moment of a whole one- or two-hour session is not as easy as we'd like. Sometimes it just happens naturally. But how can we increase the chances of it happening? Or even reach a point of mastery where this is the norm? I believe like Siegel that presence is a learnable skill, and that mindfulness practice helps us develop this multifaceted skill, as more and more coaches are finding out.

I use mindfulness to stay present for my client. If I find myself carried away on a train of thought I gently bring myself back to the present moment so that I may listen and keep my intuition available.
Steve Kennedy, an executive/business coach based in the United Kingdom

For my part I think a coach can very usefully incorporate mindfulness into their practice as integral to their developing their capacity to be present, for their client and with themselves; and this is also tied into intention. The same applies for supervisors. You can also think of mindfulness as akin to state management, and so see the Buddha as the first NLP master practitioner.
Ken Smith, coach and coach supervisor, and founder of the Coaches in Government Network which ran for five years in the United Kingdom

---

Definitions

So what is presence and how can mindfulness help here? The International Coach Federation (ICF 2010) defines presence as:

the ability to be fully conscious and create a spontaneous relationship with the client, employing a style which is open, flexible and confident.

Silsbee (2010a) defines it as:

a state of awareness, in the moment, characterized by the felt experience of timeliness, connectedness, and a larger truth.

One of the qualities of presence is deep listening but there are other qualities too, qualities which make this profound listening possible, such as warmth and openness. Silsbee (2010b), says:

> This level of openness, of listening coupled with acceptance and support, is what we call presence. Presence is beyond the skill of listening and is what allows real listening to take place.

Helminski (2000), a transpersonal psychologist and co-director of the Threshold Society, a Sufism educational organization, describes presence as follows:

> Presence is the way in which we occupy space, as well as the way we flow and move. Presence shapes our self-image and emotional tone. Presence determines the degree of our alertness, openness and warmth. Presence decides whether we leak and scatter our energy or embody and direct it. Presence is the human self-awareness that is the end result of the evolution of life on this planet.

Presence is about being open and unattached to any particular outcome. It is what Henry Kimsey-House, Karen Kimsey-House and Phillip Sandahl (and the late Laura Whitworth in the earlier edition) call 'spaciousness' (Kimsey-House *et al* 2011):

> For the coach, spaciousness also means complete detachment from any particular course of action or any results clients achieve… the spaciousness of the relationship requires that clients have many channels open to creative inspiration and must not be restricted to the coach's good ideas… Being present allows us to dance in the moment, in just this moment… To 'dance in the moment' is to be very present to what is happening right now and to respond to that stimulus rather than to a master plan.

I love the image of dancing in the moment, or of dancing on shifting carpets, rather than sitting back as the rug is pulled from under us. We often think of mindfulness as being very still and calm, and of course, stillness and calmness are part of its nature. However, we can be mindful and present when we're doing things too, when we're moving. We don't have to be serious either, we can smile and laugh and dance mindfully and with presence. Sometimes our clients will need us to hold the 'sacred space' (Campbell 2008) quietly, calmly and with stillness. At other times, they will need us to dance with them, to co-create something exciting and transformational. We can do both with mindfulness and presence.

Some people use the term 'presence' interchangeably, with or instead of the term 'mindfulness'. For me, however, they are closely related but not the same. I agree with Silsbee (2010b) that mindfulness is a route to presence.

Presence is the underlying state that we access through mindfulness and is also available to the client in the coaching conversation. Presence is the state that allows us to be the most resourceful, resilient, and self-generative person we can be, and this is, in fact, part of the promise of coaching.

Openness

To be present to and for our client requires us to be open and expansive, rather than closed and contracted. Open to ourselves and to our client; open to the wider system and to possibility, unattached to outcome, as we've seen.

I find Siegel's (2010a) exploration of primes and possibility helpful when thinking about how mindfulness can support coaching to be a much more creative and emergent process, and help us to be more present. Through this lens, we view reality shaped by probabilities, a view supported by quantum mechanics, and we're invited to picture the sense of completely open possibility within a singular plane of reality. As events happen, our position with regard to this 'open plane of possibility' shifts and we move towards a 'state of probability', which we can imagine as plateaus jutting out from the plane. He invites us to then imagine we move from open possibility to probability to activation of an actual committed event, which can be represented as a 'peak of activation' – a spike sticking out from the plane. The concept is more complicated than this, and Siegel explains it very well, but basically, in the open plane of possibility, 'a nearly infinite number of combinations of neural firings and subjective experiences are available'. And it very much behoves us as coaches to use mindfulness to hone our ability to stay within the open plane of possibility, so we are less rigid, less influenced by our moods or personalities, more able to cultivate creativity and presence in our lives.

As Siegel (2010a) says:

> being present with others involves the experience of openness to whatever arises in reality. Presence means being open now, to whatever is. We come to acknowledge our own proclivities and in that awareness, free ourselves to move from peak to plateau with ease and will.

Presence requires a tolerance for uncertainty, ambiguity and vulnerability, which some of us will inevitably find easier than others. But we can all gradually learn to loosen the grip of habit and embedded aspects of our 'personality' to become more mindful. We can all learn to monitor and modify our internal world so we can 'cultivate presence as not only an intentionally created state, but as an enduring trait in our lives,' says Siegel (2010a).

Becoming well acquainted with our own tendencies of 'neuroceptive evaulation' is helpful in developing presence, suggests Siegel, and mindfulness supports us in doing that. The brain continually monitors the external and internal environment for signs of danger – this process is called 'neuroception'. Our past experiences, especially of unresolved trauma, affect our current assessments, setting our filters and making certain actions or interpretations more likely. We look at stress in Chapter 12 but it's worth mentioning here to illustrate neuroception. If something has triggered us into the reactive state of fight–flight–freeze, it follows that we can't at the same time be in the open state of receptive presence. We shut down and disengage, and our options are limited. Not how we want to be in our coaching, and not what we want for our clients while we're coaching.

We explored in Chapter 3 what happens in the brain when we practise mindfulness, and in Chapter 12 we explore how it helps us shift to an approach rather than an avoidance state. Siegel (2010a) says because of how mindfulness awareness practices help us create receptivity and an approach state, they can be considered the basic training of the mind – he says for therapists, but I believe equally so for coaches.

He says integration is at the heart of presence: 'with integration we have openness of possibility, a fluidity of movement in and out of propensity, probability and activation, and back again to undefined, open possibility. This is the harmonious flow of a receptive state where we feel joined with others, and ourselves' (Siegel 2010a).

When I'm truly present, it feels as if I am plugged into something, to some kind of source. I certainly don't feel like I am doing all the work. Others I have spoken to describe a similar feeling. Some might interpret this as being attuned to something spiritual, God, the divine, or whatever, others might interpret it as being tuned into cosmic energy, and others still will simply see it as something physiological. One coach responding to my survey, whose reasons for practising mindfulness include being more present for their client, gave the following reason: 'to help me live in a state of grace'.

We each have our own interpretations but it seems that a sense of being tuned in somehow is pretty common. Personally, the sensation I have when I'm present with clients has the same taste or such-ness as when I'm meditating or doing something mindfully.

Presence is:

- deep listening;
- openness to possibility;
- availability;
- warmth;
- vulnerability;
- being unattached to outcomes;
- being non-judgemental;
- connectedness/interconnectedness;
- being able to stay with uncertainty/being able to dance in the moment/on shifting carpets/with the system;
- being in an 'approach' state.

Mindfulness practices

Mindfulness practices which aim to help us become more grounded, centred and open to whatever comes up will be particularly helpful when we want to enhance presence. So for example:

Three-minute breathing space (Chapter 9);

Walking meditation (Chapter 8);

Centring (see below);

Body scan (this chapter);

Witness meditation (Chapter 6).

I invite you to practise Centring (which is really a somatic/ontological practice although it is very mindful). I use this with many of my clients, both within the session and for them to do outside the session. And I use it frequently to prepare for coaching sessions and for presentations.

Practice: Centring

Come into a standing position. Take a few deep breaths. Close your eyes if you wish or gaze gently downwards.

Length

Imagine a vertical line running from your head down through your body to your feet. This line represents your dignity in the world. Stand tall, imagining an invisible thread pulling you gently skywards from the crown of your head. Your back is straight but not arched. Hunch up your shoulders, then let them fall back down so they become relaxed. Move your jaw around so it becomes relaxed. Your hands are loose by your side. Your feet are hip-width apart and have roots extending into the ground. Notice how long you feel.

Width

Move your arms out to the sides and move them up and down so you occupy space on each side. This is your width and is about your social standing, your right to be here on this planet. Notice how wide you feel.

Depth

Imagine that attached behind you onto your coccyx is a tail, a strong powerful dinosaur tail. This tail consists of all that supports you, all the learning and self-development over the years, your training and education, all those supporting you – loved ones, work colleagues. Become aware of your depth, front and back, what supports you and what goes to the front of you. Notice how deep you feel.

Tune in

Take some more deep but relaxed breaths, feeling your abdomen rise as you breathe in. Tune into what matters to you, what you really care about. Hold that deep inside you.

Wriggle your fingers and toes and gently come back to the room.

Adapted from Strozzi-Heckler (2007)

Setting up a practice

In the beginner's mind there are many possibilities, but in the expert's there are few.

Shunryu Suzuki, Zen monk

There are plenty of resources out there such as books by Jon Kabat-Zinn or Mark Williams (2011), some of which have CDs, which are useful if you wish to be guided through some of the more commonly known mindfulness practices. However, you can also read the text of the practices included in this book a few times until you are familiar with the process, then try them out. Below are some tips and pointers for getting a mindfulness practice up and running, if you haven't got one in place already. If you already have one, please feel free to skip this part.

Is meditation vital?

I believe a little mindfulness can go a long way and that very often once people have had a taste of mindfulness, they are hooked. It might take them years to establish a regular meditation practice but very often they do come back to do just that. However, like Michael Chaskalson, I believe that if we are serious about using mindfulness in our coaching work, we should have a regular mindfulness practice of our own – preferably a daily practice including meditation. I often get asked whether meditation is vital. My answer is that, no, it isn't vital to get something good out of practising, but I really do recommend it. It is very much worth the effort – if you meditate, you will reap many benefits that you won't if you don't.

It does seem somewhat hypocritical to be singing the praises of mindfulness and seeking to teach others when you aren't practising what you preach but also because if you do have an established practice, you will embody and role model mindfulness. As Chaskalson says, 'Those offering to train people to train others should absolutely at the minimum tick these boxes or they are out to lunch. And I don't see why we don't insist on people having a daily practice. I work with leaders who manage this.'

There is obviously a spectrum, with coaches and other practitioners sharing with clients various mindfulness practices they have come across here and there – and tried out for themselves at one end, while at the other are those who have set themselves up as mindfulness trainers, who may well be coaches as well, and who may be incorporating mindfulness training as part of leadership development or other kinds of programmes along with coaching, for example. Here are some tips on getting started, or on embedding a mindfulness practice further.

Setting your intent

Setting up a practice takes discipline and commitment. Jon Kabat-Zinn likens the required approach to that of an athlete's. We don't wait for it to be a sunny day to train, we train regularly.

As we know, with any behavioural change, it helps to explore first why you want to do it and what you want out of it. And as with anything that requires lots of regular practice, we have to stay motivated. Although it might seem at odds with the non-striving emphasis in mindfulness, it can help to set ourselves goals (somewhat ironically, perhaps).

Setting time aside for meditation or other practices can seem self-indulgent so it's important to keep our reasons for doing it at the forefront of our minds. Jetsun Milarepa apparently used to talk about mindfulness being like a grandfather who has to constantly watch over his spoiled grandchild of a deluded mind, to save him from disaster. Jon Kabat-Zinn talks about 'tuning your instrument before taking it out on the road' (YouTube interview). And our instrument – our mind – gets out of tune very easily so it's important to keep up our practice.

Take some time to reflect on why it matters to you to embed a mindfulness practice. Ask yourself questions including:

- Why should I practise?
- What do I hope to get out of it?
- What is the price I pay for not doing it? What do I stand to lose?
- What are realistic expectations around my practice?

Perhaps write down your reasons for setting it up in the first place and keeping it going. On the MBCT course I attended, we wrote ourselves a letter at the end about what we'd got out of the programme and why we wanted to keep up our practice. We placed the letter in a self-addressed envelope which the teacher sent to us several months later. It was a lovely idea and really served to remind me why I needed to keep motivated. We all know even the best practices slip with time, often when we most need them.

The practices

I've included most of the main practices included in MBSR and MBCT programmes. However, I've also taken the liberty of including some meditations which don't strictly fall into the mindfulness category if we take the 'purist' definition of paying attention, as discussed in Chapter 1. Once people start to explore mindfulness, including mindfulness meditation, they are usually happy to incorporate other types of meditation into what they do.

There are lots of wonderful books out there, some of which I have already mentioned. I recommend reading around the subject beyond this book. I never find it dull, personally. It's exciting getting to know our own minds and there are some fabulous mindfulness teachers who've trodden the road towards full self-awareness and present-moment awareness gently but for many years and have deeply inspiring, enormously helpful and sometimes 'mind-blowing' tales to tell and lessons to share. I wholeheartedly recommend any reader who has not participated in a programme such as MBCT or MBSR to do so – there is no requisite to be spiritual! I also recommend attending a regular group meditation class – this keeps up the motivation, and the energy and learning can be heightened when you meditate in a group.

Your approach

Approach your practice with the principles, values and intentions we mention throughout this book, including curiosity, compassion (particularly for yourself) and non-judgement. Always have a beginner's mind.

Try to practise somewhere quiet and peaceful, where you won't be disturbed by anyone or by the telephone or mobile ringing. Remember why it's important to do your practice – there are so many rewards to reap. What you get back will increase exponentially the more you practise, but even a minute is better than nothing. Pat yourself on your back whenever you set aside time to practise and remember it's totally normal for our minds to wander, that's what they do. The idea that some people have of meditating is that we clear our minds of all thoughts. I stress again, this isn't it at all. Thoughts will be there. When our minds wander, we gently bring them back to the object of focus, whatever that may be, or our intention, whatever that may be.

Reflection

Once you've finished each practice, whether it's your first or millionth time, however you 'judge' the practice to have gone (try to get out of the habit of doing this!), congratulate yourself on taking the time to practise. And then my invitation is that you take a little more time to reflect on how it went for you. Just notice what came and what comes up and ask yourself:

Did I find it easy to stay with the practice?

Was it easy to remain curious?

What was getting in the way when I wasn't able to be curious?

Was I able to bring my mind back? Without beating myself up?

What happened when I brought my mind back?

Did I notice anything unexpected?

What was I feeling? Sad, bored, happy, restless, relaxed, scared, angry, panicky?

Did I find myself interpreting or was I able to just notice?

It's good to keep a record over time of how it goes for you, and any thoughts about how your mindfulness practice relates to your coaching practice.

Do you notice your ability to be curious increasing? To focus? To be non-judgemental? To stay with something even if it doesn't really interest you?

Where is there resistance and contraction against this practice?

What else is emerging?

Remember, there are no rights and wrongs, it's not a competition.

Many Eastern meditators and mindfulness practitioners, including the Dalai Lama, are struck by how serious we become about our practice in the West. Taking it seriously in the sense of it being important to us is one thing. But we shouldn't forget it's meant to be a life-enhancing practice. One which helps us become present to the present. Enjoy!

The Body scan

I now invite you to practise the Body scan. It's one of the first exercises participants on MBCT and MBSR programmes will learn. And it's a great one for helping us develop our ability to be curious and to enquire without shutting down possibility and thinking we have to have an answer. I must confess this used to be one of my least favourite mindfulness practices. For some reason, I had a lot of resistance to it. Often when people start doing this exercise, they find it hard to do it without falling asleep. I did. It might have been because I was avoiding something but it can be very relaxing. And it is used with teenagers to help them fall asleep, as part of the Mindfulness in Schools project, although it is called Beditation rather than the Body scan and is slightly different. There is nothing wrong with falling asleep during a mindfulness practice, of course, unless you are at work, but with the Body scan, the idea is more to 'fall awake'.

When I didn't fall asleep, to begin with, I most certainly didn't 'fall awake'. I would become very aware of aches and pains, or of gaps in my awareness, or would feel 'fizzy' or fidgety, or bored. All par for the course on journeys such as these. However, as I practised more and more, I began to look forward to this particular exercise. I still fall asleep sometimes if I'm practising lying down but usually manage to avoid self-recrimination when that happens, reframing it instead as recovery time. And I do a 'bedi-tation' version if I can't get to sleep or if I wake up stressed during the night. Increasingly, however, I manage to stay awake and find I'm more and more able to approach my bodily sensations with curiosity and just 'be' with what is going on. It helps me hone this skill generally and I most definitely bring that to my coaching – I notice so much more these days.

So, if you haven't ever done the Body scan (or even if you have, lots of times), I invite you to give it a go now.

Practice: The Body scan

Find a time and place where you won't be disturbed – for 20–30 minutes or so (perhaps start with 10 minutes). Turn off your mobile and congratulate yourself for giving yourself this time. The invitation is to be open, gentle and curious, to let go and 'fall awake'.

Lying down on a mat or a firm bed, let your body relax into the floor, bed or chair, but maintaining an alert position. You might want to fetch a blanket to cover yourself with. You can also do this practice sitting up.

Relaxing your shoulders, take a few deep breaths, letting your arms lie by your sides. Gently closing your eyes.

Squeezing all your muscles as tightly as you can – your facial muscles, your eyes, your mouth, your hands, your arms, your abdomen, your buttocks and pelvic floor, your legs, your feet and any other muscle you can identify. As tightly as you can – squeezing… and relaxing.

Now, starting at your feet, turning your attention to these collections of bone, muscle, tendons. Imagining you're shining a spotlight onto your feet, just exploring gently, compassionately and without judgement what's there.

What bodily sensations are there? Tightness? Fizziness? Heat? Cold?

Can you feel anything touching your feet – a blanket, the floor, your socks or tights? Focusing on each of your toes, can you feel each one as separate units? What feelings are you noticing? Sometimes it can be hard to focus on or feel a part of your body. Try 'breathing in' to that part as you breathe out.

When your mind wanders, that's fine, accept that it's natural, no need to judge or evaluate. Don't beat yourself up. Congratulating yourself for noticing and gently bringing your mind back to the practice. Minds wander, that's what they do.

Moving on from your feet to your ankles, what can you feel? Do you notice any contractions? Any pain, any throbbing, any other sensations? Try to avoid labelling the sensations as good or bad – just being as curious as you can about what is really there.

When you're ready, moving up to your calves. Again, being curious: what sensations are here? And again, if your mind goes off, just gently bringing it back, *without judgement, with kindness, with curiosity, with compassion.*

And when you're ready, the invitation is to move up to your knees, to your thighs, to your pelvic area and buttocks, to your abdomen, your chest, your hands – including your fingers and thumbs – your arms, your shoulders.

And finishing off with your jaw, your face and your head. Just noticing, exploring, being curious, without getting caught up in storylines – so no 'I knew I should have gone to the gym'/'I'm really tense – they're working me too hard'/'What's that pain – is it something sinister?'/'I'm soooo tired, what's it all about?'

You will catch yourself bringing in judgement, or making assumptions about what you might be feeling and what it might mean. But that really isn't the point. If you find it hard, just do what you can. Be kind to yourself.

You may notice emotions carried in certain parts of the body or that certain physical sensations are linked to certain emotions. As with physical sensations, just notice what's there as your emotions arise, shift, change and fade away.

When you're ready, coming gently back to the room.

Capture any reflections in your journal.

Becoming present is the first step in attuning to others, which we will look at in Chapter 6. But first we will explore further how mindfulness can foster openness in the coaching process, along with curiosity and non-judgement, which are linked to creativity.

Curiosity, enquiry and non-judgement

05

> *Flow with whatever may happen and let your mind be free.*
> *Stay centred by accepting whatever you are doing.*
> *This is the ultimate.*
>
> **CHUANG TSU (399–295 BC), PHILOSOPHER**

Curiosity

Educator Dr William Arthur Ward has been quoted as saying 'curiosity is the wick in the candle of learning'. Curiosity – the spirit of enquiry – and non-judgement are at the heart of both coaching and mindfulness. In the last chapter, we explored presence and how mindfulness can help us stay open to possibility. In this chapter, we explore how it can support the development of curiosity and non-judgement in coaching, which are linked to presence.

Myles Downey, founder of the School of Coaching and author of *Effective Thinking*, has argued that one of the main jobs of the coach is to get clients to think. And it's not just any kind of thinking we seek to enable, it's thinking outside the box, thinking creatively, being non-judgemental and open to what emerges. If this is what coaching aims to do, we need to be curious, enquiring and non-judgemental for ourselves and our clients. Mindfulness is perfectly suited to support us in pursuit of these qualities in our coaching practice.

Enquiry

Tim Malnick, an organization consultant and coach based in the United Kingdom, has taught meditation for a decade. He frequently introduces meditation and awareness practices to leaders and groups, addressing questions of learning and change, although he tends to talk about 'awareness' or 'working with direct experience' rather than 'mindfulness'. He suggests that acquiring tools, techniques and practices is only part of the mindfulness story. An important part is that of profound enquiry.

He says: 'It's about deep enquiry into how we usually see things, and about an invitation to look at the world in a different way.' He points out that traditionally in teachings on mindfulness, the 'context and the question of *why* we use it [mindfulness] are really important'. The 'why' tends to include the development of compassion and wisdom, and an understanding of interconnectedness or interdependence, for example. However, in the context of working with leaders, 'it is about noticing some of the deeply held views we have about self, world and work and reflecting on how well they are actually working for us and others, as well as how much they actually relate to our direct experience'.

'Mindfulness involves developing a sense of openness and genuine curiosity about what arises in our experience. As we develop a practice of mindfulness, we increase our ability to be gently curious and to enquire without preconceived ideas. It can lead us into some insightful and somewhat provocative questions around our experience of work.'

As he points out, as we start to practise 'real mindfulness and gradually learn to rest in the present moment, we can find ourselves on a path along which all sorts of questions come up, many of them profound'.

Non-judgement

Being non-judgemental in order to better hold a space of enquiry for ourselves and our clients is no mean feat. As coaches, we set out to challenge assumptions in our clients, but of course, we need to role model that in the way we show up. Developing a mindfulness practice helps us suspend our judgements so we can be truly curious, and creative in our coaching. We explore non-judgement in relation to creativity in Chapter 18. Another element to this is compassion – self-compassion and compassion to others, which we can develop as part of our mindfulness practice. Again, we will explore this further later on.

As Malnick says, we come to mindfulness – and anything – with a bundle of preconceptions such as 'calm body equals good, jittery body equals bad, no thoughts is good' whereas the aim should be to just notice what is. This is where it can get a bit tricky for us as coaches and we will delve more deeply into what some might see as different foci in coaching in Chapter 6. At this stage, perhaps we can see that a lot of the time in coaching, as in mindfulness, we seek to be like a mirror or still water, reflecting what is to our client. Not necessarily trying to change anything or our own shape to accommodate what is, simply reflecting, acknowledging and accepting what is. When we're not trying to hold on ever so tightly in case a chink of something that challenges our thinking comes through, we create space for insight into what is really going on for us or around us, for ourselves and our clients. We can coach from the plane of possibility Siegel talks about.

Reflection

There is another type of reflection that's key in good coaching, and mindfulness. Like so many of us, I encourage my clients to keep a journal to aid and embed their learning, and I do so myself. Reflection is a core component in coaching – both in coaching others and in our own development and growth, as we know. So much of the deep work on the part of the client goes on outside the coaching sessions. Personally, I have learnt so much from sitting quietly down with my journal, making notes, and then looking back over what I've written before and reflecting again on that, trying out new things and recording how this went, and reflecting again. The fast train between London Victoria and Brighton on the south coast of England has witnessed numerous aha moments!

Practising mindfulness is one way to foster this ability to reflect, to slow down, and observe. It's the Observer mind or the Witness from Chapter 1 again, being more able to gather and notice data, and to get ourselves out of the way so we can actually see what's in front of our noses. It's about compassion, curiosity and non-judgement.

Murray Thomas, an executive/business coach with a mindfulness practice, who is based in the United Kingdom, says: 'In my experience, mindfulness is a key tool in helping improve self-awareness through non-judgemental reflection. The very act of reflecting in this way has enabled many of my clients to reframe their issues with more clarity and much less angst.'

The sound of silence

The first stage of learning is silence, the second stage is listening.

Maori proverb

Sometimes we can fall into the trap as coaches of thinking that in order to come from a place of curiosity – and usefulness – we need to keep bombarding the client with clever questions. Practising mindfulness – particularly solitary meditation – can help us learn to appreciate the sound and quality of silence, and be more inclined to wish that for our clients. Again, it helps us get ourselves out of the way so we can be comfortable with silence or ask the kinds of questions Nancy Kline, creator of The Thinking Environment and author of *Time to Think*, recommends such as 'What else?' or 'What more do you feel, think or want to say?' These are questions we may resist, feeling they don't allow us to show off our tricks of the trade.

Developing mindfulness can help us inhabit a less self-serving place, one from which we're better equipped to serve the client's needs and we're not trying so hard to be clever. It can help us build up our tolerance for silence – if we've been building in time in our lives to be still and quiet, the silence becomes less deafening and the urge to 'do' easier to ignore. Being silent in a coaching session can be enormously productive but it requires us to be truly present, and to be just as curious – or more so – as we would be if we were asking questions. It also requires us to be attuned to the client – more on this in the following chapter – so we can know if and when to bring an end to the silence, if the client doesn't naturally do so, for example.

Kline is a great advocate of silence and of deep listening. She says that giving ourselves and our clients the chance to see how brilliantly we can think because of our rich and radiant silence is worth the effort. 'Attention is an act of creation – in the presence of our listening and silence, clients can generate everything they need from the session,' she said at the British Association of Counselling and Psychotherapy Coaching Division's inaugural conference in London in June 2011. And in an article for *Coaching at Work* (Kline 2006), she wrote:

> Too many coaches fail to be catalytic listeners. They think that listening is linear. That it is lined up waiting to speak. Too many coaches watch for the holes, the pause, the intake of breath, the looking off into space, the slightest indication that their client is finished so that they can speak. They miss the catalyst. They miss the ignition that is inside the listening.

Mindfulness helps us as coaches to be comfortable with listening, to be properly curious and non-judgemental and to stay with the silence when it is truly golden.

The Witness meditation is wonderful for helping us develop non-judgement and openness to what is, but first I'd like to introduce you to a simple Awareness of breath practice.

Practice: Awareness of breath

Ensure you won't be disturbed for 5 or 10 minutes. Set your intention to allow yourself this time to try this practice, with curiosity, non-judgement and compassion. Make yourself comfortable, preferably in a sitting position, your back straight but not overly arched, your neck relaxed and your shoulders unhunched. Close your eyes or gaze at the floor with your eyes half-closed and without actually focusing on what is before you. Rest your hands on your lap.

Now gently bringing your attention to your breath. Just breathing normally, breathing in, breathing out, the most natural thing in the world. Without trying to change anything, noticing how you breathe. Not *thinking about* the breath, but just *being with* the breath.

Focusing your attention on your in-breath. Noticing how your breath feels as it comes in at the tip of your nostrils. Noticing any sensations there, any changes in temperature, any tickling, any other sensations.

When your mind wanders, as it surely will, gently bringing it back to the breath, using the breath as an anchor.

As you breathe in, saying to yourself, 'Breathing in'.

As you breathe out, saying to yourself, 'Breathing out'.

Bringing compassion to yourself in the practice. Just breathing and noticing what there is.

And now bringing your attention to how your chest feels as you breathe in and out.

And noticing how it feels in your abdomen as you breathe in and out.

Gently bringing your mind back when it wanders and congratulating yourself for noticing your attention has wandered.

And when you are ready, gently coming back to the room.

If you wish, you may like to capture any reflections in your journal.

In the next chapter, we will look at attunement and resonance, which practices like the Body scan (the previous chapter) also help with.

Attunement and resonance

06

> *You never really understand a person until you consider things from his point of view... until you climb inside of his skin and walk around in it.*
>
> **ATTICUS FINCH, *TO KILL A MOCKINGBIRD* (BY HARPER LEE)**

We've already talked about presence, which is of course important in both building and maintaining relationships with clients. In this chapter, we explore relationships further and how mindfulness can help us build rapport with, attune to and resonate with our clients.

I sometimes recall the English proverb 'A bad workman blames his tools' when reflecting on what worked well and what not so well in a coaching programme. When we have a sense that things could have been better – even where we have checked in with the client and they're satisfied with how the coaching has gone – we can fall into the trap of wishing we hadn't used certain tools and techniques, or that we'd used other ones or more of them. We can overemphasize the importance of the bells, ribbons and tassels, particularly when we first start coaching. However, what matters most is how we show up. It matters not one jot how many tricks of the trade we have up our sleeves if we don't get the relationship right. Yes, of course we co-create the relationship with our clients, that's part of what makes coaching exciting and interesting. But actually, the onus is on us as coaches, as supposed experts on the process, to look after the relationship. And mindfulness helps us do that.

Erik de Haan, director of the Ashridge Centre for Coaching, says the coaching relationship is the 'only genuinely effective ingredient we are able to influence' (De Haan 2008). He suggests that we can draw conclusions for coaching from research in psychotherapy about what makes a difference to outcomes.

According to a study by Hyun-nie and Wampold (2001), for instance, there is *no difference* in terms of effectiveness between different psycho-therapeutic approaches (as practised by professional practitioners rather than lay therapists). There is no single form of therapy that works consistently better than others, not even for specific client groups. What does make a difference? A reliable relationship, an 'effective personality' and consistency of adherence to a particular approach, according to research such as Rosenzweig's (1936).

De Haan says:

> It is not just about the issue or the problem, and not even just about coachees and their issues, or coachees and their organizations and their issues, it is actually mainly about the relationship. If the relationship itself is actually good, there is a better chance of change for the better – even if, for example, the question is not entirely addressed.

Working on the coaching relationship is one of 10 'commandments' for the executive coach proposed by de Haan, drawing on meta-analyses in psychotherapy and other reliable research data. Other 'commandments' include 'consider the coaching situation from your coachee's perspective', and 'try to stay fresh and unbiased'. We looked at how mindfulness can help us stay unbiased in Chapter 4, and this can be helpful when we build relationships with others. But how else can mindfulness help us attend to relationships in coaching, beyond presence, so we can better attune to others and look out on the world with their eyes?

Mirror, mirror

Historically, being good at teamwork and cooperation has helped us survive. Until agriculture hit the scene 10,000 years ago, humans cohabited in groups of up to 150 people (Norenzayan and Shariff 2008). Those who fared best in a harsh environment with scant resources and plenty of predators were those who could cooperate well with one another. Our very survival depended on being able to empathize and our neural networks have developed accordingly. Our ability to read others' internal states excels that of any other species, as far as we are aware.

We can sense and simulate within ourselves others' actions, emotions and thoughts. The very same networks that are activated in our brains when we do something apparently 'light up' when we see someone else doing it so we have a felt sense of what the other person is experiencing (Preston and de Waal 2002). These are called mirror neurons and they may be essential to how we attune to others' internal states, according to researchers such as neuroscientist Marco Iacoboni (2008).

The networks that produce our own feelings help us make sense of others' feelings. Becoming more aware of our own emotional and bodily states helps us be more aware of those of others. For those of you who are interested in the science: the more aware we are of these states, the more our insula and anterior cingulated cortex activate and the better we are at reading others (Singer *et al* 2004) A third set of brain circuits helps us read others' thoughts and beliefs, working with the other circuits so that we have an overall perception of others' inner worlds (Singer 2006).

As with much of the research in new fields such as neuroscience, it is still early days. When it comes to mirror neurons, clinical and organizational psychologist Professor Paul Brown says: 'There's an idea that because we've got mirror neurons, we will be empathetic but I don't think it's as simple as that. Our capacity to be empathetic is determined by our emotional development... the trouble is that lots of the work has originated in primates but they've no language and they're not self-reflective.' Siegel too urges us to keep in mind that the mirror neuron story is only one possible view and needs further validation but we get the idea – there is a wealth of information available to us if only we learn to pay good attention.

Defining attunement

If presence is our openness to the emergence of possibilities, attunement can be defined as 'how we focus our attention on others and take their essence into our own inner world' (Siegel 2010a). It's about taking our presence into the social sphere. As Siegel says, as signals are sent from one person to another, we have the chance to tune into and attend fully to these incoming streams of information, rather than becoming carried away by preconceived ideas or perceptual biases.

Siegel (2010a) outlines the following internal states that we need to attune to another:

- an intention to help;
- a neural stance of positive regard which probably involves the social engagement system;
- a desire to connect and assist;
- an interest in supporting another in kindness and compassion.

He also talks about a 'window of tolerance'. Outside this window, we become dysfunctional – at one end we approach chaos, at the other rigidity. When we're working with others, we need to know our own windows and note which ones restrict our ability to be present and attuned with others' emotions, and resonate with their internal states. We all have different triggers, and mindfulness helps us build self-awareness so we can recognize what these are and when we've been set off so we can be more present for the client.

One of the issues I've taken to supervision is what happens in me when I'm faced with a client who is upset. I find it easy to connect with others, to feel empathy, sympathy and compassion. However, I've had to work at staying neutral with clients experiencing strong emotions. I want to make the other person feel better. I want them to stop feeling sad or upset. Of course, actually, what I want too, is to stop them making *me* feel sad or upset. When I pay attention, I notice how I contract in my stomach, my shoulders hunch up, I catch myself leaning forwards, possibly encroaching on the client's space at times. I have to work at not getting in the way of whatever needs to happen for and in them. My ability to stay truly present, to stay on the plane of possibility and to not shut the client down is at risk. If I get too caught up in how their sadness or anger makes *me* feel, I can kid myself that I am feeling empathy and compassion, but really I might be missing vital clues from them and might be missing a wonderful opportunity for them to grow. I might intervene for the wrong reasons. Through practising mindfulness outside and within sessions, and somatic coaching and somatic coaching supervision, I've been able to work on this so that I can widen my window of tolerance in the face of sadness and upset, staying more present, and more attuned. If I'm really triggered, I have to do more than just notice what's going on, I have to take action – consciously changing my body posture, breathing into the contractions, grounding myself by bringing my attention to my feet (a part of my body that can go unnoticed if I let too long elapse between practices). I have more compassion for myself when I am finding their emotions difficult, bringing more awareness to what is going on inside me.

Access to more data

The body is a rich storehouse of memories and experiences, and it can tell us a lot if we only pay attention to it.

John Rowan (1983), transpersonal practitioner

We offer clear clues to our emotions to anyone truly paying attention. Our emotions cascade across our faces as expressions, some of which are micro-expressions that flash across the face and are easily missed (Ekman 2007) unless we practise noticing. Practising mindfulness helps us pay attention to the little details such as these micro-expressions and other bodily manifestations. We are more likely to notice that our client is shuffling about uncomfortably even though they say they are fine, for example, or we notice an almost imperceptible wince when they talk about a colleague. Or it might be that we notice more nuances in how they express themselves. Paying more attention in this way allows us to be more responsive and the client is more likely to feel we are on side. Or we're more likely to notice when the client needs challenge. We're more aware of our own reactions too – catching and monitoring ourselves so our faces don't betray a negative evaluation, for example. We're more able to nurture our relationship with the client and to be there for them because we have more access to more data. And it is not just the little details we are more likely to notice. Developing our 'attention muscle' allows us to see the bigger picture too, as we will explore further later on.

Alister Scott, a coach and co-founder of One Leadership Project, says: 'In my experience, a mindfulness practice can help breed a higher awareness of one's own "mental chatter" combined with a more acute awareness of others. These can then encourage a greater willingness to be open and vulnerable about one's thoughts and feelings. All of this can be quite challenging for other people. For example, when I'm working in groups, I increasingly experience people saying that they find my contributions intuitive and even "scary" because I've made observations about what is happening in the group, or my experience of it. Such openness can be unusual for people.

This is not all easy going – a heightened sensitivity brings both higher highs and lower lows; mindfulness means being more aware of all aspects of life – the good, the bad and the ugly. As a result, one's experience of life can become both more raw and more meaningful.'

Resonance

So we're present and attuned. What next? The next piece is resonance, where physiologically the client and ourselves become a 'functional whole' (Siegel 2010a). 'This joining has profound transformative effects on both people,' says Siegel. The whole of the body is implicated in this joining.

Speaking at the Association for Coaching's annual conference in June 2012, Professor Paul Brown, said: 'The whole of the brain is massively plugged into the heart, the gut, the lungs, the digestive system.' According to research by the non-profit Institute of HeartMath, the heart has a powerful electromagnetic field which affects our emotional interactions with others. The electromagnetic signal which our heart rhythms produces can be measured in the brainwaves of those around us (McCraty 2002). Researchers say that the brain's electromagnetic field extends a few inches from the brain but the heart's field has been measured as far as 10 feet away, and probably extends much further. Earlier research showed that when two people touched while focusing loving thoughts on their hearts, their heart rhythms started to be in sync with each other's brainwaves too (McCraty *et al*, 1998). Later research by McCraty suggests that not only does the heart receive and respond to intuitive information *before* the brain, it also has intuitive access to a field of information unbound by time and space (McCraty, Atkinson and Bradley 2004a and 2004b). We broadcast our emotional state to others and receive their signals too.

Meanwhile, research by Gerschon (1999) and Radin and Schlitz (2005) has shown the important role the gut plays too in gathering and holding information: what we might think of as our gut instinct. It really does seem to be the case that our bodies store all manner of information and have a remarkable ability to share information and get in tune with one another, and truly interact and interconnect. We can use mindfulness to further develop our ability to notice changes and information in ourselves and others.

One way we can help ourselves become more present, attuned and resonant with others is to reduce all the judgement and internal chatter, by becoming truly curious to what emerges. The following practice helps us work on this aspect. It can be tricky so if you find it so, don't be disheartened. It takes practice to tap into the Observer part of our mind, but it's well worth it.

Practice: The Witness meditation

As before with other practices, find a comfortable position, preferably in an upright position. Set your intention and motivation to be non-judgemental, curious and compassionate towards yourself as you practise.

In this practice, we're deliberately seeking to cultivate the state of mind of an Observer or Witness (not a Judge or Storyteller!).

So when you're ready, closing your eyes (or casting them downwards gently).

First noticing your breath, bringing yourself into awareness of what's happening with your in and out breaths.

When you're ready, turning your mind to what is going on within your mind. This can be a tricky concept so it's best not to overthink it.

Thoughts

Just becoming aware of the thoughts in your mind.

Noticing the thoughts that pop up or float by in your mind, without becoming engaged or caught up in them. You don't need to do anything about them or with them, just noticing them. Labelling them 'thoughts' or 'thinking'. When your mind wanders, gently bringing your attention back to the practice.

Noticing thinking. Staying with this for as long as you wish.

Images

Now becoming aware of any images in your mind. You may see images flashing in front of you as if they were being projected onto a cinema screen. Again, just noticing without judgement and with curiosity and compassion what's there in front of you, in your mind's eye.

Noticing the images. Labelling them 'images'. And bringing your mind back when it wanders, which it will naturally do.

And simply observing any images. Staying with this as long as you wish.

Emotions

Now observing any emotions that pop up in your mind. Noticing, not judging. Being compassionate and curious.

You may find you naturally flick from image to thought to emotion and back again, it doesn't matter which order. There is no order, you are simply observing what is there, the contents of your mind.

The Witness

Noticing that there is a part of your mind that is able to observe the contents of your mind, without being part of them. Noticing how that feels. Often this part of the mind is described as an ocean, deep, calm, still. And the contents are described as waves. Coming and going. Ebbing and flowing.

You may find all sorts of questions come up such as:

Am I my thoughts?

Am I my emotions?

Am I my sensations?

Who is the Witness?

What, if anything, lies beyond the Witness?

Don't overthink it, don't feel you have to answer these questions, just noticing if they come up and letting them be. Questions such as these do sometimes emerge, and you may value such an exploration. But the practice for now is just noticing, and noticing that there is part of you that can notice!

We've seen how cultivating an interest in supporting others in kindness and compassion helps us be more present with, attuned to and resonant with our client and vice versa. In the next chapter, we explore compassion in relation to coaching and mindfulness.

Compassion

07

> *Compassion and respect for the client are central to the coaching process.*
>
> **DOUG SILSBEE (2010b)**

What's love – and compassion – got to do with it? Many of us would balk at broaching the subject of compassion, or love, in a business coaching setting. However, I believe that compassion is vital to the coaching process, that we can actively cultivate and harness our compassion, and that mindfulness is one of the best ways to do this.

Historically, the drive and methods to cultivate compassion have tended to come from religious and spiritual quarters – Buddhism, in particular. Over recent decades, this has been changing. Interest in compassion is spreading to all sorts of arenas, including psychology, neuroscience, health-care, leadership, and increasingly to coaching, with people like Professor Richard Boyatzis talking about compassionate coaching.

We perhaps shouldn't be surprised. As Professor Paul Gilbert, an expert on compassion, points out, we're a species that has evolved to thrive on kindness and compassion. 'Our brains have evolved to be caring and to need caring... This caring has been such a successful strategy that it has flourished into complex potentials within the human brain, including building the competencies that gave rise to our abilities for compassion' (Gilbert 2009, *The Compassionate Mind*).

Compassion in coaching

Many of us agree that compassion ought to be a core component of the coaching process, up there with non-judgement. Yet we often think more about being compassionate towards our clients, rather than ourselves. And whilst many of us agree compassion is important, we may not be doing anything to cultivate it.

I carried out a mini-poll among 14 coaches I know. All bar one (who wasn't sure) agreed that compassion is a core underpinning to coaching. One executive coach says, 'I like to think that compassion runs through all my work, like the centre running through a stick of rock.' And a coach who works primarily with educators 'at the rough end of the chalk face' says, 'Coaching with compassion has given my sessions another dimension, it is the fuel that drives my coaching'.

Just under half of those I polled had practices in place to develop compassion, including mindfulness, 'heart connection' practices such as that practised by Sally-Anne (see the case study at the end of this chapter) and 'bringing the client into my mind before a coaching session, directing my attention to them and feeling kindly towards them'.

I am involved in a multidisciplinary eclectic group which includes Professor Gilbert – at this stage basically a group of like-minded people including leadership development professionals, healthcare professionals and coaches, exploring where we can bring compassion into work with leaders, what research and practice are out there already, and what we mean by compassion. I have been heartened by just how much is already going on across the world. But I have realized that compassion can mean very different things to different people.

Definitions

According to the *Online Etymology Dictionary*, the English noun 'compassion' came into English from the French language in the mid-14th century, from Latin *com* (together) and *pati* (to suffer) – basically, suffering with the other. This definition – this idea of empathy, of suffering with the other and feeling what they feel – is a common one.

True compassion is not dependent on how the other behaves, says the Dalai Lama:

> True compassion is not just an emotional response but a firm commitment founded on reason. Therefore, a truly compassionate attitude towards others does not change even if they behave negatively.

For Boyatzis, co-author with McKee of *Resonant Leadership*, compassion is a key component of good leadership and good coaching. Much of his recent research and writing is about this topic. His definition is wider than the traditional Buddhist and Western definition of compassion:

> Ours includes that [feeling for someone who is suffering] but it is also about whether you can open up yourself to another who is excited and joyful about the future. We base it on a continuum… If you're limited to dealing with people in pain, you're almost automatically dealing with people in stress arousal. You can give them relief but the idea (here) is that you could move them into the parasympathetic arousal system.

Gilbert says that compassion is a motivation, rather than (solely) an emotion. Like Boyatzis, Gilbert (2009) talks about deliberately seeking to activate positive emotions:

> Compassion is about stimulating the positive emotion system related to feelings of reassurance, security, safeness and calm peacefulness (as opposed to the positive emotion system linked to drive and excitement).

Gilbert describes how Buddhism, evolution, Bowlby's attachment theory and studies of the brain and positive emotion came together for him, with the insight that whichever intervention you use as a helping profession, you have to ensure the other person experiences this with feelings of kindness and warmth.

He says there is a lot of evidence that if we set out to develop compassion, learning to concentrate our attention, thoughts and behaviours on compassion, imagining ourselves as compassionate and thinking about how to be compassionate for others, we stimulate a particular system in the brain. We look at Gilbert's (2009) model of our three major emotion regulation systems in the next chapter.

To feel compassion for others requires us to first have compassion for ourselves, warts and all. The more harshly we judge ourselves, the more likely it is that we will judge others harshly and find it hard to be compassionate. We have to be willing to be open to all our feelings. This opens up a certain rawness and tenderness – what Buddhist master Trungpa Rinpoche spoke of as the 'soft spot'.

Practice: Contemplating compassion

Find somewhere peaceful where you can sit quietly for a few moments. Relax and take a few deep breaths. Set your intention for this brief practice. Reflect on the following questions:

How do *you* define compassion?

How important is compassion to you in your coaching practice?

Think of a time when you felt compassionate towards someone. Where did you feel this compassion? What did it feel like? What impact did it have on you and how you behaved at the time or subsequently?

What do you do to cultivate compassion in general before/within/after coaching sessions?

Take a few moments to sit with what has come up – be compassionate! Then gently coming back to the room, capturing any thoughts you wish to capture in your journal.

For me, compassion is:

> the motivation to empathize with another, to feel what they're feeling, to care deeply about their wellbeing, happiness and suffering, and to act accordingly... and the heartfelt emotion/s evoked within us when this motivation is activated.

Sometimes, just 'feeling the other', being present with them and what they're going through is enough. At other times, we may feel compelled to act.

Developing compassion through mindfulness

Research shows that it is indeed possible to develop compassion and loving-kindness through meditation. Professor Richard Davidson and associate scientist Antoine Lutz at the University of Wisconsin-Madison were apparently the first to use functional magnetic resonance imaging (fMRI) to suggest that loving-kindness and compassion can be learnt in a similar way as we can learn to play a musical instrument or become proficient in a sport.

And as we saw in Chapter 3, the mere act of going deep into meditation can lead to a sense of dissolution of boundaries between us and another. Quite simply, we can begin to have a sense of others' pain as our own, without even intending to.

Personally, seeing as I believe compassion is a vital underpinning to coaching, I deliberately set out to develop this through my meditation practice, through the meditation below, for example. I must confess I don't always feel close to or compassionate towards my fellow earth-dwellers – it's a work-in-progress but a very worthwhile one. It helps me come from a place of service to and love for others in my coaching – and in other areas of my life.

I invite you to put aside some time now to practise the Loving-kindness meditation, whether it's your first or thousandth time. It's one of the toughest meditations to do. Many struggle with extending loving-kindness to enemies, which is understandable, but one of the hardest elements for many is that of extending loving-kindness and compassion to ourselves. Why bother? Because to be compassionate towards, to love and to serve others, we have to be able to do the same for ourselves.

As Williams and Pelman (2011) say, 'You need to relate to the world with kindness and compassion, and you can only do this if you come home to who *you* are, accepting yourself with deepest respect, honour, and yes, love.'

Of this meditation, they say, 'In this meditation you acknowledge that however hard you find it to be compassionate to *others*, it can feel even harder to bring kindness to *yourself*.'

Practice: Loving-kindness meditation (metta or befriending meditation) (15 minutes)

Find a comfortable position somewhere where you won't be disturbed for 10 minutes or so, preferably sitting upright, with your back straight but not rigid or arched. You may like to sit cross-legged on a cushion or you may prefer to sit in a chair. If you need to do it lying down, that's OK, it's just more likely you will struggle to stay alert.

Take a few deep breaths, close your eyes or gaze in an unfocused way as if you're looking at something half-heartedly in the distance, relax your shoulders, perhaps move your jaw about to make sure it's not clenched.

Set your intention and motivation for this practice, maybe something about this being time for you, giving yourself permission to take this time out, and about cultivating compassion for *yourself* as well as others.

Turning your mind to yourself, deserving of love, just doing the best you can. Staying with this. It may be hard, sometimes we find ourselves so very hard to love and feel compassion for. If it's difficult to extend loving-kindness to yourself, just staying with that if you can, trying to avoid piling on further judgements or evaluations. If it's really too hard, moving into thinking about a loved one – a person or a pet – and then moving back to yourself. This is a very important part of this practice and you may like to just do this first step a number of times before going onto the next step.

Wishing yourself the following (you may like to change the wording):

May I be free from suffering.

May I be well.

May I be happy.

May I have love and be loved.

Welcoming each statement into your heart. Really feeling the message. Noticing how you're responding, what is going on for you. Staying with this as long as you wish before moving on to the next step.

The loved one

Now bringing into your mind somebody you love, perhaps a partner or a child or a dear friend, or even a pet, a creature you find easy to love. Imagining them in your mind's eye before you. Again, they are just doing the best they can. As you did with yourself, wishing them the following:

May you be free from suffering.

May you be well.

May you be happy.

May you have love and be loved.

Staying with this as long as you wish, radiating loving-kindness and good intent to this person. If they have done or said something to you recently that you didn't like, finding it in your heart to forgive them if you can.

Someone neutral

When you're ready, extending your loving-kindness to someone 'neutral', someone you have no strong feelings for of any kind, perhaps someone you saw at the bus stop or who was in the same shopping queue as you, or whom you saw walking their dog earlier. Visualizing them in front of you as best you can. And as you did with yourself and a loved one, saying to them in your mind:

May you be free from suffering.

May you be well.

May you be happy.

May you love and be loved.

'The enemy'

Finally, and this one can be tricky too, conjuring up in your mind someone you have negative feelings for. It's easier to start with someone you just find mildly annoying and work your way up to someone you hate or deem to be your arch enemy, if there is someone like that in your life. You may hate them or just find them rather annoying, or unpleasant.

Again, imagining this person in front of you, being their 'hateful', 'annoying, 'unpleasant' self. Reminding yourself that these are just your perceptions which may have no bearing on 'reality' whatsoever. Tapping into how they, like everyone else, are just trying their best to be happy. They want happiness just like you. Just like you, they don't want to suffer. You may like to try to imagine them when they were young or tap into how childlike we all are beneath the veneer of adulthood. If they've done or said something to upset you, trying to find it in your heart to forgive them (this may be one step too far at this stage). Staying with meaning them no harm at the very least. And if you can, wishing them what you've wished for others:

May you be free from suffering.

May you be well.

May you be happy.

May you love and be loved.

All beings

Now extending that same loving-kindness to all beings on the planet, including all your loved ones, strangers and those you find difficult, and, of course, yourself:

May all beings be free from suffering.

May all beings be well.

May all beings be happy.

May all beings love and be loved.

As I've said, this is a difficult meditation but one which can have impressive results. Relationships can suddenly take a turn for the better without us even having said anything to the other person. We can choose to extend loving-kindness to emotions we have too, our anger or whatever. Or to ourselves or others in the past or future.

I used to live in a house in Spain where each summer we'd see lots of cockroaches. I really don't like cockroaches; they are pretty much the creature on this planet I like least. So I started conjuring up cockroaches as my 'enemy' in this practice. I still don't like them, but they are no longer demonized in my mind!

Benefits

One benefit of cultivating compassion is that it helps us be more attuned – as coaches and as clients. The research by Davidson and Lutz suggests that deliberately developing compassion and kindness through meditation affects brain regions which can make us more empathetic to other people's mental states. They suggest that individuals, including bullies and those prone to recurring depression, and society in general, could benefit from meditative practices such as the Loving-kindness meditation. Their study was part of ongoing investigations with a group of Tibetan monks and lay practitioners who have practised meditation for a minimum of 10,000 hours. In this case, Davidson and Lutz worked with 16 monks who have cultivated compassion meditation practices while 16 age-matched controls with no previous training were taught the fundamentals of compassion meditation a fortnight before the brain scanning took place. The controls in this study were asked first to concentrate on loved ones, wishing them wellbeing and freedom from suffering as we did in the Loving-kindness meditation. After training, they then were asked to generate such feelings toward all beings without thinking specifically about anyone. The participants' brains were scanned as they followed instructions to either begin compassion meditation or refrain from it. During each state, they were exposed to negative, positive and neutral noises made by humans: sounds of a distressed woman, a baby laughing and background restaurant noise.

The scans revealed significant activity in the insula and in the temporal parietal junction, particularly the right hemisphere, when the experienced meditators were generating compassion and were exposed to emotional 'vocalizations'. The insula plays a key role in bodily representations of emotion including heart rate and blood pressure and in making that information available to other parts of the brain. The strength of insula activation was also associated with the intensity of the meditation as assessed by the participants. The temporal parietal junction is an area deemed to be important in processing empathy, especially in perceiving the mental and emotional state of others.

The researchers believe compassion meditation can be beneficial in promoting more harmonious relationships of all kinds.

CASE STUDY   Developing mindfulness and compassion

For Sally-Anne Airey, a coach working in the United Kingdom and Russia, developing compassion and developing mindfulness go hand in hand. Using tools such as HeartMath and a number of 'heart-opening' exercises, she has been developing a 'heart connection practice' for a number of years. Having lost her father following a massive heart attack when he was 42 years old and she was only 10 years old, she had felt distanced from her heart for years. Recently, her heart 'feels my friend'. She has found this heart connection practice very useful in Moscow, which she says is not an easy city to live in. She started to incorporate mindfulness four years ago, which she sees as 'part of the same fabric'. 'Although my mindfulness practice is relatively new, I have done quite a bit and it feels like a transformation.'

Like so many of us, Sally-Anne felt overwhelmed at times by thousands of thoughts. She had a tendency to 'overthink' and felt she wanted to explore ways to manage this tendency. She had been aware of mindfulness for years before. She used to be in the Navy – a 'very action-oriented' environment – and had for many years been attracted to the idea of mindfulness as a potential way to get a 'deeper human connection'.

By the time she went on a retreat with Thich Nhat Hanh, she was 'completely ready' for it. 'I learnt some wonderful things about stopping, about what I call pausing or pressing the pause button.'

For Sally-Anne, having a regular sitting practice is key: 'I can get to awareness more quickly. It doesn't mean I don't have difficult moments but I can spot the emotional triggers from over all the years. By spotting these triggers, I can change the patterns and start new patterns.' She finds she gets less irritated by people, realizing that she can't change them but can change how she responds. 'The only person you can influence is yourself. By doing that, change occurs around you.'

She has noticed that the people, including clients, that come into her life are open to mindfulness.

She practises mindfulness regularly, with a sitting meditation, for example. She believes there is no substitute for practice.

'I believe I have to be on top of regular practice. It's like tuning in.'

She practises mindfulness and heart practice for at least a couple of minutes before each session.

Here's what she does for those minutes:

As I breathe in, it's almost as if I'm looking deeply inside the pit of my stomach, my gut. Whatever I get when I breathe in, I embrace and accept without judging as I breathe out. And in the awareness of it, it goes. Then I breathe into my heart, I find attitude breathing quite helpful. I breathe in warmth, for example, or compassion or peace. If I'm feeling shaky, I might breathe in 'calm' and self-tolerance.

With clients, she tends to start with focusing on breathing. She asks them whether they are aware of breathing and mostly they say no.

With one client who 'was talking flat out', she intuitively used one of the pauses to ask her if she was aware of her breathing and invited her to gently breathe in and out, to notice how long the breath is. The client breathed gently and reported that she was starting to feel calmer. Sally-Anne did this for a minute then asked the client 'What do you reckon?' and the client said she 'wanted to do a lot more'. 'We talked about trying to do it three times a day, such as when she was stressed out in the Moscow traffic.'

Sally-Anne didn't use the word mindfulness with this client.

With another client who is highly self-critical, she also focused on breathing and the client responded saying he was 'doing the mindfulness', even though Sally-Anne hadn't used that word.

She hasn't yet done a sitting meditation with a client.

She uses mindfulness within the session too. 'I find it really useful to maintain presence, noticing for example that something the client is saying isn't sitting well. If I sense aggravation in me which is starting to become a judgement, I do centring and breathing, I find focusing on appreciation and compassion are two very powerful words.'

She hasn't yet used what is going on in herself as information to share with her client:

I would hope I would do that if I felt it would be helpful. I struggle with that, I think you have to be very, very careful. It's about wanting to do it from the right place, almost offering it as a 'for what it's worth'. If they're describing to me some difficulty in a relationship and are describing things, I started to experience it and shared that. In some cases it's helpful but has to be done with genuine compassion.

As Gilbert (2010) points out, compassion is 'not about submissive "niceness" – it can be tough, setting boundaries, being honest and not giving clients what they want but what they need'. Silsbee says, 'having compassion does not equate to a soft-hearted, mushy, feel-sorry-for-those-less-fortunate-than-ourselves mantra'. We need to make sure we're not being 'compassionate' to clients in order to be liked, for example.

Bringing more compassion into coaching through mindfulness can really help us to build trust so our clients can open up about what's really important to them. Dr Alister Scott, an executive coach based in the United Kingdom, who co-founded with Neil Scotton catalytic leadership organization The One Leadership Project, says: 'Mindfulness can help to bring greater listening, trust, compassion to relationships, allowing people to talk about more of the things that really matter.'

We look in more depth at working with compassion to enhance our own and our clients' relationships with ourselves/themselves and others in Chapter 18.

Better outcomes

Boyatzis and colleagues (2010) at Case Western Reserve University in the United States have carried out research into how people react to 'compassionate' and 'critical' coaching approaches. They used fMRI scans to examine neural reactions to different coaching styles. They observed brain images of people being coached by coaches intentionally using different styles – one encouraging a positive future and the other focusing on failings and what the person ought to do. A week later, those who had been coached were again scanned while they were shown videos of their previous coaches and asked to respond to a series of questions. The questions were equally divided between neutral and whatever they had been before. Neural responses to the neutral questions helped the researchers track how the interpersonal relationship was affecting the neural response.

The research suggested that when coaches use a compassionate approach to explore clients' desired positive visions with them, they're more likely to learn and make behavioural changes. The study showed that in the brains of those coached by compassionate coaches, a week or so later the parts of their brain associated with visioning, a critical process for motivating learning and behavioural change, were 'lit up' or activated.

For Boyatzis and colleagues, compassionate coaching means working with the individual's own goals but seeking to arouse a positive emotional state. Their work builds on their knowledge of intentional change theory which holds that positive emotional attractors (PEAs) and negative emotional attractors (NEAs) create different psycho-physiological states that drive a person to think about change. The idea emerged that coaches should intentionally seek to arouse PEAs in their clients, bringing about positive emotions and arousing neuroendocrine systems that stimulate better cognitive functioning and increased perceptual accuracy and openness in the client. Old-style remedial coaching which addresses weaknesses and flaws has the opposite effect, which is bad news, as we know. The latter causes people to close down and get on the defensive so they're less receptive to learning and growth. It's not about only staying with positive stories, but about showing compassion and not judging the client, say the researchers.

Richard Boyatzis on compassionate coaching

The big thing is to get people to articulate the difference between the Ideal Self and the self people think they should be, to help them deal with pain but also to help them deal with the future they would like. We tend to focus on things that need fixing, on what we call 'coaching for compliance'. We let ourselves get seduced by this, rather than 'coaching with compassion'. Basically it's down to the question I pose all the time: 'Are you seeking revenge or helping (the client) develop?' If you're coaching for compliance, you have to face up to the fact that it's not going to work… Coaching for compassion is what really separates out the really outstanding coaches… It's amazing how easy it is for people to lose sight of this when they're trying to help people. The more emotional the intensity, the more likely it is we're not going to step back and give people the space.

One of the areas around which I frequently find it hard to be compassionate towards myself, and notice clients do too, is productivity/achievement/doing versus 'just being'. Many of us cry out to have more time to ourselves to just be, yet feel the need to achieve. This is just one element of the being–doing conundrum, which I believe is a core exploration when we look at mindfulness and coaching, and indeed when we look at what it means to be human. We look at this in the next chapter.

Being and doing

08

Be yourself. Life is precious as it is. There is no need to run, strive, search or struggle. Just be.

THICH NHAT HANH, ZEN MONK

Coaching is frequently associated with doing and goal orientation, with striving for something better or different, and it often has a future focus. Mindfulness is associated with being, with the present moment and with acceptance of 'what is'. In this chapter, we explore the implications of these different foci, if indeed they are different when we scratch beneath the surface. In my experience, such an exploration is both worthwhile and necessary if we're going to bring mindfulness into our coaching practice, in fact into our lives in general.

I suggest we start by looking at being and doing. To be or to do, that is the question, or a common one at least. It's an exploration or line of inquiry that arises in many of the workshops, classes and conversations I've been involved in around mindfulness and coaching, and with clients. It's one which seems to have the potential to inspire, engage, stimulate, agitate, unsettle and annoy people. It has the ability to really get under our skin because as well as putting us on the spot about what we want to make possible through our coaching, it's about what it means to be human.

When I lived in Spain in the decade preceding the banking crisis in 2008, I frequently travelled to the United Kingdom for work. I would try to pack in as many meetings, conferences and CPD events as I could into two- or three-day visits – any longer and I would miss my young family heart-achingly. I would really step up my pace to make the visits worthwhile and it would often be exciting, stimulating and fun. Although it was tiring, I always knew I would be going back to the more relaxed, leisurely pace of southern Spanish society to recharge. For years, I felt I had the best of both worlds. Whenever I was in the United Kingdom, I would observe people, friends included, and wonder why they dashed about so, why they wore such pinched expressions, why they worried about everything and seemed to feel the need to work really, really hard, even though many of them didn't seem to enjoy it. This was before the recession, as I said. Then we moved back to the south-east of England. In a matter of only weeks, I started experiencing deep changes in how I was manifesting and feeling, and noticed them in my husband and children too. Obviously, we're all part of lots of systems. One of the systems that operate in the south-east of England, particularly near London, and many other places, of course, is one of frenzied busyness. There seems to be more pressure on people to achieve and to be productive than there is in southern Spain – that's been my experience, at least. I felt like I was being sucked into a way of being against my will. Soon I no longer noticed it. It became a way of being which wasn't about being at all, but doing. It wasn't until I started meditating again that I realized and was able to do (!) something about it.

As Kowalski (2011) says, 'It almost doesn't matter what we are busy with, as long as we are frantically doing lots of "exciting" things in the world out there. And it is really difficult not to fall for it!'

Comedienne Ruby Wax, who practises mindfulness to manage her depressive tendencies, points out that most of us worship the god of Busyness. We would usually rather be doing something, whatever it is, than 'doing nothing'. But despite our attentiveness and dedication to this 'god', we don't get nearly as much back as we put in. There are lots of reasons why we keep busy, of course. There is nothing wrong per se with being busy, the problem comes in the way we do the busyness – 'mindlessly'.

Speaking at the Mindfulness at Work conference at the University of Cambridge on 19 February 2012, Professor Mark Williams said: 'Rushing about is an illusion of creativity. We convince ourselves that it's better for us in our work to rush around to get more done but our brains think we're running away from a predator.'

Dualistic thinking around being and doing, in particular, and between the closely associated concept of non-striving and striving (not hugely helpful terms, in my opinion), are at the heart of much of the resistance people bring to mindfulness, particularly in relation to coaching. Many of us see it as an either/or. When I first started meditating, like many others I worried that I would become less sparky, less effective, less productive, whatever those words really mean. I had visions of wandering about somewhat disengaged. Would I stop caring about how well I did things? Would I stop caring at all? These are common concerns, particularly the ones around productivity and effectiveness.

Tim Malnick agrees. 'In my experience, the first question or resistance is, "If I were mindful, nothing would happen, not in the real world where I need to get things done." I encourage people to notice the deep assumptions they're in and we unpick it.'

Personally, I soon saw and found that mindfulness helped me get more, not less, done. It helped me do things better because I panicked less and could think more clearly. It also helped me decide when it wasn't right to do more, helping me to say 'no' more frequently, when I knew my energy levels were low, when I wouldn't be able do the work justice, or when it just wasn't appropriate to take on whatever it was. It doesn't always work.

I still have times when I rush around like the proverbial headless chicken, forgetting that I have these wonderful practices to draw on. However, I have no doubt that mindfulness – particularly regular meditation – has changed my relationship to doing and being, in a good way.

Lots of questions have come up for me around this particular topic, and continue to arise. I feel I have answers to some of them, for now, at least, whilst others remain tantalizingly difficult to answer (see box). It can be helpful to think of non-doing as the opposite of doing. Kabat-Zinn (2004a) talks about non-doing, saying that it has nothing to do with passive or indolent. He says it's quite the opposite: 'It takes great courage and energy to cultivate non-doing, both in stillness and in activity.'

> *The joy of non-doing is that nothing else needs to happen for this moment to be complete… Non-doing can arise within action as well as in stillness… Non-doing simply means letting things be and allowing them to unfold in their own way. Enormous effort can be involved, but it is a graceful, knowledgeable, effortless effort, a 'dooerless doing', cultivated over a lifetime.*
>
> Kabat-Zinn (2004a)

You may like to explore some questions around being and doing for yourself (we will look at exploring being and doing with clients later on). You can adapt these to use with clients too.

Exercise: Questions to explore as a coach around being and doing

- What does 'doing' mean to you?
- What does 'being' mean to you?
- Are being and doing mutually exclusive?
- How does the emphasis in mindfulness on staying with 'what is' sit with goal setting and goal achievement in coaching?
- Does encouraging clients to become more mindful and to attend more to the present moment interfere with them looking to the future, and actually getting on and changing things?
- Or does it help them be less attached to outcome and approach things more creatively?

- Does seeking to become aware of and accepting what is lead people to be more passive or does it help them effect change because they have more clarity and focus, and are more resourceful?

- If we bring more mindfulness into our lives, does this impact on our ability to enjoy the doing?

- Can you think of times when you've colluded with a client in helping them do more, even though you've wondered whether this serves them?

Doing versus being?

Dualistic thinking often gets our clients and ourselves into trouble, and how we approach the mental constructs of being and doing is no exception. Dualistic thinking is where we think of things as polar opposites: right versus wrong, good versus evil, us versus them, I versus you, the individual versus the collective, humanity versus nature, and so on. Kowalski (2011) goes as far as to say that 'splitting' is the 'main reason why things can go wrong in our relationships with ourselves, each other and the planet as a whole'. He continues: 'the mind loves to "split" – turning complexity and wholeness into bite-sized chunks that can be easily processed'.

Malnick says: 'Doing versus being is a construction of dualism. It shows how split we are a lot of the time. It also shows an interesting side of what (many) people think mindfulness is. They think it's the opposite of doing lots of stuff, which is understandable given where we're at with the frenetic busyness world view. Most people experience it as a dualism... I push back... asking "When you're really busy and your mind is really full, are you more or less effective?" Often, lots gets done but it's not effective.'

Many coaches, myself included, see the need for more equilibrium, believing that mindfulness can offer a way to bring in more being. As Barbara Babcock, a life/business/executive/wellbeing coach based in the United Kingdom, says, 'I think mindfulness can offer a balance to the "doing" aspect of coaching. It is the being aspect of coaching which complements the doing in my view.'

Michael Forlenza, executive director of the Professional Coach Certification Program at Duquesne University's School of Leadership in the United States, agrees that mindfulness helps to counteract an overemphasis on doing and helps our clients be more reflective and thus better equipped to work out what they want. He says, 'I see that there can be a tension but I don't necessarily see that as problematic.'

The key here is that of course we can be more mindful when we are engaged in activity. This was the mind-blowing realization that struck me when I was struggling as a hard-working single mother all those years ago.

I didn't have to drop everything to stay sane (just as well when in charge of a young baby!) I could learn or relearn to disengage from frantic, frazzled mode and become calm and peaceful whilst still doing what I needed to do. And I was in a better position to judge what I needed to do.

That said, if you meditate frequently, you can reach a state, even if for a few moments only, of pure being, where you are not in doing mode at all. This offers a very welcome break from all the activity and thinking. We can then resume activity, recharged.

Langer (2005) says that 'action is the way we get to experience ourselves. And so, we act not to bring about an outcome but to bring about ourselves.' We are action-seeking creatures. But there are other ways to bring about ourselves, including meditation. I would argue that we are most likely to bring about ourselves when we pause for breath, when we go to what Amy Salzman calls our 'still, quiet place'.

All too often, we use activity to become 'mindless', to escape ourselves. As one executive coach, who is based in the United Kingdom and who also advises boards, CEOs and chairmen, points out, doing can be a way to run away from being and ourselves: 'There is a reason we are called human *beings*, not human *doings*... Activity is not a sign of effectiveness, just activity where you can hide from issues.'

Walking is an excellent activity that we can do mindfully in a non-doing sort of way.

I invite you to stop reading now and do some walking meditation. This is a standard meditation for many monks. It can be a good way for those of us who are resistant to sitting meditation to gain the benefits of meditation. And it is easy to incorporate into our lives for those of us who are able bodied.

Practice: Walking meditation

Make sure you are not going to be disturbed for 10 minutes or so (or you can try with less time, five minutes for example). Set your intention to allow yourself this time to practise. You may like to set an alarm to ensure you stick to the time you've allocated for yourself or you may like to just see how it goes. Your aim is purely to 'be with' the walking. You're not trying to get anywhere, you're merely attending to the activity of walking. You can walk anywhere you want, in the countryside, around a large room, along your street. You can walk as fast or as slow as you want. I like to walk slowly, except if I am in a group walking meditation session where I don't want to test others' patience! You may like to coordinate the walking with the breath, as Thich Nhat Hanh suggests. For example:

As you lift your foot, saying to yourself in your mind, 'breathing in' and keeping that focus on the in breath until you breathe out, saying to yourself in your mind, 'breathing out' as you place your other foot on the ground. Then repeating. You might like to say just 'in' and 'out'.

Or you can choose to focus on particular aspects of the walking – how your feet meet the ground, bringing your attention to your heels, your toes, the balls of your feet.

What is it feeling like as you lift your feet?

What are you noticing as your feet touch the ground?

Or you might like to focus on your body as a whole.

What are you noticing with each footstep?

Are any emotions coming up?

Are you noticing any thoughts popping into your mind?

You may notice irritation – perhaps you feel you should be rushing somewhere or that this is a 'waste of time' or you may feel impatient. Or happy. Or elated. Whatever it is that you notice, just notice it. If it is a 'pleasant' sensation, just noticing and not trying to hang onto to it. Noticing and letting go.

Letting go

How long will we fill our pockets like children, with dirt and stones?
Let the world go. Holding it, we never know ourselves, never are
airborne.

Rumi, Persian poet and mystic

As well as being helpful in building our ability to be non-judgemental, exploring how to let go can inform our journey of discovery around being and doing. It may be an oft-cited cliché in many New Age circles but many mindfulness teachings emphasize this part, some even saying it is this that's most important. According to Ajahn Sumedho (Kornfield 2000), an American abbot in the Theravadan Buddhist tradition, 'For minds obsessed by compulsive thinking and grasping, you simplify your meditation practices to just two words – "let go"... For years I did nothing but this in my practice. Every time I tried to understand or figure things out, I'd say "let go, let go, let go" until the desire would fade out.'

Jack Kornfield (2000) says: 'In the inevitable rising and falling, the cycles of expansion and contraction that come as you give birth to yourself, there may be moments to push, to strive toward a spiritual goal. But more frequently the task is one of letting go, of finding a gracious heart that honours the changes of life.'

What do we mean by 'letting go'? Kabat-Zinn (1994) says, 'letting go means just what it says... It is a conscious decision to release with full acceptance into the stream of present moments as they are unfolding. To let go means to give up coercing, resisting, or struggling, in exchange for something more powerful and wholesome which comes out of allowing things to be as they are.'

Practising letting go helps us loosen our grip on our perceived need to be busy for the sake of it, for example. Letting go of what no longer serves our clients, or ourselves, is a big part of coaching, as we know. The first step in letting go is setting the intention, and then being able to notice what is there, before letting it go. What are the stories we're telling ourselves? What are the assumptions we're holding? What are the addictions and obsessions that have a hold over us? What ideas do we cling onto? What judgements are we reluctant to let go of?

Mini practice: Letting go

I invite you to try letting go now, just for a few minutes, wherever you are. Sit comfortably in your chair, both feet on the floor, legs uncrossed, back upright but not arched. Loosen your jaw, gently close your eyes. Take three deep breaths. Scan your body for contractions and wherever you find them, tighten that part of the body as much as you can… squeeze, and relax. Loosely pay attention to your breathing, using the breath as an anchor and say to yourself, 'Letting go, letting go, letting go'. Now coordinate this with your breathing. Breathe in and as you breathe out, say to yourself, 'Letting go'. Do this a few more times. Notice what happens, how you feel. And when you're ready, gently come back to the room. And take the opportunity to capture any reflections.

Our inability to let go easily gets us into sorts of trouble and is partly to blame for the overconsumption we see in our world, for example. We have a tendency to grasp, to hang on, to hoard: emotions, stories, stuff. I watched a very sad programme the other night about someone whose house was filled to the brim and to get into his kitchen, this poor chap had to go through a 'death tunnel'. Obviously this is at one end of the spectrum but many of us suffer from an inability to let go easily. Building up an ability to let go into the moment helps us be more comfortable with the idea of non-striving, of non-doing.

It's also helpful when exploring this topic to look at what happens emotionally.

Emotion regulation systems

At a gathering of alumni from Michael Chaskalson's Mindfulness for Coaches programme, Chaskalson suggested Professor Paul Gilbert's model showing the interaction between our three major emotion regulation systems (Gilbert 2009) (see Figure 8.1) can be useful in looking at the topic of being and doing. I have since tried this out with clients and it has proved a helpful way to explore doing and/or being, and how we can use mindfulness to nourish ourselves.

Gilbert, professor of clinical psychology at the University of Derby and an expert on shame and compassion, developed a model depicting our three major emotion regulation systems, as shown in Figure 8.1. The model is based on research including that by Depue and Morrone-Strupinsky (2005) which suggested we have at least three types of emotion regulation systems, which interact. We can think of the threat and self-protection system as red; the incentive, resource-seeking, drive-excitement system as blue; and the soothing, contentment and safety system as green. Mindfulness can help us operate more within the 'green' system, but also helps us operate mindfully within the 'blue' system. So although we're trying to spend more time just 'being', we're not avoiding 'doing', just doing 'doing' mindfully.

FIGURE 8.1   Types of affect regulation system

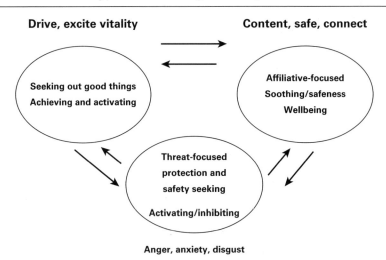

SOURCE: Gilbert 2009, *The Compassionate Mind*; Constable; reprinted with permission

Own goals?

Another potential conundrum is that of striving and non-striving.

Most of us will be familiar with the GROW model made famous by Sir John Whitmore, in which goals feature as a core component (Goals;

Reality; Options; and Wrap-up or Will), but there is an ongoing debate about whether goal setting and goal achievement are all they're cut out to be. The likes of David Megginson, professor of HRD at the Coaching & Mentoring Research Unit, Sheffeld Hallam University, have voiced concerns that goals are not the be all and end all, and can actually cause problems. Writing for *Coaching at Work* in May 2007, Professor Megginson said that 'goals can be inhibiting, unnecessary or irrelevant'. He is currently researching coaching and goals. Then we have people such as Dr Anthony Grant, director of the Coaching Psychology Unit at the School of Psychology, University of Sydney, who often points out that humans are goal-setting creatures, that setting goals is part of our nature. In the same issue of *Coaching at Work*, Dr Grant said that one of the problems is that many coaches don't understand the psychology of goal theory and how to apply it to coaching. He agreed that goals can hinder the development of coaching and mentoring but says this is only if practitioners are rigid and not used to working with goal theory, and that 'goals can indeed close the door on potential opportunities, but only if coaches allow themselves to be locked into preset goals'.

Denmark-based coaching academic Henrik Leslye quite rightly points out that 'coaching is so much more than just action/goals' while UK-based executive coach and coaching consultant Diane Newell, formerly the managing director of the European Mentoring & Coaching Council, questions the view that coaching is focused on goals and actions: 'It has a change focus which is not quite the same.' Derek Watson of Mindful Leadership in the United Kingdom says: 'Goal/outcome focus is a Western construct that does not apply globally.'

So the debate around goals in coaching rages on. I personally think that we place too much emphasis on traditional goal setting and goal achievement at times in coaching, particularly when we're expected to justify coaching expenditure to coaching sponsors. And this can blind us to what else our clients might need – such as silence, deep exploration, reflection time, being heard, learning how to be more grounded and centred, although I recognize that these can be goals for the client.

Whatever our stance on the place of goals within coaching, mindfulness has plenty to offer here. Leadership coach Fiona Parashar has outlined a positive psychology-based model for energizing the goal-setting process, which included co-creating a new language with alternative words such as dream, agenda or best possible self (2009). Her model includes a mindfulness element, which she describes as 'slowing to speed up'. Her research with seven experienced executive coaches led her to conclude that 'helping clients make a genuine connection to their goals through centring, mindfulness or an invitation to be present, seemed to increase engagement'.

Of course, setting up striving as one polarity and non-striving as another is once again dualistic thinking and it can be fruitful to enquire around that. Another related and potentially interesting concept to explore is that of ambition. We live in a world of wanting.

Malnick says:

I often work with people around the question of ambition. So much of our contemporary work and organization discourse assumes some idea of personal ambition and organizational progress. The idea that we are working, putting self effort into something that will arise at some point in the future. And that it will somehow be better than now. Pretty much every idea of growth, goals, targets assumes that view of the world. It's interesting just to notice that, to notice what a strong story it has become.

We explore the nature of desire and wanting in Chapter 16.

Acceptance

Acceptance is an important aspect of mindfulness, and of coaching and other helping professions. We can't make changes if we don't first accept our present reality: that's the starting point for any journey. Roberto Assagioli, founder of Psychosynthesis, distinguished between inner qualities which reside in our lower subconscious and those emanating from our higher unconscious or superconscious. These so-called 'lower qualities' include anger, confusion, control, cynicism, dishonesty, greed, guilt, suspicion, worry, whereas 'higher qualities', which are related to our spiritual goals, ambitions and values, include compassion, stillness, humility, love, peace, strength, awareness, surrender, wisdom and acceptance (Kowalski 2011). Kowalski points out that non-acceptance stimulates and embeds the following 'lower qualities' in our psyche: anger, envy, frustration, guilt, resentment, revenge and worry. He says non-attachment often leads 'to lethargy and inactivity because of the immensity and impossibility of trying to change the past and build a different future on that basis. Non-acceptance of what is leads far away from the Now.'

Acceptance sometimes gets a bad press and can be associated with stagnation and weakness. But becoming more mindful and accepting of what is certainly doesn't mean not taking appropriate action when something needs to change or not standing up for oneself. It certainly doesn't mean being or encouraging our clients to be overly passive, victims even. This might sound obvious but one client I worked with – a Buddhist – really struggled with this at first (see box).

CASE STUDY   Not being a doormat

Here's Paul's story of how he resolved the tension between his desire to be accepting as well as compassionate but not wanting to be a 'doormat' or victim:

When I first came to coaching, I was being bullied at work by my boss. I'd been raised in a tough East End of London environment and had been into fighting when I was young. I was known on the street as someone you didn't mess with. It was all about respect. If someone didn't respect me, I fought them until they did. That was the currency. It didn't matter that I was clever then. It was my fighting ability that mattered. As I grew up, I stopped fighting but I still felt people had to respect me or else. I had lots of ways of making sure they did and I wouldn't put up with any nonsense. Then I became a Buddhist and really got into mindfulness and compassion. The trouble is at first I thought I just had to sit back and take it. I didn't stand up for myself and I ended up taking time off from work with stress. I just felt like a real doormat. The coaching really helped me realize I had to take a stand. The mindfulness helped me not blow my top and to accept that I couldn't change my boss. My boss is very childish, insecure I suppose, he shouts at everyone when they don't do things just so, really bullied me. I meditated almost every day during a really difficult period when everything came to a head. But I didn't take it personally. I didn't shout. It's hard to explain but it's about accepting what you can change and knowing when you can't change things, like the Serenity Prayer. I have left that job now but with my head held high and no baggage, and a really good reference from my boss.

Since the coaching, this client has left his employer and set up his own business. His boss has been sacked. Paul continues to meditate.

Back to the future

The other piece of the puzzle is the present moment 'versus' the past and future. Living more in the moment is a goal expressed by many of the coaches and clients I speak to, as we see in the *Mindfulness in Coaching* survey (Chapter 21). Modern-day thinkers including Eckhart Tolle, author of *The Power of Now*, urge people to live in the 'now' and we are reminded at every turn, it seems, that the present is all there is. However, it's not easy to inhabit the present, as we all know.

What is the present anyhow? Is there such a thing? It's a slippery subject. Yet however many knots we may tie ourselves in as we explore this conceptually, on some level I think we all appreciate that truly, that's all there is. Like being and doing, the past and future are mental constructs. When we think about what happened in the past, we think about it in the present, in the now, ditto with the future. Again, it's not easy to describe the 'now', it has to be experienced and it's linked with being, with tapping into a continuum of moment-to-moment awareness. When we manage to pull this off, it can be wonderful, we can feel much more alive.

Mindfulness is not about only attending to the present, of course. As Professor Mark Williams said at the Mindfulness at Work conference, mindfulness is not about *not* remembering and *not* planning, 'it's about *knowing* that you're remembering and planning'. In what he calls 'driven-doing', we start to overthink, overstrive and get lost in the past and future rather than see them as past and future.

Mindfulness doesn't require us to forget about the past or future; it's about being able to switch off from thinking about the past and future when we want to (we explore this in more detail in Chapter 12 on stress) – which isn't always easy. And it's about us developing the ability to be more mindful when we do have to attend to the future or the past.

Chartered occupational psychologist and coach, Sarah Dale, who is based in the United Kingdom, says: 'It's about mindful planning – not that you never think about the future but that you are mindful about how you do that, which seems to bring down the adrenaline/anxiety levels about it.' And coach and psychologist Lynne Spencer, who is also based in the United Kingdom, says, 'It's a complex link for those who are unfamiliar with mindfulness, but it can be very future-oriented if properly harnessed.'

Pressing pause

So to conclude this chapter, mindfulness is about helping us and our clients pause for breath when we need to, but be more able to do what we need to do mindfully. It's not about disengaging from the future, or forgetting the past, but about being able to attend to the present more effectively and with more joy and connectedness. Goals are fine – particularly if they are to be mindful! However, achieving for achievement's sake or ticking off the list of goals outlined at the outset solely to satisfy a sponsor surely doesn't make sense.

I remember interviewing Julie Starr, author of books including *The Coaching Manual*. She told me about one high-achieving client who came to coaching to help her become more productive. After telling Julie all she was doing and sharing what she would like to do more of, Julie looked at her and said: 'When is enough, enough?' Mindfulness can step in and say to us 'Enough is enough!'

Being able to recognize when we're out of balance, when we're doing too much is important both for us as coaches, and for our clients. In the next section on working with mindfulness in coaching and mentoring, we will look at how we can use mindfulness to support us directly as coaches, and how we can support our clients, including working with stress management, resilience and wellbeing.

PART THREE
Working with mindfulness in coaching and mentoring

As we explored in the last section, I believe having a mindfulness practice will make you a better coach, helping you bring and enhance qualities such as curiosity, openness, non-judgement and compassion, and helping you be present and attuned to the client. In this section, we will delve into how mindfulness can develop, support and nurture you directly as coach, moving on to how you can support your client through mindfulness.

Developing, supporting and nurturing the coach

09

When I first started exploring how mindfulness and meditation can inform coaching practice, most coaches I asked about this would either look surprised and say, 'Hmmm, I hadn't really thought about it' or 'Well, I get a lot out of meditation myself but I wouldn't dream of talking about it with clients.' But times really have changed and more and more coaches are adopting mindfulness practices to help them be better coaches.

In this chapter, we look at how to use mindfulness to prepare for a coaching session, enhance performance within the session, after sessions and to help us take care of ourselves.

Session preparation

We all know how important it is to be in the right headspace when we meet with a client and most of us hopefully will endeavour to prepare in some way rather than dashing from session to session. It's not always possible or easy to make time for this, of course. We might have allowed time before a session with a client but get caught up in something unforeseen or hear some bad news, for example. Mindfulness can be immensely useful in helping us be calm, relaxed and present for the client we are about to coach.

Sarah Dale says: 'Meditation as part of my preparation for coaching sessions can be very helpful in achieving a calm and present state of mind for the session itself.'

Another coach, who uses practices including Centring, Mindful breathing and 'mindfully checking-in', says:

I meditate before the session and 'open myself' – the client feels this and they become still, relax and open up too. I [have] always found meditating for 5 to 10 minutes before a client session, holding them softly in my mind, has led me to insights of where to probe with them I would not have experienced from 'logical work'. The clients became still and opened. There formed a safe space in which to explore sensitive issues when they sensed no stress or judgement in me. Exceptionally productive sessions.

Here are some practices I find particularly effective and easy to do in a short period of time:

The Mindful minute (this chapter);
Conscious breathing (this chapter);
The Three-minute breathing space (this chapter);
Centring (Chapter 4);
Loving-kindness meditation (Chapter 7);
'Mindful awareness of whatever I'm doing'.

If you're willing, please join me in enjoying a Mindful minute now. Whether it's the first time you've done this or not, I invite you to approach this practice with curiosity, non-judgement and openness. I find this practice (introduced to me by Michael Chaskalson) to be very popular with coaches in the Mindfulness for Coaches workshops I run, and with clients, probably mainly because it only takes a minute!

Practice: The Mindful minute

If you're doing it for the first time, you will need something to time yourself with, or ask someone else to time you.

Sit (or stand) comfortably in a relaxed but upright position, feet flat on the floor, hands in your lap if you're sitting or relaxed by your side if you're standing, shoulders and jaw relaxed. Close your eyes or relax your gaze and bring your attention to your breath. Start the timer and just allow yourself to breathe normally. The idea here is not to do anything other than count how many breaths you take in a minute. Don't force the breath, just breathe however you normally breathe, counting at the end of each out breath. By the end of the minute you will know how many breaths you take in a minute. The number varies significantly according to the person. It doesn't matter, it's not a competition in how deep your natural breathing is. When you reach the end of the minute, note which number you reached. Obviously, if you already know how many breaths you tend to take in a minute, don't bother timing yourself. This is a fabulous exercise to do when we haven't got much time. We can allow ourselves to have lots of Mindful minutes throughout the day without feeling guilty. It's a great one to share with clients too. Who can truthfully claim that they haven't even got one minute to spare throughout the day?

With acknowledgement to Michael Chaskalson

Practice: Conscious breathing

The best way to make the most of the exercise above is to breathe consciously. In his books, including *Peace Is Every Step*, Thich Nhat Hanh suggests one way to do this is to say to yourself as you breathe in, 'Breathing in, I know that I am breathing in.' And as you breathe out, say, 'Breathing out, I know that I am breathing out.' Once this is established and you are focused it is possible to reduce the silent affirmation to 'In' and 'Out'. Our breathing, which is likely to be shallow and fast if we are feeling stressed, will become gentler and more peaceful. I have practised the Mindful minute or just become conscious of my breath in all sorts of locations on the way to meet a client or to a business meeting – on a London Underground escalator, on the tube or train, in a lift in the client's building...

In *Peace Is Every Step* (1991), Thich Nhat Hanh writes:

It is a joy to sit, stable and at ease, and return to our breathing, our smiling, our true nature. Our appointment with life is in the present moment. If we do not have peace and joy right now, when will we have peace and joy – tomorrow, or after tomorrow? What is preventing us from being happy right now?

The Three-minute breathing space, Centring and variations such as Focusing can also be very helpful. I find the more we practise centring ourselves, the more we are able to make 'short cuts' when we are short of time. For example, if we are overly caught up with our thoughts and feeling scattered just before a session, we might quickly bring our attention to what is going on in our feet, for example, becoming aware that we *have* feet, in the first instance, and that they are in contact with the ground beneath us, supporting us. Or even just thinking 'Feet!' whereas in a longer practice, we would pay attention to all sorts of sensations: what is the temperature of our feet – hot, cold, neutral? How does our footwear feel against our skin? What other sensations are there – tingling, throbbing, other kinds of pain? And so on.

Or if we're feeling intimidated by the prospect of meeting a new client or we're coaching a client who tends to trigger a lack of confidence in us, we might attend to 'our line of dignity', making sure we are standing tall and upright. Again once we have a solid practice, we can make short cuts when we need to and think 'Stand tall, with dignity,' for example, finding whatever cue works for us to 'come to our senses' and get grounded.

The Three-minute breathing space too is designed to be practised at different moments during the day, building on a solid underlying practice, rather than waiting until we're tearing our hair out. As Williams and Penman (2012) point out, 'one of the great ironies of mindful awareness is that it often seems to evaporate just when you need it the most... when you're under pressure, the last thing your mind wishes to be is mindful'.

In spite of only being three minutes long, it can be surprisingly effective, even for those new to mindfulness. One client trying it for the first time reported: 'I feel calmer. My breathing has slowed down. It felt like longer than three minutes.'

Practice: Three-minute breathing space

Ideally, make sure you're somewhere where you're not going to be disturbed (for only three minutes), although this practice can be done anywhere (such as the tube or the toilet before a client meeting!). You can do it sitting, lying or standing. Adjust your posture so your shoulders are relaxed, jaw loose, back erect but not arched. Gently close your eyes or gaze softly downwards. Set your motivation for the practice.

In this practice, you start with a wider perspective, then narrow it down to the breath, then back out again to your whole body/mind, the room and so on. You might like to think of an hourglass as an image.

Awareness

So, during this first minute, you take a wider perspective, doing a bit of a 'weather check'.

What are your thoughts?
What are your feelings?
What are your bodily sensations?

Gathering

During the second minute, take a narrower perspective, focusing on the in and out breaths, gently breathing without forcing the breaths. Use the breath as an anchor.

Expanding

For this last minute, widen your perspective once again, getting a sense of the whole body, the environment around you, any sounds, any smells and so on.

Your mind will wander! Just gently bring it back with no judgement, just curiosity. Congratulate yourself for giving yourself this time.

Adapted from Jon Kabat-Zinn. This practice is taught on MBCT and MBSR programmes.

Mindfully doing what we're doing anyway

Just as it's hard to argue that we can't find even one mindful minute, the argument that we haven't got time to do something mindfully that we're doing anyway is pretty indefensible, although it really can feel that way sometimes! However, if we can just persuade ourselves that it's worth a try even when we don't feel like it, it can really help. It's particularly useful when we are genuinely time-challenged before a session to help us get into the right state. We might walk – or even run, if we're really late – mindfully to a client's offices. We might make ourselves a cup of coffee or tea mindfully or mindfully eat. We can do absolutely anything mindfully and ideally, that should be our aim.

Within the coaching session

Passmore and Marianetti (2007) concluded that training in mindfulness can help coaches in four areas:

- preparing for coaching;
- maintaining focus in the session;
- remaining 'emotionally detached';
- teaching mindfulness to clients.

Maintaining focus is an important one – this is about the increased focus and concentration that come about through single-focus practices such as watching the breath. The more we practise bringing our wandering minds back to a single focus, be that on our breath, a candle, sound, whatever, the more we will be able to do this at will.

As well as being commonly used to describe an inability to connect emotionally as a coping strategy, the term 'emotional detachment' is used to describe an ability to maintain boundaries and psychic integrity. We need to be able to avoid becoming so emotionally entangled with our clients that we experience flooding of emotions which get in the way of us serving our client. If we're sobbing with our client over their redundancy news, or are angry and itching to ring up their boss to give them a piece of our mind, we're no good to them at all. What we're talking about here is being able to manage our emotions and responses within the session so we can empathize, feel compassion and care for our client whilst at the same time being objective and grounded. Practising mindfulness supports us in doing this more readily, offering us some emergency strategies to employ in the moment. And as we'll explore later on, self-management is a core skill we can help clients with using mindfulness – but we need to role model it ourselves. If we suddenly find it is all becoming too much, we might take a mindful moment to focus on our breath, using it as an anchor, or feeling our feet on the floor… bringing our attention to our senses in some way: coming to our senses.

One potential problem is that people who have a tendency to feel detached may be more likely to be attracted to types of meditation that may increase this sense of detachment. This is important to bear in mind with clients, which we will explore later, but it is also something to watch out for as coach. If you have a tendency to be detached from others or disengaged, it may be worth ensuring you incorporate practices such as the Loving-kindness meditation or grounding practices such as Centring.

Sometimes, if I am going to be coaching on the telephone from home or can find somewhere quiet to sit before a session, I practise the Loving-kindness meditation, or parts of it. Like Sally-Anne Airey, I will bring my client into my mind and heart, wishing them happiness, wishing them well and so on. As we saw in the last chapter, actively cultivating compassion through meditation helps us be more empathetic. This can be particularly useful if we are finding working with a particular client difficult, or if we feel we are in danger of colluding with a client against others in their system.

CASE STUDY   Mindfulness for self-management

I had one client, 'Denise', who was having problems with her boss, Anna. Her boss took her work very seriously. She had no children, worked late into the night most evenings, was always on her Blackberry texting Denise – 'I know you're at home but if I don't text you about this now, I'll forget!' Or 'Sorry to bother you but I just have one teeny question I need an answer to.' She would say to Denise that she understood her going home 'early' to her young child and that she didn't want her to get too overworked whilst piling project after project onto Denise. I only had Denise's story to go by – perhaps Denise was exaggerating. Either way, there was a lot we could work on including helping Denise manage her responses and being clearer around boundaries with Anna. The thing was, I had grown very fond of Denise and I could feel flickerings of anger towards Anna. Denise's husband had taken time off work due to stress and her mother-in-law was ill. She had a lot on her plate and was concerned that her husband might lose his job, which made her nervous about her own job. Anna really wasn't helping matters, I felt. However, I knew I really wasn't going to help matters either unless I reached a state of non-judgement. So before the next session, I practised the Loving-kindness meditation and held Anna in my mind for some of it. When we had our session, sure enough Anna came up. But we were able to explore the situation with much more compassion. How lonely Anna must be feeling in her current role – her sidekick was off with cancer, funding was drying up, she had put so much into the organization over the years and now its future was looking a little uncertain, she had had a divorce a few years back and so on. How difficult it must be for her to be understanding around Denise's different demands given that her focus was so much on work. How actually she might be struggling to cope herself and might not be able to stop herself easily from reaching out for help to Denise. My client and I were able to explore further how firmer boundaries might be helpful for Anna – Denise likened her to her own young child needing to know where he stood. We explored whether it might be helpful for Denise to disclose the difficulties Denise was experiencing at home and that it could be helpful to renegotiate Denise's roles a little, possibly adding additional areas where she might be able to support Anna in exchange for offloading some of the projects onto someone else. All this exploration would of course have been desirable and possible had I not done the Loving-kindness meditation before the session. However, I found it much easier to stand in Anna's shoes and help Denise do the same through having dispelled any anger, replacing it with compassion. And of course, it's possible to conjure up compassionate feelings within a session too, especially the more we practise this outside the session.

Denise reported back in the following session that she had had a 'highly satisfying' discussion with Anna, in which there seemed to have been some shifts in their relationship. We did a little more work on this – I had taken it to supervision and my supervisor had suggested using the lens of transactional analysis, in particular the Drama triangle (Karpman). Denise realised that she did cast herself as the Victim sometimes with Anna as Persecutor, and as Rescuer at other times too. This opened up a discussion about Denise being a bit of a martyr sometimes in different settings, which Denise recognized and found helpful. And of course, sometimes Anna was the Victim, such as when Denise got 'all huffy' and so on. I didn't actually suggest Denise practise the Loving-kindness meditation although I could have done and have done with other clients.

Again, it is possible to have mini-meditations along the same lines as the Loving-kindness meditation.

Regular mindfulness practice helps us be more grounded and centred, it helps us be more resilient in the face of deep suffering. We need to care deeply for our client but to remain strong and available for them. We also need to practise equanimity and remember our client is part of a wider system. It's not just about them or us.

Empathy

As Michael Chaskalson points out in *The Mindful Workplace*, perhaps even more important than the areas cited by Passmore and Marianetti (preparing for coaching; maintaining focus in the session; remaining 'emotionally detached'; and teaching mindfulness to clients) is the ability to empathize with our client, which is enhanced by mindfulness. Through being ourselves, accepting who the client is and being empathic, we create conditions for change and transformation in our clients. Also linked to empathy is our ability to set aside our egos within the session, by which I mean the selfish self-obsessed part of ourselves. We often say things like 'It's all about what *you* want from the coaching' or 'It's *your* agenda that matters here' and in 'pure coaching', we know we must resist at all times the urge to share our own stories unless we feel there could be some vital pearl in there for the client, and even then to ask permission and to offer it as a suggestion. Some counsel that it's best never to offer anything up from your life while others point out that it's a way to be congruent and authentic, and to create rapport. And others find clients want a mix of mentoring and coaching, or pure mentoring where wise counsel is actively sought. In all cases, however, it's got to be about the client. Yet of course, we always bring ourselves to the coaching, in reality. I think it's important to explore this, and mindfulness can be a platform from which to do so. Practices such as the Witness meditation can be useful here in examining what and who we are, and combining mindfulness within approaches such as existentialism, or transpersonal coaching can be useful, including work on sub-personalities (Chapter 19).

Practices such as the Loving-kindness meditation, the Tibetan Buddhist practice of *Tonglen* and certain contemplative prayers are aimed specifically at us moving away from a model in which we are at 'the centre of the universe', helping us to develop compassion and empathy. And as we saw when we explored the neuroscience of mindfulness, meditation in general can lead us to feel more interconnected. Feeling calmer and more relaxed too means we are less likely to be self-centred – we all know how, when we get stressed, we tend to become more focused on ourselves. There are evolutionary reasons for that which we will explore in the next chapter.

I would add another two to Passmore and Marianetti's list: creating/maintaining rapport and accessing useful data – these inhabit the arenas of attunement and resonance we explored in earlier chapters. John Rowan, transpersonal psychologist and co-founder of the Institute of Psychotherapy and Social Studies, has described rapport as 'being connected to the other person, relating well to the other person, being on the same wavelength, being able to communicate well... where rapport exists, the client feels accepted, welcomed and included' (Rowan 1983). We all know how important it is to create rapport in the first session. Although he is talking about humanistic counselling and therapy, much of Rowan's thinking and approaches can be applied to coaching and, as he says, in talking about entering into a relationship with a client, 'at this stage I feel that rapport is virtually the only thing I can achieve, so I may as well achieve it well. And I do it by mirroring the client.'

Although neuro-linguistic programming (NLP) has attracted criticism over the years from some quarters, it underpins many coaches' practice and concepts such as 'matching', 'pacing' and 'mirroring' are widely understood. 'Matching' is when we copy someone's physiology, 'mirroring' is when we match what the other does with a mirror image – raising our left arm to mirror their right arm, for example – and 'pacing' is when we copy the other person's language.

Even for those who are not fans of NLP and for whom the idea of consciously copying someone doesn't sit well with values of authenticity and genuineness, if we think about how we create rapport when it works well, we will probably notice that we naturally match, mirror and pace, at least to some extent. If our intention is to help the client feel 'accepted, welcomed and included', we will not tend to act or speak in a way we think they might find jarring. If a client is softly spoken and measured, I will naturally find myself speaking more softly and holding myself in a more measured way. If a client is ebullient and bouncy, I will find myself bringing those aspects of myself to the fore. Practising mindfulness helps us to do this more accurately.

Access to more data

Within the coaching session, we pay attention both to what is going on in the client before us and within us. Neil Scotton says:

> There are times when I catch myself trying to analyse and be clever and I do this more and more. I catch it, stop myself and pay more attention to the language, the pauses, the person in front of me… reaching a level of profound listening and just being there for the person. I'm getting to the stage where it can happen really quickly. Maybe that presence is a manifestation of mindfulness.

Some of the best coaching can come about from noticing a small body movement in our client. Mindfulness helps us notice by improving our attentional focus as well as developing the Witness function so we can observe while we are doing whatever it is we're doing. If we practise mindfulness regularly, we'll become more and more able to tune into the slightest change in our own bodies. We might notice a little flutter in our stomach and be curious about that. Or that our shoulders are hunching ever so slightly and wonder why that is. Or that an emotion has washed over us that we don't recognize as our own – shame, for example. Of course, whatever we notice could be our own stuff. Or perhaps not. But the more we notice, the more data we have at our disposal to be curious about. It can be immensely powerful in coaching to share what is going on for us with our client. This is connected to empathy as the more attuned we are to our client's inner world, the better able we will be to work out what is coming from them, from us, and/or from the both of us. It is about the sensitive, active listening at the core of good coaching. And mindfulness can significantly enhance our ability to do this. Scotton says, 'This includes noticing "What am I paying attention to in the way I'm listening/watching/noticing" and "What's happening in the relationship between us?"'

Scotton recalls how in a session, he noticed how his breath had become tight. He focused on his breath going in and out, which allowed him to 'reconnect with the client'. His mindfulness practices include meditation: Centring, the Body scan, Mindful walking, Mindful eating and Tai Chi. Scotton says:

> I am noticing that the difference between 5 and 15 minutes is highly exponential. It leads to a spaciousness in a number of ways. It allows me to be more present for the client… it enables me to let go of being anything and paradoxically enables me to just be… it's cumulative, the more you do it, the more aware you are.

After the coaching session

Mindfulness and reflection go hand in hand. Some sort of contemplative practice allows us to be better able to notice and reflect on what has happened with our client, within ourselves and in the wider system. We might find all sorts of insights or issues come to the surface during mindfulness/meditation which we can explore with our coach supervisor, or just that generally being more attentive means we are aware of more. We can bring that sense of curiosity and enquiry we talked about earlier to what is going on in our coaching, as long as it's combined with a sense of letting be and we gently avoid getting overly caught up in thinking.

Setting aside reflection time after coaching a client can be very useful and I find it is greatly enhanced if I do a practice such as a quick Body scan. What is going on in my body after the coaching, what sensations am I noticing as well as what thoughts? I might notice that as I think about the client, I am feeling agitated, or my stomach has contracted, or whatever. Sometimes, scanning the body will throw up some interesting sensations which give us all sorts of clues, both to what is going on with the client, perhaps something under the surface we hadn't picked up on in the session, or in ourselves that we might like to take to supervision.

Now we've explored how mindfulness can support us, let's look at how it can support our clients directly.

Introducing mindfulness to clients

10

*"We don't beat drums, we don't sing songs;
we teach right-brain skills in a left-brain way.*

JEREMY HUNTER, MINDFULNESS TRAINER

One of the questions I most commonly come across around mindfulness in coaching, even amongst coaches with a deep mindfulness practice is: 'How on earth do I introduce it to clients?' Some find it difficult to make the leap between finding mindfulness helpful for themselves and being able to offer it explicitly to clients. This is often due to a concern about how the client will view mindfulness (this came through in my survey – see Chapter 20). This is a valid concern but there are ways to address it and to make the best possible case for mindfulness, as we'll explore.

However, even more important to consider is whether it's appropriate to introduce mindfulness. Is it useful? Is it appropriate? Is it right for the client? If the answer to these questions is yes, then we can think about how to do so.

Appropriateness

Obviously, mindfulness is just one of many possible approaches to use – as well as depending on the coach's preference and training, it will very much depend on the client, their agenda and the context as to whether mindfulness will be appropriate as an explicit approach. Not everyone will be drawn to it and some may be highly resistant.

Executive coach Linda Woolston says, 'Most clients think mindfulness is great... [but] some would look at you as if you were bonkers.' Others will assume they are too active, too busy, too all sorts of things, to meditate and practise mindfulness.

Detachment and disengagement

Clients can sometimes be afraid that if they practise mindfulness, they will become disengaged and not enjoy life to the full, whereas I would argue that mindfulness is about the opposite, enabling us to live life joyfully and more completely. That said, as we cultivate equanimity and being less judgemental, through our mindfulness practice, we may come across as less passionate to others, perhaps. And in some people, meditating may fuel a sense of disengagement (see Mark's case study, Chapter 12). This is easy to redress and there are other kinds of practices designed to increase the sense of connectedness directly such as Loving-kindness meditation, which is what Mark practises to counteract the disengagement he says he's prone to.

With other types of clients, such as those for whom mortality is at the forefront of their minds, it may be appropriate to explicitly use mindfulness practices to help them work on non-attachment.

Difficult emotions

Some people have concerns about meditation stirring up or bringing to the surface unpleasant feelings that might be hard to address in the coaching. Of course, it may well do so, just like any other approach with the potential to go deep. We do need to tread very carefully – as we would expect to anyway – with any client who presents in a highly traumatized state. Hunter says with someone in such a state, 'just watching what's going on might not be enough. They need other tools.' However, difficult emotions are part of us and mindfulness can help us deal with them, as we explore in Chapter 17.

Overcoming resistance

I'm not advocating becoming a mindfulness warrior, set on overcoming obstacles to clients adopting mindfulness, come what may. However, where we genuinely believe that mindfulness may benefit our clients yet we anticipate resistance to them exploring it, it's worth giving some consideration to what the obstacles may be and how we may deal with them if and where appropriate.

Misinformation

We may find clients are misinformed about what mindfulness is. They may think mindfulness is about emptying their minds, for example – which it isn't. They may think mindfulness has to be spiritual – of course, it can be, but it doesn't have to be. They may think it's only for Buddhists. Or they may think it's something only for depressed people, for example. They may not realize it has a wealth of research backing it up, or may not appreciate how it may be helpful with specific issues. They may not realize they can be mindful without sitting on a cushion.

Speaking the client's language

As always, it's important to speak the client's language and to speak to the individual's or organization's needs and interests. One coach shared that, with many of her clients, talking about resonance versus dissonance in leadership was a way into talking about mindfulness. Certainly talking about mindfulness within the various leadership models can work very well (Chapter 15).

Many clients respond very well to hearing about the neuroscience behind mindfulness, or some of the research into its benefits (Chapter 3).

Other clients might respond well to gadgets such as HeartMath's emWave2, a device to help people manage stress, or RESPeRATE, a device designed by Israeli manufacturer InterCure to lower hypertension. I've spoken to coaches who use these as ways to introduce mindfulness, encouraging clients to slow down.

What's in a name?

Sometimes it's the label itself that's a problem. One public sector client said she felt mindfulness was exactly what she and her colleagues needed to manage the widespread changes afoot in the organization. However, she feared that within the current climate of austerity, the press would have a field day, running newspaper headlines such as 'Local council staff zone out at taxpayers' expense' or 'Council squanders taxpayers' money on meditation'.

Some, like Tim Malnick, talk about awareness rather than mindfulness, others about presence, managing emotions, self-awareness or emotional intelligence. Apparently when Google first ran mindfulness training as an MBSR offer, it didn't manage to attract many participants. However, when it rebranded its Search Inside Yourself programme as a way to develop emotional intelligence, bingo. Many of its engineers were all too aware of their deficits in this area and were happy to sign up. The programme was set up by a long-standing employee, Chade-Meng Tan, who said that for many high achievers, stress can be a badge of honour.

For Professor Jeremy Hunter, it's self-management that has been the way in. Hunter was one of the pioneers in introducing mindfulness practice, attention training and emotional management into a management context. As well as running a coaching practice, he created and still teaches on these topics on executive management and MBA programmes at the Peter F Drucker and Masatoshi Ito Graduate School of Management at Claremont Graduate University in the United States.

Linking mindfulness to self-management

Professor Jeremy Hunter says:

Peter Drucker wrote about the importance of managing yourself. And I suddenly realized that mindfulness could be the basis of a practice of self-management... it could be the basis for teaching people to manage themselves, not in a spiritual context, which wouldn't be appropriate in a business school setting.

Although he was sure he was onto something, it was vital to get the tone right.

The business world is very conservative. My operating assumption was that I had to be able to engage Orange County right-wing evangelical Christian businessmen as well as left-wing Toyota Prius drivers. Both had to say, 'God, that was really great.' I like to say, 'We don't beat drums, we don't sing songs; we teach right-brain skills in a left-brain way, it's all based on finding a new basis of attention and understanding that your attention is malleable and changeable.'

His pilot was a big hit and he still teaches The Practice of Self-Management and The Executive Mind, a series of executive education programmes dedicated to managing oneself. Students learn practices such as seeing where their attention goes when they're stressed or when they're multitasking, for example.

It's really pragmatic, we look at results – what are these effects and are those the ones you want? And how does attention perform under stress?... Then we look at what are the motions of the mind that create and recreate the process and start to see how we're habituating our experience to produce that kind of result. For most people that is a revelation.

His students say what they get out of his classes is the 'realization that they have more choices than they thought they had' and 'that enhanced level of attention'.

Mindfulness gives you greater control over your attention, it gives you choice over how you use that freedom which is exceedingly rare and precious. Actually, the whole institution of coaching is an expression of that as well. Here you are engaging with that person to live life better.

The real action is practice

Another obstacle to clients (and ourselves!) embedding a mindfulness practice is 'non-compliance'. However passionate we may become about mindfulness, the fact is that without practice, it won't have much of an impact. Reading about it is all well and good, and can go some way to changing our mindsets. But as Chaskalson says, 'the real action is practice'. Some clients will have resistance to any kind of regular practice, whatever it is. We need to recognize that for many of us, too, particularly some of our busy working clients, setting aside time to practise can feel impossible.

The fact that it takes time to develop mindfulness is a potential barrier to introducing it into organizations. As Jean de Bruyne, a business coach and psychologist based in New Zealand, says, 'Most organizational (corporate) clients want immediate change and action, and therefore the idea that mindfulness takes time to develop is not something that they want to sometimes focus their energies on.'

In Chaskalson's experience, expecting clients to practise for 30–45 minutes daily has proved unrealistic. He has shortened his teaching sessions too. He now asks people to practise for 20 minutes daily. As he says, 'you have to approach working with mindfulness in organizations differently to a self-referring public. If we encourage people to do just eight hours of practice, we can shift the needle.'

Sometimes it's about being patient and sowing seeds which flourish far and wide later on. Chaskalson, for example, worked with one individual in an organization of 100,000 employees. Gradually this rippled out, with more and more individuals coming forward for mindfulness training/coaching, enabling him to set up a mindfulness group.

Making the business case for mindfulness

We've already started to look at how mindfulness can be helpful and we will continue to look at benefits and applications in this section. However, I thought it might be useful at this point to consider how we can make the business case for mindfulness in coaching, either as external or internal coaches, or as leaders/managers using a coaching style, or anyone else who uses a coaching style, perhaps within teaching or mental health (there are more and more examples of mental health professionals adopting coaching principles).

As coaches, we might be first approaching coaching sponsors who won't be the people we'll be coaching. And obviously it will depend on the perspective of the coaching sponsor as to which benefits we emphasize if we want to roll out formal programmes which include mindfulness.

Running mindfulness programmes

We might be called upon as coaches to offer coaching programmes with a heavy mindfulness bent. If we wish to use the MBSR/MBCT offerings to inform programmes we run, it's important that we have completed such a programme as they are highly experiential and just reading about them really won't cut it! It can be helpful – and some say highly advisable – too to undergo mindfulness teacher training such as that offered by Bangor University.

Jane Brendgen identifies seven core elements within the MBSR/MBCT template (Mindfulness at Work conference, 2012, Cambridge). They are:

- formal practices;
- experiential learning;
- inquiry;
- underpinning themes;
- group discussion;
- meta-structure;
- the teacher's qualities (embodying mindfulness).

If we think about offering mindfulness to different populations, there will be different themes that appeal or have relevance and usefulness, depending on the group – stress, pain relief, self-management and so on. If people are going to be bothered to practise, they need to see the relevance – be it a group or an individual client. We will be looking at mindfulness in relation to specific issues in the following chapters.

Making the case for mindfulness with clients – some tips:

- Make it relevant: highlight the potential benefits of interest to specific clients.

- Highlight the research backing up mindfulness.

- Use appropriate language – you may wish to talk about awareness or presence, for example.

- Keep it secular: avoid getting into spirituality unless the client wishes to.

- Be realistic about how much time people will be able to or want to set aside for practice.

In the next chapter, I share a model for starting to introduce mindfulness to clients.

The FEEL model

11

I developed the following model to illustrate what we're trying to do in mindfulness. I find it useful to share with clients or to have in mind when I am working with a client, and others say they have found it useful too.

FEEL: a model for applying mindfulness

Focus;
Explore;
Embrace;
Let go.

The model

Focus

This is about us setting, then acting upon, our intention to shine a searchlight onto something – our thoughts, our feelings, our bodily sensations including sound and so on. It has been likened to a bee landing on a particular flower. The more we practise 'attentional control', the better we become at it. And it is a very useful 'muscle' to strengthen. We can shift our focus from one object to another. The nature of this focusing is like that of someone tracking an animal in the jungle, treading gently but with heightened awareness, with lightness of touch but sharp and steady focus. Maintaining our focus, we expand to exploration.

Explore

This is about us gently allowing ourselves to explore what is arising and emerging, with compassion, curiosity, non-judgement and openness to possibility. Think of the child engrossed in playing with something new and open to new information and new insights. We're seeking here to activate the 'approach system' which we look at later on.

Embrace

This is a reminder to us to turn towards whatever is there, be it pleasant or unpleasant, without judgement and without grasping or pushing away. Thich Nhat Hanh brings to mind the image of gently cradling a baby – the baby is the subject of our attention, perhaps a thought, a feeling or a bodily sensation. So for example, we might turn our attention (our Focus) to our emotions and in exploring (Explore), we might become aware of anger. And instead of engaging with this, or activating the inner critic, or such, we hold this anger gently. We might label it – there's anger – creating a helpful distance between us and it. Again, it's about approaching with kindness rather than avoiding.

Let go

This is about us not holding on tightly to anything. Just witnessing what is there and letting go. This can be hard when we are experiencing something very pleasant – it is not uncommon to experience blissful states through meditation. Or we could just be feeling wonderfully relaxed. Don't chase it!

Using FEEL

Let's imagine we have a client, 'Matt', sitting in front of us who is sharing how they're struggling with a particular work colleague, how fed up this person is 'making' them feel. They tell you some stories of recent encounters with their colleague, and behaviour they've found unacceptable. It's beginning to feel like a bit of a rant.

How might we use mindfulness here?

Perhaps Matt isn't even aware of his feelings of anger, even though it might be obvious to us, or we might have a pretty strong hunch. We can use FEEL to help him investigate and sit with what's going on for him.

'Matt, I hear that you've been finding it very difficult lately with this colleague and how fed up you're feeling. I wonder if you'd be willing to try a little exercise to explore what's going on for you in a bit more depth?'

'Yeah, sure.'

'OK, so I'd like you to get into a comfortable position and take a few deep breaths, just natural unforced breaths. Closing your eyes, if you're willing. And when you're ready, shining a spotlight onto your feelings, tuning in and shining a light onto what's there.' (Focus)

'And when you're ready, I invite you to gently explore these feelings. (Explore) Here are some questions you might like to consider – just exploring for yourself without trying to change what's there, you don't have to answer me.

'What kind of feelings do you notice?

'Where do you feel them in your body?

'Are they new feelings or familiar feelings?

'Are there any thoughts associated with these feelings?

'Whatever's there, I invite you to just sit with these feelings. Trying not to be too harsh with yourself, not judging yourself at all. Turning towards and just gently holding the feelings that are there. (Embrace)

'Now I invite you to explore whether you would like to and whether you can let these feelings go (Let go), or at least to loosen their grip. Don't feel you have to, the invitation is there if you want to.

'And in your own time, gently come back to the room.'

Don't rush Matt to speak, he will probably need some time to land. Invite him to share what came up during the practice, and to capture it in his journal.

Transformation can happen at any time. Just focusing on something (pain, anger, sadness or whatever) can mean it's suddenly no longer there or has transformed into something else. This can happen as we explore it too; it might elude us or become something else. It might shift as we embrace it gently and let it be, or in the final stage, let it go. The point is not to force anything. Also, although I have described a linear model, it is pretty fluid. We move around through focusing, exploring, embracing and letting go as different things arise.

It is likely to be easier to do the above with a client with whom you have been explicit about being informed by mindfulness. It might feel too directive for some.

Another way in which an opportunity for mindfulness might be created here is if you spot body language in your client which suggests 'hot' feelings, a disorganized state. Perhaps they are waving their hands around or tapping their feet or screwing up their face. Using FEEL, you can act as a mirror to this body language, bringing the searchlight onto this (Focus). You can then 'Explore' this with them, asking probing questions, trying to get them away from conceptual experience – the mental chatter – to direct experience if you can. You might ask them to describe what this hand waving is, for example, how it feels when they're doing this, what shape it has, is there any colour and so on. Other approaches and underpinnings you already have in your practice framework may inform this exploration – gestalt, narrative, use of metaphor, clean language, for example.

CASE STUDY   Noticing what's there

A powerful session with one of my coaches, who is informed by gestalt and mindfulness, came out of her spotting me twisting my hands around and her going straight in with questions about what this was. She didn't seek to interpret, just kept on asking questions – and it did have a shape of sorts, a colour, even a name. And something really shifted that I don't think would have shifted if her line of enquiry had been about the issue I had presented with. In focusing on this 'thing', I was taken away from my logical brain which was trying so hard to work it all out, but frankly, getting nowhere fast. I am not suggesting this would work for everyone but it is a way of bringing in mindfulness. I then found myself sharing the Thich Nhat Hanh holding-the-baby metaphor, talking about how I didn't want to push this thing away, that it had served me well many times (Embrace) but that actually it was time to let go (Let go). But I knew I couldn't do this immediately, I needed to be patient.

I think we have to be careful here, however. Whilst we can encourage clients to sit with unpleasant feelings, to turn towards them in exploration (activating the 'approach' mechanism), there may be times when what comes up for them is too uncomfortable. Again, it comes down to boundaries and being able to spot our limitations. But it is also about taking the lead from the client. It might not be appropriate to suggest they embrace something, of course. And we might need to tread carefully when we ask about the possibility of letting go of something – it may still serve them well, or just not be the right time. It's that lightness of touch we're after here, being able to create and enjoy some distance, to recognize we are not our thoughts, our feelings and so on. It's freedom and the sense of letting go that come with that knowledge or recognition of not knowing what we're after.

Another opportunity for mindfulness with a client experiencing anger might be a mindfulness practice we suggest we do in the session. We might suggest we do an Awareness of breath meditation (Chapter 5), for example, to move them away from being agitated into a more creative, resourceful space in which we can then explore what is going on around this for them.

We can also, as we've said before, use mindfulness to tune into what is happening within ourselves (FEEL), to access data which may be useful. So we might describe to the client how their being angry affects us. This may provide them some useful insights into how they impact on others around them. It might be news to them, for example, to hear that showing anger can make people shut down – they might only see a lack of responsiveness and interpret this as people not caring or bothering. Or we might share that their anger makes us feel nervous and that we think if we were a colleague, it would affect our performance at work, and so on.

We might share some mindfulness strategies they can employ outside the session when they get angry – coaching them for mindfulness.

And, of course, within the session we will be able to practise mindfulness ourselves, especially if we are triggered, which will in turn allow us to be more resourceful for the client.

As I said, it's about spotting opportunities for mindfulness, rather than being wedded to mindfulness.

Client issues

In the following chapters, we will look at some other potential opportunities for mindfulness by looking at some client issues and coaching themes where it can be particularly helpful.

In Figure 11.1 overleaf, I list some of the many issues and goals coaches, including myself, have found mindfulness to help with. In the next chapter we start to look in detail at what mindfulness has to offer to those working with the common issues of stress and work–life balance.

FIGURE 11.1   How mindfulness can help: presenting client
issues/goals

Live more in the present
Improve performance
Deal with chaos and change
Find meaning and purpose
Accept how things are
Be more self-accepting and self-compassionate
Have higher self-esteem
Manage anger
Resolve/manage conflict
Improve difficult relationships
Improve ability to communicate
Achieve better work–life balance
Improve clarity
Improve focus and concentration
Increase working memory capacity, planning and organization
Enhance problem-solving ability
Enhance ability to make decisions
Be better able to think medium and long term
Improve creativity
Increase emotional intelligence, including empathy, emotional regulation
   and social skills
Develop greater presence
Enhance self-awareness
Enhance awareness of others
Enhance ability to recognize, slow down or stop automatic and habitual
   reactions
Recognize and overcome self-limiting beliefs
Develop authentic leadership
Be more aligned with values
Be more intuitive
Increase wellbeing
Tackle sleeping problems
Eat mindfully
Become calmer
Tackle stress and anxiety
Manage mild depression
Improve resilience

Stress, anxiety, depression and work–life balance

12

Stress is one of the main curses of modern times – study after study high-lights its ubiquity. In February 2012, management group Kenexa High Performance Institute reported that workplace stress was at a four-year high. The United Kingdom was found to have the highest level of stress, according to the report, *Stress: What's the impact for organisations?*, a four-year study of 60,000 workers in the UK, the United States, Germany, China, Brazil and India. The report found there had been a marked increase in workplace stress in every country, industry and job type. The main causes of employee stress were found to be work–life conflict, poor leadership and management behaviour, lack of job security, lack of team cohesiveness and dissatisfaction with level of pay.

Stress overtook musculoskeletal problems as the top cause of absence, according to another study (Chartered Institute of Personnel and Development 2011). Some 39 per cent of employers reported that absence due to mental health problems had risen over the preceding 12 months. Again, management style was highlighted as a major cause of stress, along with workloads and considerable organizational change and restructuring. Dealing with sick days costs employers an average of £673 per absent employee a year, up by £73 from 2010, said the report.

It's no surprise, then, that more and more coaches are facing stressed-out clients, and are often personally experiencing higher levels of stress. Those of us who manage or lead using a coaching style, or who coach internally, may be particularly vulnerable in these challenging times. We may find we're coaching others who are stressed while operating in the very same system which is causing stress to our clients. Many of us are coaching people who are fearful for their future, who have concerns about being made re-dundant or who have been made redundant. Or perhaps they are struggling because they have remained in post and are suffering from survivor's syndrome, as well as having much more to do within a difficult environment. Clients may come along with other goals to work on but very frequently, once coach and client get chatting, stress rears its head, or at least a desire to get more work–life balance or not to feel so overwhelmed. According to Professor Stephen Palmer, director of the Centre for Stress Management and of City University's Coaching Psychology Unit in London, 'Research, including ours, highlights how coaching can reduce stress and enhance wellbeing while we've found that stress management is the most common health goal in coaching' (*Coaching at Work*, 2011). He predicts a rise in health and wellbeing coaching, recommending approaches including solution-focused coaching, cognitive behavioural coaching and mindfulness.

Helping clients – and ourselves – manage stress is one of the most important ways in which mindfulness can contribute in coaching. More than half of coaches using mindfulness with clients use it to help their clients with stress, according to my *Mindfulness in Coaching* survey (Chapter 21). However, before we look at how mindfulness can help, let's examine what stress is and how it impacts us.

The good guy and the bad guy

Of course, there is 'good' stress and 'bad' stress. Some stress can help improve our mental and physical performance, what endocrinologist Hans Selye (1975) termed 'eustress', from the Greek 'eu' which means good. This is the opposite to distress, which is what we're concerned about here. Stress can come from being in a situation where our capability is being underused, as well as when we're overloaded, or feel that way. We've all had periods when we are bored 'out of our minds' – not very mind-full. Time seems to go incredibly slowly and we perhaps can't understand why we feel stressed. Ideally, what we're aiming for is what Mihaly Csikzentmihayi calls 'flow', which requires the perfect ratio between challenge and resources.

How stress affects us

Stress can be fine in the short term. In the long term, it's bad news. Stress activates corticosteroids, our immune system is attacked, and we produce fewer neurons whilst older neurons are stimulated. Our brain tissue shrinks and we are less able to learn. We are more likely to feel anxious, nervous and low in mood. We are more likely to perceive the world around us as negative and threatening in general.

When we feel under stress, messages are carried along neurones from the cerebral cortex (where thought processes take place) and the limbic system to the hypothalamus. The anterior hypothalamus produces sympathetic arousal of the autonomic nervous system (ANS), an automatic system that controls the heart, lungs, stomach, blood vessels and glands. The ANS consists of the sympathetic nervous system (SNS) and the parasympathetic nervous system (PNS).

The parasympathetic nervous system is designed to work in tandem with the SNS, acting as an antidote and allowing us to recharge. When our PNS is activated, our hippocampus is aroused, helping with our memory and learning capacity. We are more likely to feel joyful, positive and optimistic. Neurotransmitters including endorphins are produced, which increase wellbeing. Our PNS aids relaxation. It conserves energy levels. It increases bodily secretions such as tears and saliva to defend the body and aid digestion. It sends its messages via a neurotransmitter, acetylcholine, which is stored at nerve endings.

The sympathetic nervous system gears the body up for action in stressful situations, by, for example (Palmer 2000):

- increasing strength in our skeletal muscles;
- increasing heart rate;
- increasing sugar and fat levels;
- reducing intestinal movement;
- inhibiting tears, digestive secretions;
- relaxing the bladder;
- dilating pupils;
- increasing perspiration;
- increasing mental activity;
- constricting most blood vessels but dilating those in heart/leg/arm muscles.

Palmer explains that the main sympathetic neurotransmitter, noradrenaline, is released at the nerve endings and that the stress response also includes the activity of the adrenal, pituitary and thyroid glands. Once the sympathetic nervous system is activated, it instructs the middle part of the adrenal gland, the adrenal medulla, to produce adrenaline (preparing the body for *flight*) and noradrenaline (preparing the body for *fight*). They increase the metabolic rate, as well as the heart rate, and the pressure at which the blood leaves the heart; they dilate bronchial passages and coronary arteries, and the skin blood vessels constrict. Gastrointestinal system activity is also reduced (producing the sensation of butterflies in the stomach).

Meanwhile, the pituitary, an endocrine gland close to the hypothalamus in the brain, is activated by the anterior hypothalamus. The pituitary releases adrenocorticotrophic hormone into the blood. This activates the adrenal cortex, the outer part of the adrenal gland, which then synthesizes cortisol. Cortisol raises arterial blood pressure, mobilizes fats and glucose from the adipose (fat) tissues, reduces allergic reactions, reduces inflammation and can decrease lymphocytes which work on bacteria, for example. Hence, the immune system can be compromised when we are exposed to raised levels of cortisol over long periods. The adrenal cortex releases aldosterone which increases blood volume and subsequently blood pressure. Prolonged arousal over long periods can bring about hypertension.

The pituitary also stimulates the thyroid gland to secrete thyroxin, which increases the metabolic rate, raises blood sugar levels, increases respiration/ heart rate/blood pressure/and intestinal motility (which can lead to diarrhoea). And the pituitary also releases oxytocin and vasopressin which contract smooth muscles such as the blood vessels. Vasopressin increases blood pressure by making the blood vessels more permeable to water.

The parasympathetic nervous system should help us become calm again. However, in many of us our stress response is maintained. This can lead to:

- lowered immune system;
- raised blood pressure, and possibly hypertension and headaches;
- malfunctioning adrenal gland – tiredness, weak muscles, digestive problems, dizziness, and sleep disturbances.

Biological responses to stress (Palmer and Dryden 1995) include the following:

- diarrhoea/constipation/flatulence;
- frequent urination;
- allergies/skin rash;
- high blood pressure/coronary heart disease(angina/heart attack);
- epilepsy;
- dry skin;
- chronic fatigue/exhaustion/burnout;
- cancer;
- diabetes;
- rheumatoid arthritis;
- asthma;
- flu/common cold;
- lowered immune system;
- poor nutrition, exercise and recreation;
- organic problems;
- biologically based mental disorders.

Seeing the whole picture

The more stressed we are, the less we are able to see the whole picture. We literally get tunnel vision. As Professor Mark Williams said at the first

Mindfulness at Work conference (February 2012): 'We're like a rabbit going into a tunnel, it's not 'hello sky, hello trees'. We go straight into the tunnel.'

Williams tells a charming little story about gazelles. These graceful creatures spend most of their time grazing on the African savannah. If a lion shows up, they all run off. Five minutes after charging away from a life-threatening predator, with their amygdalas going crazy, the herd members are calmly grazing again. The gazelles can switch on their fight–flight–freeze mode when needed, and they can also switch it off. Humans, on the other hand, have evolved something pretty special – the ability to bring the past into the present and to look to the future. The past, for example, still holds its ability to shame us and give us pain in the present, and we can learn powerful lessons about how to act in the present by looking to our past. However, sometimes what we recall really isn't relevant to the current situation, and more importantly, we sometimes lose the ability to switch off. And despite our 'superpower' of being able to tune into the past and future, we still suffer from what are sometimes called 'amygdala hijacks' when we think there is danger.

At these times, our old primitive brain overrides our newer brain, and again, at times, we can't then switch it off again so we remain on hyperalert. Many of us will have suffered from being in this state at one time or another, or will know people who have. It's not much fun. You lose the ability to prioritize, everything seems difficult, dangers and problems seem to lurk at every corner. Making even minor decisions becomes hard.

Approach and avoidance orientation

We've evolved over time two different neurological processes: the behavioural inhibition system (the avoidance system) and the behavioural activation system (the approach system) (Gray 1981). There are times when tunnel vision is just what we need but it's often not appropriate and we want to be able to choose to see the wider picture when it serves us. Often what serves us best is to be approach-oriented. The approach system is reward seeking and is associated with feelings such as hope and joy whereas the avoidance system, on the other hand, holds us back from moving to goals. Instead of seeking rewards, it is sensitive to danger or punishment. This system correlates to right prefrontal cortex activation. It is associated with emotions such as fear, anxiety and disgust. Being able to experience these emotions can be very helpful but we can develop a chronically overactive avoidance system, leading to anxiety and depression, and stamping out creativity.

Many people who become anxious also become depressed. The Mental Health Foundation (MHF) (2010) explains that someone who is suffering from depression 'will experience intense emotions of anxiety, hopelessness, negativity and helplessness, and the feelings stay with them instead of going away'.

Although as coaches we have to be careful about overstepping our boundaries, and treating depression is certainly beyond the scope of coaching, the truth is that many of us will face clients who are actually depressed or who are moving towards depression. One in 10 people will experience depression at some point, says the MHF, and we do seem to be seeing a rise in depression. One possible indicator that this is the case is the increase in how many antidepressants are being prescribed. In 2011, almost 50 million prescriptions for antidepressants were handed out by doctors in the United Kingdom, a rise of 9 per cent compared with the previous 12 months.

Working with mindfulness helps us and our clients manage stress, and also in preventing us getting depressed in the first place, and preventing a recurrence (half of those who have become depressed will do so again, according to the MHF). Before we look at what mindfulness can offer here, let's explore another mental process which, like approach and avoidance orientation, can be helpful but problematic.

Discrepancy-based processing

Another process that can be enormously helpful but which presents us with lots of problems too is discrepancy-based processing. This is our ability to compare where we are now with where we want to be and where we don't want to be. It is a wonderful faculty to have but it can be problematic. It's automatic, it's conceptual and it looks out for discrepancies, keeping in mind what to avoid, and using both past and future (remembering and planning). And as Williams says, it depletes our energy.

Williams explains how it can all go wrong when we apply problem solving to our moods and feelings and we can end up going round and round in circles. For example:

Where am I now? Overstressed.
What/where do I want to be? Respected and do well.
What do I want to avoid? Feeling low, weak, undervalued.

'Doing mode has to hold them all in mind... it only works by going round and round to get a solution but the problem is if you do this with your feelings, the feelings get worse,' says Williams.

Discrepancy-based processing is all well and good unless it affects our original state for the worse. In this case, the 'where am I now?' – perhaps a slight feeling of tiredness, or maybe no sense of tiredness at all – is exacerbated.

With your mood, if you're holding two states in mind, it makes you feel more depressed. You redouble your efforts and drive yourself further down. So discrepancy-based processing volunteers to help with tasks it can't help with. It creates the next round of ruminative worrying but you think your mood is naturally declining, you don't realize the problem solving makes it worse.

Whatever we call anger, sadness, disgust, fear and happiness, most psychologists agree they have a signalling function, says Williams.

> They signal that something needs to change (in the case of) the negative ones while happiness says carry on as you are... All signals need to switch on when they're needed and off when not needed.

How mindfulness can help

There is a lot of research underlining how over-planning, ruminating and fretting triggers the 'stress response', which brings with it self-defeating physical, emotional, psychological and behavioural aspects that can lead to physical and mental illness (Palmer and Cooper 2007), and showing how learning to experience life from moment to moment can create calm and wellbeing.

Developing mindfulness skills helps people become more engaged in their work, more energized and less anxious, sleeping better and suffering from fewer symptoms of stress, according to the MHF (2010). Connecting with the present, the 'here and now', stimulates a very different physiological response, as we've explored. Of course, it's not just individuals who stand to benefit – feeling calmer, more in control, and experiencing heightened wellbeing, for example. Those around them, their wider system including employers are likely to reap benefits including greater clarity, improved decision making and judgement, and better relationships. Improvements in relating to others was one of the benefits highlighted at Transport for London (TfL), which has run stress reduction programmes incorporating mindfulness tools for a number of years. Although not directly related to coaching, I've included a case study from TfL (below) as it illustrates how powerful mindfulness can be in helping employees deal with stress, and increasingly coaches are being called upon to offer stress-tackling coaching interventions.

CASE STUDY   Transport for London (TfL)

'I have learned to smile again and to laugh about life': this was one of the comments from a participant on a stress reduction programme which included mindfulness techniques, offered to Transport for London (TfL) employees. According to an internal review carried out in 2003, mental health is one of the top two health issues affecting staff working at the local government body responsible for most aspects of the transport system in Greater London in England. Employees working at TfL face a high number of stressors, including lone working (train operators), dealing with customers (station staff), shift work, suicides and 'near misses' on the underground, workplace violence, and delays and extra workload associated with upgrades and ongoing organizational change.

The stress reduction programme takes a 'psychoeducational approach'. TfL explains that as well as teaching mindfulness techniques, it teaches employees how to interrupt the stress cycle by taking control of physical symptoms; how to map the factors causing stress and take control; positive thinking, being responsive not reactive; and enabling lifestyle changes to support a healthier approach to life and work (TfL 2012). According to TfL, which presented on the programme at the United Kingdom's National Health Service's quarterly Health Work and Wellbeing forum on 13 June 2012, participants generally respond positively to mindfulness techniques, finding them 'very beneficial'. The tools offered are 'seen to be powerful self-awareness tools' and it apparently helps that the programme offers 'an eclectic mix of mindfulness activities to suit most people'. However, TfL says that 'occasionally we have to encourage participation as some people may not understand how it works'.

The programme, which involves two hours a week for six weeks for cohorts of 6 to 10 participants, has delivered impressive results. Among those who have attended, absenteeism due to stress, anxiety and depression dropped by 71 per cent for the following three years. Some 84 per cent of participants 'are relating to others better'; 82 per cent have increased their amount of exercise; 77 per cent have improved diet (including drinking, smoking), and 54 per cent have improved sleeping patterns.

Meditation can help to strengthen our approach pathways, switching off overactivated avoidance pathways, as long as we do it with kindness. Research such as that by Urry *et al* (2004) has found that electrical activity of the left front area of the cortex increases after mindfulness meditation training. And this left shift is thought to reflect a shift towards the approach state of the left hemisphere.

Remedial coaching

We can think of remedial coaching as avoidance-orientated. Clients who come for remedial coaching may be more likely to come to the coaching in a more anxious, less flexible state. They're here because they're a 'problem'. So right from the start, remedial coaching is going to make it hard for clients to work from their most creative, flexible state. Obviously, we can always reserve the right to say no to such coaching. At the very least, we can ensure we do it ourselves in a mindful, approach-orientated way. Even if we don't do remedial coaching, there are many times when we have to deal with problems in the coaching – negative feedback from work colleagues; the threat of demotion; genuine concern about redundancy; relationship issues. A sense of feeling trapped – which many of our clients will present with – is a sure activator of the mind's avoidance system and depressor of its approach system. Clients who feel deeply trapped will often feel exhausted and helpless.

CASE STUDY Trapped

Chandrika was exhausted and felt there was no escape from her current situation. Her workaholic perfectionist tendencies had delivered the goods in the past – she had a well-paid senior role in an investment bank and was known as someone you could rely on. She always worked long and hard hours. She had always worked hard – her parents had pressurized her to do so. Her parents had drummed it into her that they worked so hard so she could go to private school and that she needed to honour this by getting the best grades, going to the best university and so on. But she was tired. She wanted out but couldn't see how. She was getting into all sorts of negative thinking spirals and if she wasn't careful, she was going to fall into deep depression.

There is a lot that coaching can offer to someone like Chandrika. A cognitive behavioural coaching approach helped her explore some of her self-limiting beliefs ('I must be perfect all the time') while a transactional analysis lens helped her become aware of her Be Perfect driver. Mindfulness was introduced to Chandrika within coaching sessions and as homework. It helped her put in place some practices to recharge, and to step away from 'doing' mode as it was the wrong tool for the job here. The more she had thought about being free, the more aversion she had been feeling towards her current state and the more she had wanted to get out whilst feeling more and more trapped. Round and round and round the maze she had been going. Mindfulness also helped her turn towards and observe her negative thoughts, to see her thoughts as mental events.

The great god of busyness

Sometimes we might encounter resistance from a client (and ourselves) to mindfulness because they associate it with doing nothing. As Langer points out (2005), we tend to see inaction as a lack of a particular action – not checking our e-mails, not writing that report and so on. It can be helpful to reframe so we're seeing ourselves instead as choosing to go down another route – relaxing, refreshing, renewing, reflecting, or even actively 'doing nothing'.

Gilbert's three-circle model showing our three-affect regulation systems is useful here (Chapter 8). Michael Chaskalson has suggested having this as a frame of reference when we think about being and/versus doing or talk about this with our clients. We sometimes need to operate in the 'red zone' – this is our protection system. But we also need to operate in the other zones too. The function of the incentive, resource-seeking, drive-excitement system is to give us positive feelings so we seek out resources for ourselves and others so we can survive and prosper. This is our activating, go-getting system. In manic depressives, it can be out of kilter, shifting from too high to too low and vice versa. But the rest of us can have problems too. When we are thwarted in attempts to get what we want, the threat system can be activated.

The third system, the soothing, contentment and safety system, is when we're not striving for anything; we're peaceful and content. This is the zone we inhabit when we're meditating. Gilbert (2010) says, 'When people practise meditation and "slowing down", these are the feelings they report, not wanting or striving, feeling calmer inside and connected to others.'

It can be helpful with some clients, particularly those who appear to be trapped in a cycle of intense productivity with little time for anything else, to explicitly explore their relationship with being and doing.

Questions to explore with your client around being and doing:

- What does 'doing' mean to you?

- What does 'being' mean to you?

- Are being and doing mutually exclusive?

- Are there times when you are 'doing nothing'?

- Are there more helpful ways to frame 'doing nothing'? Such as non-doing? Or resting? Or recharging? Or contemplating? Or being?

- What happens when you aren't doing? What thoughts, bodily sensations and emotions are you aware of? What storylines?

- If you focus more on the present moment, how will that impact on you looking to the future, and making things happen? Could focusing more on the present moment with mindfulness help you become less attached to outcome and to approach things more creatively?

- Does seeking to become aware of and accepting 'what is' mean you end up being more passive or will it help you effect change?

- If you bring more mindfulness into your life, how will this impact on your ability to enjoy the doing?

Tim Malnick says:

As we start to practise mindfulness, we may have to question quite deeply what it means to live a life or lead an organization based on a seductive myth of a never quite arriving future. We may start to see that ambition, as a direct experience, keeps us in a state of permanent dissatisfaction to some extent. It is important to emphasize that this is not an ideology, nor is it a moral question of ambition being good or bad. It is simply that through practices of mindfulness we may start to question areas of our work and life that we just never noticed before, but that have been powerfully and quietly driving a lot of what we do!

As coaches and/or clients, we may gradually become less bothered by success, developing a genuine sense of curiosity about those moments of tightness where we are holding onto something tightly. Our work and our mindfulness practice become less about success and failure. One of the things we may start to see is how we beat ourselves up and how claustrophobic that makes everything [feel].

Examples of coaches using mindfulness to help clients explore being and doing

I used a centring practice yesterday with a client. She has a hectic working life, running from meeting to meeting. Often our coaching sessions start before we have even reached the meeting room with her offloading all the stresses and things that have happened since we last met. She is increasingly aware of how thinly she is stretching herself and how she is operating from a place which drains her and from which she is not able to find the resources she needs to keep going. Centring at the beginning of the session allowed her enough breathing space to identify more thoughtfully what she actually wanted to use the time for, and that we need to spend more time on how she FEELS about her life, not just how to do it all more effectively.

Kate McGuire, life/executive coach based in the United Kingdom

I used mindfulness with a client who felt much of what was going on around her was out of her control and that this was causing her a lot of stress. She was willing to accept that the past can't be changed and the future will by its nature always contain things out of our control. She identified activities she could do which enabled her to be more in the moment. She connected to the feelings of peace and contentment that she associated with one of these activities she had recently been engaged in. This helped her to better understand how mindfulness could help her.

Beverley Grant, executive coach based in the United Kingdom

Yesterday I coached a client who is at a career crossroads. We are working on the long term; however, she is on a short-term contract and is catastrophizing about the near and distant future. We discussed ways in which she might reduce her anxiety and be more trusting, accepting about the future. She also said she wanted to learn to be more in the present. One of the pieces of homework is to download a guided meditation on acceptance and listen to it on a regular basis.

Marianne Craig, career and personal coach based in the United Kingdom

Applying breathing techniques to help a client through an event they are anxious about (eg presentation, meeting with conflict, etc).

Katherine Tulpa, co-founder of Wisdom8 and
an executive/team coach based in the United Kingdom

CASE STUDY   Getting some balance

Mark, a partner at a law firm, worked with UK-based executive coach Linda Woolston initially through the Alliance. She introduced him to mindfulness as a way to carve out more space for himself in the midst of a tough demanding job and a young family.

Linda, quite early on, perceptively picked up that one of the things blocking me was managing conflicting demands between my busy work life and busy home life with two young kids. The one thing I sacrificed was time for myself. Linda asked if I'd ever thought about meditation. I said, 'No, I'm not sure where I would find the time but I'm open-minded.' She said, 'It doesn't have to take a lot of time, it could be a minute. Are you willing to give it a try?' I said, 'Yes, sure, let's try it and see how it goes.' I practised it [the Mindful minute, Chapter 9] every day and even on that basis, I found I was getting some value although it was difficult to put a finger on what it was. The next time I saw her, I said, 'That's great, I'm actually interested in taking it a bit further' and she said, 'There's someone I know . . .' My coaching with Linda carried on and to some extent in parallel, I saw Michael Chaskalson [mindfulness trainer/coach] and did the mindfulness on a one-on-one basis. I did feedback to Linda. With Michael it was an introduction to mindfulness but very much approaching it in a working professional environment. I was very drawn to someone with a very nice manner and very knowledgeable, approaching it not from a spiritual religious level. From a work level, I could already see it was benefiting me and in a broader sense, I felt very fortunate to have that opportunity. Over time, I became more interested in the Buddhist background but at the beginning, it was lots of science and the thinking behind what we were doing, how we could be physically changing how the brain is wired. For someone like me, approaching it from a more emotional [stance wouldn't have worked], lawyers [look at] cause and effect, I like the logic, I found myself immediately comfortable. We did 25-minute sitting meditations, talking through the benefits, then embarked on a series of sessions on CDs. I found at a quite early stage of the process that I was getting a lot of benefit, in terms of everyday living and yes, it did manifest itself in a work context, thinking back. I used a lot of the coaching with Linda to explore whether I should make a career move but what was driving me to get the original coaching with her was a sense that someone who is calm and undemonstrative had become more tense, bottling things up, not shouting but allowing myself to get more worked up over things that didn't matter. Even early on in the mindfulness practising, I was catching myself, for example, with external stimulus such as e-mails feeling an emotion such as anger, irritation and rather than setting these in train, I was recognizing these signals and developing the ability to just calm myself. I found even early on I developed that knack quite well. It made a big difference in an obvious way and with the wider benefit of feeling more philosophical about life and work, and the relative unimportance of things in the office, maintaining a general sense of calm. I felt better able to glide through the day so I kept it going with Michael, having follow-up sessions, topping up the practice and exploring some new techniques. I did one long-weekend silent retreat in Bangor with Buddhist mindfulness-based meditation. It was my first experience of 'hard core'. I was fine with it, initially I found it a bit odd that it was silent, you couldn't even look at anyone and it was quite intense in terms of the programme, up early, doing sitting and walking meditation but it was a profound experience, deepening my practice. I was feeling an enormous sense of calm, almost to the sense of detachment. It was very useful in terms of deep-cleaning my mind, I'd like to do it again. I was approached by headhunters and I am pretty sure that I was much better able to deal with the whole stressful process of making a career move in a more positive way, and just in terms of weighing up opportunities, the ability to take a step back and view things. Over the course of the last year, I've been doing less but I still practise meditation – it was six or seven times a week, now it's two or three times a week. I feel it's enough to keep me topped up. Michael said even doing the original [eight-week] course makes a difference, it stays with you. It's still very much part of how I go through life. I will do some Mindful walking or take Mindful moments in the office, a bit of a check-in with myself. Interestingly with the meditation, having started it off at home, it will now tend to be at lunchtime, on a bench or in a local church for a particularly productive recharge. Where mindfulness comes in as a lawyer is the ability to listen to clients for what they're wanting, I'm better than I was, my mind has decluttered to an extent because of the practice. I've always been very disciplined but I am better able to concentrate, better able to come up with solutions quickly, more focused. It's improved relationships – really early on, I'm sure some people won't have noticed a big difference because I was bottling things up but my wife noticed I was less inclined to get snappy about things, more inclined to let provocation wash over me. I'm not a complete angel but it has certainly made a big difference. With a young family, you get disturbed nights – it's fulfilling on one level and frustrating on another. I'd noticed a couple of times I'd got irritated with the kids, I felt afterwards, 'That was a bit harsh, I should have been able to stop myself.' The meditation process helped a lot. But there was something negative – the flip side to taking some emotion out of exchanges can be a sense of detachment. I'm not the most emotional person. I'm naturally drawn to meditations like counting the breath but I try to intersperse this with the Loving-kindness meditation which I am not so drawn to. Mindfulness isn't something I broadcast at work although I have spoken to a couple of the other partners about the process. It's a different culture, it's less the done thing here.

Tips for working on stress

- Discuss how widespread stress has become in our society and what happens when we get stressed to help take the sting out of what is already an unpleasant, and sometimes terrifying, experience. Questions such as 'Why is this happening to me?', 'I bet everyone else is coping, am I really weak?', 'I know I shouldn't be feeling like this, why can't I stop it?' and so on can start to lose a lot of their power.

- For clients who want the science, share what some of the research in neuroscience is suggesting around how mindfulness can help.

- Start each session with a short mindfulness practice – it can be just the Mindful minute or the Three-minute breathing space (Chapter 9) to help the client 'land' and bring your client (and you) into a more resourceful state.

- Encourage the client within and/or as 'homework' to sit quietly whenever they feel a 'stress attack' coming on and really notice what is happening in their body, feelings and thoughts. Where are they feeling it in their body? Where are there contractions? What feelings are coming up? What thoughts are coming up? What do they feel about these feelings? Remind them to be curious, non-judgemental and compassionate.

- Discuss doing and/versus being, how it's not about not doing, but about doing mindfully, as well as doing more being! Share Gilbert's three-emotion regulation systems model from Chapter 8.

- Encourage reframing.

Homework for the client

Try out this cognitive behavioural coaching-based exercise, which has a mindfulness element, for yourself. Then try it with clients. Invite your client to keep a record, perhaps in their journal, or using the following.

Unpleasant events record

Try to be aware of unpleasant events in the moment, as much as possible. Use the following framework to prompt your exploration and awareness, and write it up later, so you can track changes.

What is the event?
Are you aware of unpleasant feelings actually while the event is happening?
What is going on in your body?
What moods, feelings and thoughts come up for you around this event?

And later: What are your bodily sensations, feelings and thoughts as you record the event and what it prompted in you retrospectively?

You can unpack this in a subsequent session. It's helpful to have some grasp of cognitive behavioural coaching (see Chapter 19).

Encourage your client to track any differences. Invite them to notice any recurring themes. Which kinds of events trigger which kinds of responses? Remind them to be curious, open, non-judgemental and compassionate to themselves, to just notice what is without trying to change anything.

You might like to suggest, if you are not an MBSR or MBCT teacher, that clients suffering from stress or at risk of depression attend a local eight-week MBSR/MBCT programme. The MHF is among bodies which have called for mindfulness-based therapies to be made available on the UK National Health Service, particularly for those with recurrent depression. And the large majority of general practitioners (72 per cent) think mindfulness meditation would benefit the mental health of their patients, according to the MHF (2010). However, at that time, only 20 per cent of GPs said they had access to MBCT courses for their patients and further cutbacks in mental healthcare funding has no doubt exacerbated the problem of a lack of access. If clients can't get onto programmes for free, it's worth their paying out themselves. Prevention is far better than cure, particularly as cures can be elusive in the arena of mental health. The MHF has ploughed on in subsequent years with efforts to increase access, offering an online mindfulness course. Research with the University of Oxford published in the *British Medical Journal* in May 2012 showed average reductions of 39 per cent in course participants' perceived stress and that the course offers comparable benefits to face-to-face therapy. However, I really valued the group discussion element of the MBCT programme I participated in, as did a number of my fellow participants.

I'd also like to emphasize again the importance of us as coaches being clear about when to make or recommend a referral to a GP, clinical psychologist or other specialist help. We need to bear in mind the past history of the client and the pervasiveness of their symptoms. And we need to make sure we are ourselves in a resourceful place.

Recommended mindfulness practices

Mindful minute (Chapter 9) – stressed clients will feel they have no time for anything but can't deny that a minute really isn't very long!

Body scan (Chapter 4) – to help the client become more aware of the impact of stress on their body.

Centring (Chapter 4) – this is a wonderful practice for clients whose stress is inhibiting their performance – they can do this before stressful situations as an alternative to the Mindful minute, or Watching the breath.

Watching the breath (Chapter 5).

Loving-kindness meditation (Chapter 7) – this is helpful for clients who are being really hard on themselves, and probably taking it out on others.

Obviously there are links between stress, depression and anxiety, and resilience, happiness and wellbeing. However, I think the latter three topics warrant their own treatment because if we can build resilience and sow seeds for happiness and wellbeing early enough, using tools such as mindfulness, we can hopefully avoid high stress levels, burnout, depression and anxiety. We look at how in the next chapter.

Resilience, happiness and wellbeing

13

Before we explore what makes us resilient and how mindfulness can help our clients build resilience, let's look at what we mean by it.

Definitions

Neenan (2009) defines resilience as:

> the ability in the face of difficulty to retain flexible cognitive, behavioural and emotional responses.

Davidson (2000) defines it as:

> the maintenance of high levels of positive affect and wellbeing in the face of adversity.

Davidson says: 'it is not that resilient individuals never experience negative affect, but rather that the negative affect does not persist'.

Reivich and Shatte (2002) see resilience as 'the ability to persevere in the face of stressors and bounce back from setbacks'.

And Clough and Strycharczyk (2012) define mental toughness (which they see as broader than resilience) as: 'The quality which determines in large part how people deal effectively with challenge, stressors and pressure… irrespective of prevailing circumstances.'

What makes us resilient?

Dr Suzanne Kobasa at City University of New York has studied all sorts of people who might be expected to lead stressful lives, including lawyers, bus drivers and call centre staff. She found that those who got sick often had a different psychological characteristic to those who stayed healthy. She called this psychological hardiness. She says 'stress-hardy' individuals have high levels of the following psychological traits:

- control (holding a strong belief that we can influence our environment and make things happen);
- commitment (feeling engaged in what we're doing, and trying hard);
- challenge (seeing change as a natural component of our lives which can offer opportunity).

Israel-based medical sociologist Dr Aaron Antonovsky has studied people who have survived extreme stress, such as Holocaust survivors. The core important traits he identified were:

- comprehensibility (holding an inherent sense of coherence, feeling we can make sense of our internal and external worlds);
- manageability (feeling we have sufficient resources to cope);
- meaningfulness (feeling that the demands and challenges we face are ones in which we can find meaning and can commit to).

Research by Campbell (2009) based on 25 interviews with leaders, came up with some surprising results. She found that resilience:

- can be learnt;
- is not confidence;
- is about both being able to control *and* letting go of the need to control;
- includes speed of bounce back;
- includes a full recovery of energy;
- includes pacing so that around a third of an individual's energy is used for sensing, prioritizing and refreshing.

Meanwhile, Clough and Strycharczyk (2012) have come up with the following model, proposing that overall mental toughness is a product of four pillars:

- challenge: seeing challenge as an opportunity;
- confidence: having high levels of self-belief;
- commitment: being able to stick to tasks;
- control: believing that you control your destiny.

According to Strycharczyk, resilience tends to embrace the last two – control and commitment – whereas mental toughness embraces all four.

There are recurring themes in all of these models around the importance of people believing there is meaning in their lives; that whatever is happening is understandable, to them, at least; and that they can manage and have some control over their lives. Attunement to others is important too.

> Personal experience and scientific observation each confirm the importance of interpersonal attunement for our sense of wellbeing – and our growth toward resilience.
>
> Siegel 2010

How mindfulness can help

There is nothing either good or bad, but thinking makes it so.

Hamlet, Act 2, Scene 2

People are not afraid of things, but of how they view them.

Epictetus

There is a story from Buddhist teachings about the Two Darts. The Buddha apparently told this story (the Sallatha Sutta) to distinguish between how an 'untaught worldling' – very quaint terminology for a layperson untrained in mindfulness – and a 'well-taught noble disciple' respond to anything painful. When something bad happens to any of us, we are struck by a first dart – the actual event. However, how we respond next is up to us. We can either be neutral in our response – just noticing the painful feeling or whatever. We can purposefully seek a positive response. Or we can also strike ourselves with a second dart – the mental response we have to that first event.

Positive emotions and reappraisal

We can all think of times when we've actively sought to stimulate a positive emotion to make us feel better. We might go to see a comedy or arrange to see some friends if we're feeling low, because we think doing so will make us feel happier.

Our ability to regulate emotions is essential to our wellbeing and our resilience and mindfulness can really help here. Richard Boyatzis says, 'When we encourage those we're coaching to discuss problems, we can see their energy draining – their thought–action repertoire contracts. Mindfulness is an excellent strategy to help us regulate our emotions.'

Researchers such as Barbara Frederickson have discovered the central role positive emotions play in our success and wellbeing, and our resilience. Frederickson's Broaden and Build theory (1998) of positive emotions says that the experience of positive emotions broadens people's momentary thought–action repertoires, building their enduring personal resources. Frederickson describes this as 'the discovery of novel and creative actions, ideas, and social bonds, which in turn build that individual's personal resources'. Garland *et al* (2010) say mindfulness and Loving-kindness meditation are ways to generate positive emotions which may counter the negative affective processes implicated in depression, anxiety and schizophrenia.

Actively developing positive emotions is linked to the ability to reappraise, which mindfulness helps with. Positive reappraisal is an adaptive process by which we reconstrue stressful events as benign, valuable or beneficial. The ability to reappraise in a positive light has been associated with positive health outcomes.

Stepping back

One of the ways in which mindfulness helps our clients – and ourselves – reappraise or reframe is because it helps us reflect and stand back so we can see the view from the balcony, rather than the dance floor (Heifetz 1994). There is a body of research and thinking including from people such as psychologist Chris Argyris and the late anthropologist Gregory Bateson which emphasizes the importance of stepping back. Argyris has defined learning as the detection and correction of error, saying that single-loop learning occurs when errors are corrected without altering the underlying governing values, while double-loop learning occurs when errors are corrected by changing the governing values and then the actions. We have to step back in order to get a different perspective, which then helps us change our values and behaviours. Bateson, who helped to extend systems theory/cybernetics to the social and behavioural sciences, also advocated stepping outside in order to develop the capacity to learn.

So one of the key ways mindfulness can help clients build resilience is in developing some distance from whatever is going on from them – tapping into the Observer mind we explored earlier. They can then get things into perspective and have greater choice over whether to accept things as they are or reframe them. We make sense of the world through language and sometimes giving something a different label can create a shift. Or just detaching from language and allowing ourselves to feel and notice without judgement can help us see things differently.

Research by Baer *et al* (2006) on mindfulness traits showed that observation is an independent variable only in people who had formal mindfulness training. It was interwoven with being non-judgemental, being non-reactive, acting with awareness and being able to label and describe the internal world. So basically, becoming mindful means we can 'see' much more.

Evaluation

Nothing is inherently anything, it all depends on our evaluation. Langer (2005) says, 'If we can only learn to think mindfully about how evaluation works on us, we won't have to be held hostage by it. When we are evaluative, we confuse the stability of our mind-sets with the stability of the underlying phenomenon.'

We see things differently, according to our motivation and our vantage point. And people see the same information differently too. We make sense of the world through language, through the labels we put on things but unless we are mindful, we get 'mindlessly' caught up in all sorts of labelling. We mind-read, we imagine we know how others feel or see the world because we know how we might feel in a similar situation, leading us to imagine people are more similar to us than they really are: Lee Ross's 'false consensus effect'. Research shows us that the false consensus effect is widespread and that we overestimate how many others would feel or act how we would feel or act.

There is a lot of research out there showing how much power our frames of reference have over our attitudes. One study, for example, by Fazio *et al* (1981) asked people questions which led them to give introverted or extroverted answers, regardless of whether they were actually extroverted or introverted.

One of the wonderful things about great literature, theatre and cinema is how we're helped to stand in another's shoes, to see the world through their eyes. Sometimes, we find sympathy and compassion are evoked in us for characters towards whom we would expect to feel negatively. In Milton's *Paradise Lost*, for example, we find ourselves identifying with Satan. And as we began to explore in earlier chapters, mindfulness helps us suspend our judgement towards events, experiences and people. Instead of mindlessly and hastily jumping to conclusions, we can stay with not knowing for longer, and can access more information.

Am I sure?

There is another Buddhist story about a man being sent into a panic because he sees a snake on the path in front of him. He then realizes that it is not a snake at all, but a coiled rope. The lesson, of course, is that we rush to evaluate, to interpret and to label. If we are mindful, we and our clients can be open to more possibilities and options, and make better decisions. We are sense-making creatures but all too often in our mindlessness, we shut down possibilities, believing the sense we have made of an event or an experience was the only sense to be made. What we really need to do is slow down, suspend our judgement; we need to come to our senses. We can take some deep breaths, attend to the here and now, ground ourselves, and then ask ourselves, 'Am I sure?' How many times have we had the experience that we are absolutely convinced we didn't do something only to realize we have, for example?

We know we tend to prefer action to inaction. If through mindfulness, we seek to suspend our snappy evaluations, would that hold us back from action? It can do, but Langer says that if we accept that evaluations are products of our minds, rather than things having intrinsic meaning, we can eliminate evaluations and take action without worrying about negative evaluation. She says that hidden within the fear of inaction is the evaluation that making the 'wrong' decision may be costly.

Garland, Gaylord and Park (2009) propose that the mechanism which allows us to shift from a 'stress appraisal' to a positive reappraisal involves the meta-cognitive mode of mindfulness, a mode which allows us to see and experience thoughts as transient, psychological events rather than the truth.

Nelson, Stuart, Howard and Crowley (1999) describe meta-cognition as 'a meta-level of awareness which monitors the object of cognition while reflecting back upon the processes of cognition itself'. Once again, this is the Observer mind we explored earlier.

Attentional control

Practising mindfulness helps us develop our attentional control and this is an important ingredient in resilience and in high performance. Dr David Marchant, senior lecturer in sport and exercise psychology at Edge Hill University, writes in 'Developing mental toughness: improving performance, wellbeing and positive behaviour in others' (2012): 'If there is one factor that underpins people's ability to perform at their best, whatever their occupation, whatever the situation, it is their ability to focus and control their focus of attention effectively.' He says that although attentional control is well understood in sports, which is where the most valuable research has been carried out, it has been an underdeveloped area of application in the occupational world until now.

Numerous studies suggest that mindfulness can make a big difference to our resilience levels. Jon Kabat-Zinn's team, for example, scored people who had completed the eight-week MBSR programme on the resilient traits identified by Kobasa and Antonovsky that we looked at earlier. Participants felt happier, more energized and less stressed. They felt their lives were more meaningful and that they had more control over their lives. They were more likely to see challenges as opportunities rather than threats (Weissbecker *et al* 2002; Dobkin 2008). It's exciting that the traits mentioned above are not set in stone and that they can be developed or enhanced in just eight weeks. We looked at the approach system earlier, which can be developed through mindfulness – this appears to be important in building resilience.

Tips for working with resilience:

- Discuss with your client what resilience means to them and explain some of the common themes.
- Explore with the client how resilient they think they are and what they have in place to help them, suggesting mindfulness as another tool to have at their fingertips.
- Share some of the research on how mindfulness helps with resilience.
- Suggest you end with a practice such as the Three-minute breathing space to help them recharge before they go back into the fray.
- Encourage them to become familiar with their thoughts, emotions and bodily sensations so they can nip things in the bud when they feel their energy is depleting, or they are being triggered.
- As before, explore doing versus being and discuss how it's normal for us as human beings to want to be active, but that to be resilient, we need to pace ourselves, with minor fluctuations in energy demands rather than massive peaks and troughs.
- As before, encourage reframing and help them build a wider repertoire of positive emotions.
- Explore how your client deals with uncertainty and complexity (see Chapter 14).

Recommended mindfulness practices

Mindful minute – this can easily be built in throughout the day as part of everyday routine.

Three-minute breathing space – again, as it's only three minutes, it is a fabulous practice to do in addition or as an alternative to the Mindful minute as part of everyday practice. Resilient people pace themselves and these mini practices help us do that.

Awareness of breath.

Centring – this practice can be employed easily before demanding situations, as a matter of course.

Loving-kindness meditation – ensuring we are compassionate towards ourselves and others can keep those twisted storylines at bay and help us not jump to conclusions.

Health and wellbeing

So mindfulness helps with wellbeing and happiness levels because we're more likely to be able to reappraise positively. We've seen how mindfulness can help us manage stress, and we know from countless studies what a killer stress can be.

We looked at some of the research into the impact of mindfulness and meditation on our health in Chapter 3. To recap, we saw that mindfulness decreases cortisol; calms the autonomic nervous system; boosts the immune system; and improves a range of medical conditions including type II diabetes, cardiovascular disease, asthma, premenstrual syndrome and chronic pain. It can also work wonders on psychological conditions such as anxiety, insomnia, phobias and eating disorders, which can all take their toll on people's health.

Better outcomes

Mindfulness training combined with coaching helps clients attain their health-related goals, particularly if clients receive mindfulness training first, according to a study in 2008 by Australian researchers (Spence, Cavanagh and Grant 2008) (see box).

Mindfulness and health goals

Research by Dr Gordon Spence, Dr Anthony Grant and Dr Michael Cavanagh from the Coaching Psychology Unit at the University of Sydney found that mindfulness helped clients resist the temptation to sabotage their progress toward goals. 'Many people find their psychological struggles hardest to resolve,' they said.

The three coaching psychologists took 45 coaching clients and put them into three groups. One group was given four weeks of mindfulness training. This was described as mindfulness meditation or attention training to help people reach 'the awareness that emerges through paying attention on purpose, in the present moment, and non-judgmentally to the unfolding of experience moment by moment', followed by four weeks of one-on-one coaching. The second group received coaching followed by mindfulness training while the third group received eight weeks of health education focused on principles of exercise and nutrition management.

After eight weeks, the clients who received mindfulness training followed by coaching had goal attainment that was 'significantly greater' than clients who received education and direction.

Clients in the group that received coaching first and mindfulness training second fared better than the education-only group, but their results were not as significant as the meditation-first group, according to the research.

Making Australia Happy

Mindfulness and coaching were at the heart of another Australian research project, Making Australia Happy, an ambitious initiative launched in 2010 to improve the wellbeing and happiness of as many people in Australia as possible. More than 45,000 have taken the Happy 100 Index constructed by Dr Anthony Grant, director of the Coaching Psychology Unit of the University of Sydney. The Index is a composite of the Depression Anxiety Stress Scales, Positive and Negative Affect Scales, the Satisfaction With Life Scale and the Warwick–Edinburgh Mental Wellbeing Scale. Dr Grant led the team of experts which also included Russ Harris, general practitioner, mindfulness expert and author of *The Happiness Trap*, and Anna-Louise Bouvier, a physiotherapist and mind–body specialist.

The initiative was backed up by a TV show which charted the progress of eight participants from one of Australia's least happy regions. As well as showing decreases in levels of the stress hormone cortisol, tests run by the experts recorded an overall increase in the hormone melatonin, which helps with sleep and immune function. Volunteers with unhealthy blood pressure and cholesterol levels showed a significant drop, comparable to what would be expected if they had taken medication, while their pain thresholds increased.

All the volunteers recorded a significant reduction in the level of neural activity after the eight-week period (around 50 per cent), which is positive. When participants' levels were first measured, the average was 48, with 50 as neutral. Nearly two months later, it had gone up to 72, then to 84 at the end. And 24 weeks on, it was still at 80, demonstrating that the impact was not short-lived.

It became clear on the programme that physical aspects of lifestyle including diet changes, increased exercise and more sleep can make a huge difference to happiness and wellbeing, and that interventions need to be customized for the individual. For some of the participants, mindfulness was more important.

The green zone

We've seen that mindfulness helps us operate from the soothing, contentment and safety system of Professor Gilbert's model. The calm, peaceful types of feelings from the 'green zone' are associated with higher wellbeing and lower depression, anxiety and stress than the positive affect from the 'blue zone', according to self-report research by Gilbert et al (2008).

Gilbert suggests that if there are different types of positive emotions with different brain systems underpinning these, it makes sense for those in the helping professions to focus on how to stimulate capacities for the positive emotions associated with calmness and wellbeing. Practising mindfulness and cultivating compassion help to stimulate these capacities in our clients (and ourselves).

When we learn mindfulness, we learn to navigate to the content, safe, connect system. This is the system that's nurtured by caregivers when we are young. And Gilbert (2010) says, 'When people practise meditation and "slowing down", these are the feelings they report; not wanting or striving, feeling calmer inside and connected to others.'

We've also seen how mindfulness can help us become present, attuned and resonant with others, which also contributes to wellbeing. Feeling cared for, accepted and having a sense of belonging and affiliation with others are fundamental to the development of our physiology and our wellbeing, according to Siegel (2007).

The Five-a-day model for mental wellbeing

Another model which can be useful when looking at wellbeing and mindfulness is the Five-a-day model. The United Kingdom's 2008 *Foresight Report on Mental Capital and Wellbeing* (**www.bis.gov.uk**) led to the development of this model for maintaining mental wellbeing, although it contributes to improvements in general wellbeing. Here are the five ingredients:

- Connect (with people around you).
- Be active.

- Take notice.
- Keep learning.
- Give.

Dale and Lancaster (2012) suggest mindfulness as a way to take notice and also suggest coaching while walking as a way to Be Active into the session. Mindful walking (Chapter 19) can be useful here.

Mindful eating

Sometimes our clients will identify losing weight as one of their goals and/ or leading a healthier lifestyle. Bringing mindfulness to how they look after themselves, to how they nourish themselves can deliver impressive results. A good place to start is the Raisin meditation (Chapter 1). It doesn't take long to eat a raisin mindfully but it is a very different experience from just wolfing down handfuls without giving them much thought. By the time you get to tasting the raisin and letting its flavour burst through your mouth, it can taste very different from how it usually tastes. This can be done within the coaching session or set as homework – although I find the latter is a bit hit and miss. Clients seem to engage more in mindful eating if you do it together the first time.

You can then encourage the client to try eating at least one meal mindfully each day – they will probably find this is the meal they enjoy the most, and will probably relish the peacefulness of the experience. There might be affirmations they might want to play around with too – for example, something around treating their body well, gaining the nourishment they need. They can then build up to trying to approach all eating with mindfulness. They will probably find they feel fuller after eating more slowly, and might find their digestive system is very appreciative of them not rushing their food.

This approach can also be used with people who find they don't eat enough or the right kinds of food, encouraging them to really savour the experience of eating.

You might like to recommend clients struggling with this issue read the following book, which also includes a CD: *Mindful Eating: A Guide to Rediscovering a Healthy and Joyful Relationship with Food*, by Jan Chozen Bays. We often tend to lay the blame for obesity at the door of processed food and of course, the type of food we eat is a real problem. However, Bays says that mindfulness addresses eating disorders at their source – food in itself is not bad or good – 'the source of the problem lies in the thinking mind and the feeling heart'.

With mindful eating, we are truly present to the joy of eating, savouring all the different sensations, textures, feelings, noises even. We so often guzzle down our food without thinking and leave the table only to feel hungry soon after. If we eat mindfully, we learn to eat with moderation and self-compassion. And for those of us who really love our food, we get to really enjoy it to the full.

Tips for working on health and wellbeing

- Work with the client using the Five-a-day model as a way to enhance wellbeing and underline the importance of 'taking notice' using mindfulness techniques.
- Suggest clients introduce Mindful eating, short practices such as the Mindful minute and the Three-minute breathing space, and Mindful walking (if they're able bodied) into their regular routines, building in time each day to slow down.
- Explore the health benefits mindfulness brings and look at how the client is already helping themselves.
- Use mindfulness to explore and challenge assumptions the client may hold so they can usefully reframe.
- Combine mindfulness with approaches such as cognitive behavioural coaching; techniques such as motivational interviewing, and models such as Prochaska and DiClemente's transtheoretical model of change (six stages: pre-contemplation; contemplation; planning/decisions; action; maintenance; and relapse), which can be useful in health and wellbeing coaching.

Part of how we build resilience is about how we deal with complexity, change and uncertainty, which we will look at in the next chapter, along with systems thinking.

Uncertainty, change, complexity and interconnectedness

14

> *If there is no doubt, there is no choice.*
>
> **ELLEN LANGER**

> *The more we can encourage those we coach, our business clients, our direct reports and so on, to stay with not knowing, to be curious and not to make assumptions, the more we will help them tap into choice and possibility. Their worlds will be full of so much more potential.*
>
> **DANIEL SIEGEL**

In this chapter, we look at how mindfulness can support us and our clients in accepting and dealing with uncertainty, change and complexity. We also look at how mindfulness practice can help us appreciate interconnectedness, enabling us to take a more systemic approach to life and work.

Uncertainty

In the Western hemisphere in particular, we seem to be obsessed with trying to predict the future. Risk assessment is integral to organizational processes and we're always trying to come up with ever more sophisticated models for solving problems and predicting what will happen next. When these fail, we feel out of control and as if our world has been turned upside down.

Often we take out our anger and fear on those we charged with being the crystal-ball gazers. Those who 'got it wrong' are made to suffer. And if we 'get it wrong' ourselves, we become full of self-recrimination. We do all we can to 'get back to normal' – a 'normality' where we 'know' exactly what is going to happen. A normality that doesn't really exist.

Kowalski (2011) says, 'trying to predict the future on the basis of past experience... has developed into something of a cultural obsession in many areas of our lives... the assumption seems to be that predictability is normal while unpredictability needs to be avoided and "repaired"'.

This is nonsense, of course, but it doesn't stop us doing it. There is arguably more of an emphasis in Eastern cultures on 'going with the flow'; however, trying to make predictions is partly to do with how human brains work. Our brains crave certainty; they hate change. Change is unknown and therefore seems dangerous. We're sense-making animals, we look for patterns and seek to predict wherever we can. We experience pleasure when our predictions are correct. As David Rock explains in *Your Brain at Work*, the ability to predict and then obtain data that meets those predictions generates an approach ('toward') response. One of the reasons people enjoy games like crosswords is the rush they get from 'creating more certainty in the world, in a safe way' (Rock 2009). Yet of course the only certain thing is death; uncertainty is very much part of the rich and colourful tapestry of life.

There is a link between the concepts of autonomy and certainty. We like to feel we have control or agency over our lives. Many studies, including Marmot *et al* (1997), have shown that having control or feeling like we have control positively affects our ability to manage stress, our wellbeing and our resilience, as we explored in the last chapter. Feeling or finding we have choices makes all the difference to our ability to cope and flourish because it shifts us to an approach response.

Staying with the unknown

One of the problems for many clients, leaders for example, is that they are expected to *know*; we expect them to be decisive, to *lead* us. In seeking to preserve what is often an illusion of being certain and ultra decisive, people can shut themselves down to possibility. They want to look like they know what they're doing, even if they don't. They don't want to appear vulnerable and wavering, so they become 'black and white' in their thinking. They become 'mindless'. It's understandable, but often not very fruitful. Others, overwhelmed by the unknown, may become 'scattered' or burn out. So one aspect of working with uncertainty through mindfulness is becoming comfortable with not knowing. This was exactly what 'Tom' needs to do.

CASE STUDY   Desperately seeking all the information

'Tom' wants to work through coaching on speaking out and challenging others. It emerges that he feels he needs to have *all* the information at his fingertips before making any moves. He feels that if he only had more time and/or were more intelligent, he'd know everything he needs to know to inform his assertions, challenging of others, and actions. The trouble is, he'll never be informed enough for his liking, partly because no, there isn't enough time; partly because he sets himself ridiculously high standards, but also because it's impossible to know and predict *everything*. We're working on what 'good enough' looks like. We're working with mindfulness so that Tom can scan himself and his environment, picking up more nuances and 'hidden data' to help him keep better informed. We're working on him being more compassionate towards himself for 'not being perfect' (using the Loving-kindness meditation, for example). And we're working with mindfulness to help Tom accept that life is uncertain and changing (using meditations including Awareness of breath and the Body scan).

Mindfulness is also helping Tom recharge during the day. We sometimes practise a short meditation during coaching and he now builds in Mindful minutes and Three-minute breathing spaces into his working week, with longer meditations at the weekend when he can. More than anything, practising meditation is helping Tom 'roll with the punches'. He is beginning to accept that he really can't know everything there is to know, and that actually that's OK. Even more than that, sometimes the right thing to do is stay with not knowing.

Default modes

Mary Beth O'Neil, author of *Executive Coaching with Backbone and Heart*, talks about how, in times of acute anxiety, we tend to go into our default modes. Mine, for example, is to feel scattered, indecisive and ungrounded, whereas when I'm not anxious or stressed, I'm very comfortable with ambiguity, with shades of grey rather than black and white. We all have our own default modes. Some of us become more rigid and inflexible when anxious and faced with uncertainty. So part of it is about using mindfulness to build self-awareness. Which mode do you default to under stress? Can you spot the triggers and the signs that this is happening?

Clarity and decision making

For those of us working with leaders, or who are leaders, we know just how tough it is being in a position where the focus is on getting results and fast, and on snappy decisions. Nobody wants an indecisive leader. But people do want someone who doesn't just charge from one thing to the next, without thinking it through, who just reacts rather than responds, who makes a decision just for the sake of being seen to make a decision. Sometimes, the way forward really isn't clear. Encouraging clients, including leaders, to be mindful can help them take the time they need – even if it's just five minutes somewhere quiet – to just be, and often the solution will come to them seemingly out of nowhere. We've all had that happen, I am sure.

If instead of becoming more 'black and white' and rigid, a client has become more scattered in the face of uncertainty, mindfulness can sharpen their focus and increase clarity about the way forward. Moving into approach state will help them feel more confident and better able to trust their own decisions, while the meta-cognitive aspect of mindfulness will help them notice and gather more data, and be more intuitive. And apparently, those who meditate are better able to make rational rather than emotionally charged decisions, according to research by Kirk *et al* (see box).

The Ultimatum Game

Imagine one of your friends has just won £100 and offers you a few pounds. Would you take his offering? According to research carried out over the last three decades, only a quarter of us would accept, even though it seems the logical thing to do. The rest of us would decline because we see the offering as paltry and unfair. But apparently, if you're an experienced meditator, you're much more likely to accept, according to Kirk *et al* (2011). Their research shows that experienced meditators use different areas of the brain when they are faced with 'unfair' choices. This allows them to make decisions rationally rather than emotionally. Apparently, human decision making is often viewed as a competition between cognitive and emotional processes and we deviate from rational processes when we include emotional factors in our decision making. The researchers used computational and neuro-imaging techniques to study the neurobiology of social cognition and decision making in 26 Buddhist meditators and 40 control subjects. The participants played 'the Ultimatum Game', in which the first player proposes how to divide a sum of money and the second can accept or reject the proposal. The researchers' hypothesis that successful regulation of negative emotional reactions would lead to increased acceptance rates of 'unfair' offers by the meditators was confirmed. But there were surprises in the neuro-imaging results – the meditators engaged different parts of the brain than expected. The anterior insula in the brain has been associated with the emotion of disgust, playing a key role in marking social norm violations, rejection, betrayal and mistrust. In previous studies of the Ultimatum Game, anterior insula activity was higher for unfair offers, and the strength of its activity predicted the likelihood of an offer being rejected – this was the case with those in the control this time too. However, the meditators' anterior insula showed no significant activation for 'unfair' offers, and there was no significant relationship between anterior insula activity and offer rejection. 'Hence, meditators were able to uncouple the negative emotional response to an unfair offer, presumably by attending to internal bodily states (interoception) reflected by activity in the posterior insula,' say the researchers. Apparently, meditators activate an almost entirely different network of brain areas. Instead of drawing on areas such as those involved in theory of mind, prospection (looking forward in time) and episodic memory, meditators draw upon areas involved in interoception and attention to the present moment. 'This study suggests that the trick may lie not in rational calculation, but in steering away from what-if scenarios, and concentrating on the interoceptive qualities that accompany any reward, no matter how small,' say the researchers.

Change and impermanence

Though nothing can bring back the hour
Of splendour in the grass, of glory in the flower;
We will grieve not, rather find
Strength in what remains behind.
William Wordsworth (1770–1850)

My late mother often used to remind us that 'this too shall pass'. Nothing stays the same from moment to moment. With each moment, we are made new once again.

Impermanence is a core concept in many teachings on mindfulness, particularly those of Buddhist origin. Nothing lasts forever, everything changes. We can see impermanence all around us but it's a slippery concept to hold onto nevertheless because we find it disturbing. If we are impermanent, that means we are going to die! Much of the behaviour we find unacceptable in others (and ourselves) is due to fear of change and we can turn to meditations such as the Loving-kindness meditation to encourage compassion towards ourselves and others.

Through mindfulness, we can contemplate the true nature of things and how everything passes. This helps us stay with what is – difficult emotions, difficult situations, pain, disruption – in the knowledge that it will change. Working with mindfulness on accepting impermanence as natural helps us let go to welcome in the new. We looked at letting go in Chapter 8.

If we think of this in terms of the FEEL model, we *focus* or tune into what's actually happening, *explore* what's going on right here, right now (not in the past or future!), gently *embracing* or cradling whatever comes up; then we can *let it go* and move on if that what's needed, being open to what emerges. It can be helpful in times of disruption and change to do practices such as the Awareness of breath (Chapter 5).

Ebb and flow

We can use the breath as our anchor – everything may be changing around us but our breath is still there as long as we live. Through our breath, we can become more acutely aware of the ebb and flow of life, how it is a continuous flow of receiving and giving, taking in and giving out, of change. We talk more about this ebb and flow in relation to gestalt in Chapter 19.

Change is very often difficult, even when we seek it out. Fritz Perls, who co-developed gestalt, observed that trying to force change – even if we desire that change – sets up resistance to the change, consciously or unconsciously. Surrendering to the flow of our breath, of life, helps us to go with the flow in general, and to be more accepting of change.

Paying attention to this relationship we're in with our environment is very much part of mindfulness. We're in a constant dance of change. Any attempts to make things including ourselves solid, rigid and unchanging are bound to fail.

One of my meditation teachers was talking the other day about hedges versus solid walls. She was pointing out that in addition to being hospitable to all sorts of wildlife rather than being a man-made block of 'dead' bricks, hedges can withstand strong winds because of the space between the leaves. When we erect big strong hard walls, we can be more susceptible to coming crashing down when the winds of life build up into a full onslaught. I always think of bendy young trees too and how we benefit from being flexible in our approach to life. Mindfulness helps us be spacious, bendy and flexible.

Building mindfulness into our lives, particularly when all around feels uncertain and hard to understand, helps us recharge. We allow ourselves to disconnect, albeit temporarily, from the hustle and bustle and nourish ourselves so we're better able to go back into the fray. We can remember that we are more than our thoughts, more than our pain and pleasure, more than our performance targets, more than our ability to second guess what the world is going to throw at us next, more than the snip-snappy decisions required of us. Through pausing, by anchoring ourselves through our breath or attention to our feet and the earth, we can access inner peace, just for a while. The world around us may seem crazy, frantic and chaotic but we can be the peace within the storm, we can rest in the eye of the hurricane through mindfulness practice. This too shall pass. There is only now.

Complexity

The world we live in is highly complex and seems to be getting more so. Many of us, particularly leaders, feel very insecure, stressed and afraid in the face of this complexity.

Behind closed doors in intimate conversations with their coaches all over the world, many leaders are confiding their fears – of failure, of ridicule, of isolation, and of the sheer complexity, ambiguity and speed of the world around them. These are fears we all share at times, of course, but leaders are highly visible and the challenges they face in these times are immense – the world in which they lead is highly complex, increasingly uncertain and very demanding.

We know that feeling stressed and fearful is not conducive to clear thinking, to high productivity, happiness and wellbeing. And dealing with complexity can be highly stressful. Neela Bettridge says the leaders she coaches and for whom she consults report experiencing 'stratospheric levels' of stress. Deep-seated anxiety is crippling many of our leaders, rendering them 'mindless'.

Neela Bettridge says:

With all this noise and interference, how do we deal with complexity without losing the plot? How do we engage people who are difficult to engage with? How do we see what is really in front of us?... It's a business extension of mindfulness. What is my leadership presence? What is my signature? What is my purpose? How does that play itself out? How do I want it to play out? How do I remain present with all this noise?

I think if people are more able to be mindful and aware of their leadership presence, they are much more able to deal with complexity. One of the things that tends to happen is the rabbit-in-headlight syndrome. Mindfulness helps leaders be more emotionally detached and pick their way through complexity.

Bettridge uses mystic Ken Wilber's four-quadrant integral framework with leaders to explore what needs to be done around sustainability on an individual and organization level, to great effect, especially when combined with mindfulness. Wilber's model uses four lenses: interior individual (intentional); exterior individual (behavioural); interior collective (cultural); and exterior collective (social).

Ben Bryant, professor of leadership and organization, and Jeanny Wildi, research associate, both from IMD, the executive education organization, say, 'In the wake of these overwhelming demands emerges an organizational culture of fear – we become anxious about our own competence and we become afraid of making mistakes and incurring the judgment of others. Because we feel overwhelmed by this rapidly evolving complexity of organizational life, our capacity to access mindfulness is overlooked.' Bryant and Wildi say that although our minds are well developed to cope with all this complexity, 'simply coping' doesn't often lead to optimal effectiveness.

One of the problems is that when we seek to cope with this complexity, we approach it cognitively, and we tend to think we need to gather as much information as possible. In our bid to make sense of our worlds, it's natural to scan our environments for data but when we're dealing with highly complex situations, this can be a fruitless mission.

Being well informed is a good thing, obviously, but the combination of a cognitive approach and information overwhelm can be paralysing. Also, we can feel overwhelmed and use 'cognitive shortcuts' because we feel we don't have enough time to work through all the aspects of an issue.

As Bryant and Wildi say, 'Managers become more impulsive, and in so doing, they rely on familiar scripts, schemas, mental models, rules of thumb, habits, and routines that help them make sense of their environments. Relying on impulses is not the same as relying on intuition, however. In taking cognitive shortcuts, managers' actions tend to become "mindless".'

So one way of helping clients overwhelmed by complexity is to use mindfulness to move them from fearful avoidance state into approach state, as we explored in Chapter 12. We also know that mindfulness can help us think more innovatively, and more strategically, as research at the Institute for Mindful Leadership confirms (see box). This aspect is very useful when we're helping clients grappling with complexity.

Strategic thinking

The Institute of Mindful Leadership carried out two studies in 2009 and 2010 into 'mindful leadership'. One surveyed 80 'mindful leaders' from 12 not-for-profit organizations. Of these, 93 per cent said mindfulness training had a positive impact on their ability to create space for innovation; 89 per cent said it enhanced their ability to listen to themselves and others; and nearly 70 per cent said the training made a positive difference in their ability to think strategically.

Janice Marturano, vice president, public responsibility, and deputy general counsel for General Mills and director of leadership education, Center for Mindfulness, partnered with Saki Santorelli, executive director of the University of Massachusetts Center for Mindfulness, to develop a popular four-day programme called Cultivating Leadership Presence through Mindfulness. Since 2006, more than 140 people including directors have gone through the programme at General Mills. Another 150 or so have attended other mindfulness courses such as Mindful Leadership at Work, which consisted of a weekly session for seven weeks. And since 2008, more than 20 external organizations have sent along participants too. According to Marturano, leaders attending the programmes soon came up with ideas about where else mindfulness might be brought into their organizations, sharing their experiences with other leaders, particularly where they have found better ways to lead in the face of change and uncertainty.

Reframing

Mindfulness actually helps us make decisions more quickly through helping us to let go of our evaluations, as well as more rationally, according to research by Langer. Participants in one of her studies were encouraged to reframe positive as negative and vice versa and in doing so, released the grip evaluations had on them (Langer 2000).

We can help our clients and ourselves deal with both uncertainty and complexity through reappraisal, or reframing, which we looked at earlier. John Blakey now often responds with humour to leaders' comments about feeling like they've been on a roller coaster, not because their struggles are a laughing matter but in service of them reframing how they view things. He makes comments such as, 'That sounds exciting. I'd have to go to Alton Towers (a theme park in the United Kingdom) and pay lots of money to go on a roller coaster. Which one were you on – Nemesis, Oblivion?' He points out that the sensation of things rushing past us can be seen as similar in both scenarios – the difference is in how we frame it and in whether we have trust – if we feel safe, we can enjoy the sensation.

'I think in business we're going to have to have people get used to being on a roller coaster and build in that it's a huge challenge but have a mind-set reframe, otherwise I can't see how people will stay resilient,' says Blakey.

Seeing as the world will continue to be complex and uncertain, and may well get more so in years to come, it makes sense to develop our ability to reframe as quickly and smoothly as we can, in or shortly after the moment. It makes sense to let space in around us and breathe into what's happening, giving ourselves the gift of pausing for breath, so we can re-engage with a different storyline if we need to in the face of all the unpredictability and multilayeredness.

I see a link here too with the suspension of evaluation and judgement we talked about earlier in the section on creativity, and with the Two Darts story. The first dart is the reality of so much happening, so quickly; the second is how the leader, or any of us, frames this. We can choose our responses through training our minds.

Systems and interconnectedness

> A human being is part of the whole… he experiences himself, his thoughts and feelings as something separated from the rest – a kind of optical delusion of his consciousness. This delusion is a kind of prison for us… Our task must be to free ourselves from this prison by widening our circle of compassion to embrace all living creatures and the whole of nature in its beauty.
>
> Einstein (cited in Kabat-Zinn 1991, p 165)

Just as everything changes, nothing exists in isolation. Dualistic thinking, 'splitting', which I mentioned in Chapter 8, is one of the mental processes that can get in the way of us appreciating interconnectedness.

Kowalski (2011) says, 'So we split ourselves from the "world out there", from each other, and then we proceed to split ourselves and the outside world into smaller clearly defined bits. What gets lost in the process is a sense of wholeness and oneness.'

As we've touched on before, mindfulness – meditation in particular – helps us experience this sense of oneness. Kowalski (2011) says that although we have complex processes of production and information exchange linking us together, 'our growing interdependence has not yet found its way into our consciousness, which is still mainly dominated by the individualistic thinking of "me" and "other"'.

Feeling at one with the universe is commonly reported as an experience resulting from meditation in the literature. Another cause of much of humankind's suffering is this illusion about the solidity of boundaries between ourselves and others, ourselves and the universe.

Macy and Johnstone (2012) talk about widening our sense of self, about transforming 'the expression of selfishness by widening and deepening the self for whom we act'. Viewing the self as a separate entity with a clear outer boundary is only one way of seeing the self. They say:

> When we identify with something larger than ourselves, whether that
> be our family, a circle of friends, a team, or a community, that becomes
> part of who we are. There is so much more to us than just a separate
> self; our connected self is based on recognizing that we are part of many
> larger circles.

As Macy and Johnstone point out, seeing ourselves as separate entities as opposed to connected parts of a larger whole leads to a preoccupation with how well our own self is doing compared with others, whilst seeing ourselves as part of a larger whole doesn't mean losing our individuality. 'Quite the opposite: it is through finding and playing our unique role within a community that we feel more strongly part of it' (Macy and Johnstone 2012).

Practice: Contemplating interconnectedness

If you have a flower to hand or an image of a flower, put it where you will be able to see it.

As with earlier meditations, get into a comfortable position, back erect, shoulders relaxed and so on. Taking a few deep breaths and setting your motivation for the practice.

Then bringing to your mind or actually looking at the image of a flower.

Thinking about how many conditions have come together for the flower to bloom. Clouds and rain; sunshine; earth and minerals; oxygen; perhaps a farmer… without these, the flower would not be here. If you think about it, you can 'see' all these elements in the flower. They are part of the flower. They are within the flower. The flower does not exist in isolation.

Now thinking about yourself. Contemplating all the conditions and causes that came together for you to exist and to continue existing: your parents; the water you drink (the clouds, the rain, the treatment of the water, the plumbing); the air you breathe; the food you eat (the clouds, the rain, the sunshine, the gardener, the delivery trucks, the shop workers); and so on. Just like the flower, you don't exist in isolation.

Thinking about all the hard work that goes into producing the many goods you use.

Thinking about the impact you have on others with everything that you do.

Thinking about how others support and nurture you.

What does this interconnectedness mean for you? How does an awareness of interconnectedness impact how you act?

Dancing with the system

Senge (1990) and others have explored systems thinking in relation to business but as Blakey and Day (2012) point out, many still see it as an academic concept rather than a principle to live by or by which we should conduct our coaching. They talk about 'dancing with the system', which is about 'listening at a deeply intuitive level and responding on behalf of the system's will, insight, and purpose'.

How can we promote this type of listening in ourselves and others? Through building awareness, through cultivating mindfulness and thus an ability to notice.

Some of the systems thinking concepts explored by Blakey and Day (2012) resonate for me with the type of thinking and being that we develop in mindfulness: an appreciation of interconnectedness and of the bigger picture:

- suboptimization (the awareness that systems are often embedded in other systems, which are themselves further embedded in other systems);

- emergence (the idea that complex systems have the capacity to exhibit new behaviours and that such behaviours can be triggered by small changes in the detail of the situation – the 'butterfly effect');

- fractals (used to describe how the examination of a small-scale component of a system can reveal information relating to the system as a whole.

Keep it simple

The temptation when we're working on complexity with clients is to get complex, to use detailed models to try to cover all eventualities. Models such as Wilber's can be very useful but as Blakey warns, we need to be careful when working with intellectual models or intellectualizing in general as this can mean our clients don't become aware of what they're feeling. We can use mindfulness to help our clients not get stuck in thinking mode, and to bring their emotions in all their glory to the foreground.

Blakey likes to be aware of three levels, what he calls 'thinking brain', 'heart brain' and 'infinite brain' – the last being a way for him to cover anything spiritual. He says, 'If I find people are getting overwhelmed or things are getting too complex, I'll ask simple questions like "How do you feel?" Often they'll answer "What I really think is . . ." So I ask them again, maybe four times and they might say "I feel despair." And something shifts into heart brain or infinite brain.' He continues: 'For coaches who are open to "infinite brain", it's a real goldmine to investigate and work in.'

CASE STUDY   Focusing on feelings

David, a leader in a medium-sized organization, is struggling to stay calm and focused, and to get a handle on all the complexities in his world. He realizes that silo thinking is not going to help the organization survive, and in a recent address to employees he urged them to consider the bigger picture and to communicate more with one another so they can appreciate how what each department does impacts on other departments and beyond. In board meetings, he urges fellow executives to keep well informed of all that's happening in the world at large and not to have their heads buried in detail. He reads widely on systems thinking. He thinks he has to have all the answers and his brain is working overtime to find solutions to all manner of problems. He wants to use the coaching sessions as time in which to explore which are the best solutions to the most immediate problems. There are many 'immediate' problems. It takes courage not to get drawn instantly into helping David come up with solutions, and to share what you're feeling: afraid and as if you're in a whirlwind. You ask him what he's feeling and he starts telling you what he thinks. You suggest a brief exercise, inviting him to come into the present moment, to pay attention to his breath and to his feet on the floor. He's very fidgety at first but does settle. You ask him what he's feeling. 'Actually, I'm feeling really scared,' he says, sounding surprised. You respond: 'You're scared. OK, just sit with that feeling of scared for a few moments.' You stop talking for a few minutes, then say: 'Be kind to yourself and avoid the temptation to judge this feeling.' Asking, 'Where are you feeling this fear in your body?' Again, sounding surprised, he says: 'In my gut. Actually it's just here, where I've been having all that pain.' You invite David to describe what's he's noticing about the fear. 'What does the fear look like?' 'How big is it?' 'Does it have a colour, a smell, a taste, a texture?' Just as we would in a Body scan, you invite him to shine a spotlight on the object (Focus) – the feeling – then Explore and sit with it, Letting go into the experience (you will offer him the option of letting go of the fear, perhaps transforming it into something else, later). 'It's like the pixels you used to see on low-definition televisions but there's more red than any other colour. It's a bit blurry. It smells sharp and tangy. It's in the way,' and so on. You notice David sounds a bit breathless.

You invite David to do a Centring practice, to become grounded and to focus on his breathing, without forcing it, leading him through the practice. He's struggled with breathing in the past. Having never paid attention to it before your sessions, he'd got into the habit of shallow breathing. After his breathing deepens and slows, you ask him to share what he's noticing. 'It's not as bright now. I can see past it. I don't feel as frightened now but it's still there. I hadn't realized it was there at all.' You invite David to explore whether he can let go of the feeling or to transform it or the way he's framing it. You ask, 'What are you noticing right now about how you're perceiving this fear? Is another way to feel/see this fear coming up for you?' David says, 'Well, I'm assuming it's a bad thing. I don't have to experience it as a bad thing, I guess. I could see it as something different. As a warning system, maybe.' And so on. You explore with David what it would be like to let go sometimes, to not be in problem-solving mode. He seems a bit baffled but agrees to try out some practices at home.

Tips on using mindfulness to help clients deal with complexity, uncertainty and change

Introduce mindful practices to help the client:

- Move towards the 'approach' state which is partly what they're craving anyway in their search for elusive certainty (explain this to them).

- Normalize their desire to feel in control, explaining how our minds work. Discuss where they feel they are on a scale of 1 to 10 (1 = not feeling in control and 10 = feeling totally in control) and how important feeling in control is to them. Explain how mindfulness can help them 'gain control' by helping them be more choiceful about their responses and storylines, boosting resilience and creativity.

- Discover through mindfulness their 'still quiet place' within that they can trust and rely on.

- Manage their egos so that they're more able to overcome fears of rejection, failure, embarrassment and more able to be comfortable with taking risks and 'making mistakes'.

- Stay with not knowing and the unknown.

- Become less attached to outcome, letting go of constant evaluation, letting go full stop.

- Access more information (not just intellectual) so they can make better decisions.

- Think more strategically.

- Come up with more innovative and creative solutions.

- Move away from a solely intellectual response.

- Be present with all their emotions – unpleasant and pleasant.

- Reappraise and reframe.

- Recharge and manage stress.

- Be more flexible and adaptable.

- Be more grounded and centred.

- Open out to the natural ebb and flow of life and embrace change and impermanence as natural.

We've talked a little about leaders in this chapter as they are so often in the firing line when it comes to dealing with complexity and change. In the next chapter, we focus solely on leaders, exploring where mindfulness fits into some of the currently popular leadership models and looking at how some coaches are using mindfulness in their leadership coaching.

Working with leaders

15

Great leaders face sacrifice, difficulties, and challenges, as well as opportunities, with empathy and compassion for the people they lead and those they serve.

BOYATZIS AND MCKEE (*RESONANT LEADERSHIP*)

The old models have failed us, we need a paradigm shift and new kinds of leaders to lead and enable the change required. As we seek to shake off the shackles of the old command-and-control leadership paradigm, and move towards more collaborative, sustainable, coaching-style organizational cultures, what we need are leaders who really get this. We require leaders who are emotionally intelligent, who are self-aware; conscious and compassionate leaders, leaders who are mindful.

We need the 'resonant leaders' described by Boyatzis and McKee (2005), people who can inspire those around them, who can create resonance in their relationships, their teams and organizations.

What makes a leader resonant?

Resonant leaders, say Boyatzis and McKee, are in tune with those around them, with others' thoughts and emotions. They are emotionally intelligent: they either intuitively understand or have developed the following competencies: self-awareness, self-management, social awareness and relationship management. Key to this resonance, according to Boyatzis and McKee, are hope, compassion and mindfulness.

Great leaders are awake, aware and attuned to themselves, to others and to the world around them. They commit to their beliefs, stand strong in their values, and live full, passionate lives. Great leaders are emotionally intelligent and they are mindful: they seek to live in full consciousness of self, others, nature and society.

Since writing their book, Boyatzis tells me he has now added playfulness as the fourth component.

Resonant leaders are approach-oriented (see Chapter 12), displaying the emotions associated with this orientation such as curiosity, kindness, openness, compassion, non-judgement and tolerance. They energize and inspire those around them, whereas dissonant leaders suck the energy out of employees, displaying avoidance-oriented feelings and behaviours including aversion, intolerance, irritability, fear and control.

Dissonance and burnout

Dissonance is the default, according to Boyatzis and McKee, partly because organizations will put up with dissonance if they think the bottom line is unaffected. With a focus on short-term results, it is hard to be mindful. It is also because all too often people are afraid to tell leaders that they are creating toxic environments. And according to experts such as Boyatzis, McKee, and Gilbert, without intervention, human systems naturally drift into the threat-affect regulation system. Leaders, and those around them, have to work hard at creating systems in which affiliation is the norm. Boyatzis and McKee (2005) say that without intentional effort to move into resonance or remain there, 'we can miss opportunities for personal transformation, and our relationships will slide into less effective and less fulfilling interactions. On the path to resonance with self and with others, hope is the driver, compassion enables it, and mindfulness makes the path smoother and more understandable.'

The trouble is that even the best, most visionary, most resonant leaders burn out, particularly in these times of unprecedented change and demands. They can get trapped in what Boyatzis and McKee call the sacrifice syndrome, and dissonance takes over from resonance. And it spreads like wildfire. Dissonant leaders fly off the handle easily, they expect way too much from those they work with, they feel and instil fear. They operate in the 'red zone' too much of the time – the threat-affect system – and drag those around them into the red zone too. But though they may be in company when it comes to the emotional system they're in, they're pretty much on their own when it comes to everything else, much of the time. It's a lonely place to be, at the top, and very often their relationships outside work suffer too.

Burnout

We hear terrible tales of what happens if leaders carry on in this way. There has been much in the press about the situation in Japan, for example, which even has a word for death from overwork: *Karōshi*, with its government now compiling statistics on those falling victim to it. According to the International Labour Organization, 28 per cent of Japanese employees worked 50 hours or more per week in 2001, a percentage significantly higher than many European nations, although on the same level as the United

States; however, many overtime hours worked in Japan are unrecorded, so the Japanese may still be working the longest hours. In 2005, the Japanese Ministry of Health, Labour and Welfare reported 328 Japanese employees who suffered the fate of *Karōshi*. The number is a little more than seven times higher than the recorded result in 2000.

And it's not just in Japan that leaders and others are feeling under pressure to put in many hours. In the UK, in November 2011, just eight months after taking one of the biggest jobs in British finance, Lloyds chief executive Antonio Horta-Osorio was forced to take sick leave following a diagnosis of extreme fatigue and stress due to overwork. At the time, he said he was 'unable to switch off'. The announcement of his sick leave wiped nearly £1 billion off the state-backed banking group in one stroke – so it's not just the individual who is affected. The taxpayer, who owns 40 per cent of the bank, was left £372 million worse off. Horta-Osorio returned to work in January 2012.

Before launching his mindfulness-based programme, Professor Hunter carried out research among serious mindfulness practitioners who were also knowledge workers including *Fortune* 500 CEOs, architects and writers. And one of the things that emerged, he says, was: 'Their lives were so complicated and they were pulled in so many directions. They'd say, "If I didn't have these practices, I think I'd be dead."' Sometimes these people meant this literally, showing Professor Hunter their medical records.

However, it's precisely these high and sustained levels of stress that could be the motivation for leaders and leadership practitioners to 'leave their comfort zone in search of the next big leap in leadership', according to Love and Maloney (2009). They say that we've seen extensive adoption of emotional intelligence and social intelligence techniques, hypothesizing that many existing leaders have attained some degree of self-awareness and ability to self-manage. This work has laid a strong foundation for future growth in leaders but the current level of leadership development can be viewed as having hit a plateau, they say. In addition, those who have developed better self-awareness and self-management may be driven by unaddressed chronic stress back to 'less conscious thinking and behaviour'. Love and Maloney say leaders are really struggling with 'the ability to focus, be present, and to think as creatively and deeply as their business requires'. They suggest that by introducing leaders to mindfulness, they might 'cross a breakthrough point on a continuum of higher mental states of leadership', such as 'greater capacity for present moment awareness, compassion, ethical decision making, and systemic/integrative thinking'.

More mindful leaders

Leaders can be somewhat coy in coming forward to admit they've been practising mindfulness but the number is growing. As well as training many coaches in mindfulness including in-house coaches at GlaxoSmithKline (see case study), executive coach Michael Chaskalson has led 'mindful leadership' training in the Cabinet Office and Home Office, as well as at KPMG, PricewaterhouseCoopers, the Prudential and the London Business School.

Coach and organization consultant **Tim Malnick** says:

Many of our current notions of leadership emphasize a story of personal control – over ourselves and to some extent over events. But when we practise mindfulness, if we are genuinely open we may see that actually we can't control our thoughts or our experience from moment to moment. This is quite curious and can be quite exhilarating for some people. We may start to explore leadership as 'the art of letting go' – a courageous practice of surrendering our endless judgements, hopes and fears as a way to be fully available and present to what is actually arising in each moment. This is a quite different view of leadership enabled by a personal practice of mindfulness.

CASE STUDY   GlaxoSmithKline

GlaxoSmithKline brought in executive coach and external mindfulness trainer Michael Chaskalson to train its 270 Job Plus leaders-as-coaches in mindfulness. Job Plus coaches are employees who have been trained to coach and who have clients in the business. The initiative was led by Sue Cruse, director of health, sustainability and performance. All the coaches followed an MBSR-style eight-week course, committing to individual practice. 'Not all of them were engaged but most of them got a lot out of it. It was quite a challenge, it's a bit "Marmitey", some people loved it and said it was brilliant; some people loved Michael and the idea of it but said "It's not for me,"' said Sally Bonneywell, vice president, coaching. 'Not being able to find the time to do this amount of mindfulness training was the excuse for some. Other people said they got lots out of it and that it helped them with calmness, [feeling] energized and grounded. We now teach the Mindful minute on the Job Plus coach training programme as a way of getting into and being available for coaching before we do it. We say anyone can find a minute. People report that it helps them be more mindful. Some people have signed up to do an online (mindfulness) course.'

Now let's take a brief tour around some of the currently popular leadership approaches to see where mindfulness fits in.

Mindfulness within leadership models

Leadership used to be all about the Great Man, someone who had been born with certain innate characteristics such as the charisma and heroism deemed to be requisites for great leadership. The focus then shifted to a set of desired behaviours, capabilities and competences, which could be cultivated. It then moved to situational leadership – the leader inspiring followers to be at their best – and more recently to what leadership coach Graham Lee has called 'the interior model of leadership'.

According to Lee, who spoke on mindfulness within leadership at the Mindfulness at Work conference in February 2012, the leadership 'approaches' most commonly cited by the senior HR professionals and leaders he talks to regularly are emotional intelligence and Jim Collins's Level 5 Leadership. The latter model combines deep personal humility with intense professional will.

And as Lee says, the two underpinnings of these approaches – emotional intelligence and humility – are changing the way people see leaders, and mindfulness is at the heart of both.

'The core notion of humility overthrows the idea that we need a charismatic leader; it's the opposite. Level 4 leaders are charismatic; they get things going but have no capacity to sustain... Mindfulness stands on these two pivotal ideas in leadership – humility and emotional intelligence. Interior leadership is different from exterior leadership,' says Lee.

In my own conversations with leadership coaches and leaders themselves, I'm also finding (as does Lee) that the following models – particularly Boyatzis's, Collins's (2001) and more recently Scouller's (2011) – have a lot of traction. They are proving to be fertile ground for discussions and explorations around how mindfulness can help leaders.

Resonant leadership

We touched on Boyatzis's model of resonant leadership earlier. This model sees leadership as inherently stressful, with leaders all too often falling into what Boyatzis *et al* (2012) call the sacrifice syndrome and into damaging vicious circles which lead to dissonance, a shrinking of perspectives, poor decision making and volatile emotions/reactions.

Here mindfulness is about renewal. Leaders are encouraged to actively cultivate the positive emotions of hope, compassion, playfulness and mindfulness. As Lee points out, mindfulness is not a formalized component; however, leaders are encouraged to pause and to attend to the here and now.

For dissonant leaders either to become resonant for the first time or to rediscover resonance, they need to set aside time to recharge, and to develop and cultivate skills and practices which can act as an antidote to the stresses and strains of leadership. Given our exploration earlier in the book of approach and avoidance, we can see that mindfulness can help leaders develop the ability to actively and purposefully switch to an approach mode. It can offer them strategies for renewal, so they can be more resilient and less likely to burn out. We all need these, but most leaders are highly time pressured and they have to make a deliberate effort to build in time for renewal; it really won't happen otherwise.

Three levels of leadership

The three levels of leadership described by Scouller (2011) are: the personal (in the centre); the private (the next layer); and the public (outer layer). Scouller's model proposes that leadership presence is about healing of psychological divisions, and a sense of wholeness and integration. It's aligned with Lee's interior leadership model. Here, it's about leaders developing self-mastery:

- gaining control over distracting mental habits;
- stopping identifying with thoughts and impulses that pull towards past or future;
- dissolving limiting beliefs of the false self.

The three components are:

- dis-identification;
- mindfulness;
- self-inquiry.

Theory U

Otto Scharmer's Theory U (2007) holds that what we pay attention to and how we pay attention on an individual and collective basis are key to what we create. Scharmer believes we all have a blind spot which gets in the way of us being able to fully pay attention. His theory takes us through a process to enable us to connect to our 'essential Self' in the realm of what he calls 'presencing' (combining the present with sensing). And this apparently helps us see our blind spot and pay attention (be mindful) so we can open our minds, hearts and wills, shifting our awareness, and helping us create a different future.

In some ways, we can see Scharmer's 'U' as a map for mindfulness within groups. Moving down the left side of the U requires the group to open up and deal with the resistance of thought, emotion and will; moving up the right side requires the integration of thinking, feeling and will in the context of practical applications and learning by doing.

The process seeks to develop the following leadership capacities (adapted from Otto Scharmer's website):

- Holding the space of listening (to others, to oneself, to what emerges from the collective). This requires the creation of open space in which others can contribute to the whole.
- Observing (suspending the 'voice of judgement' to allow movement from projection to true observation).
- Sensing (connecting with your heart).
- The preparation for the experience at the bottom of the U – presencing – requires 'the tuning of three instruments': the open mind, the open heart and the open will.
- Presencing (connecting to your deepest source of self and will – allowing the future to emerge from the whole.
- Crystallizing (accessing the power of intention).
- Prototyping (integrating head, heart and hand).
- Performing (playing the 'macro violin' – performing at a macro level).

Authentic leadership

Lee and Roberts's Authentic Leadership model (2010) also has mindfulness at its core. Here, it's important to adopt a reflective stance which involves:

- standing back; paying attention to one's focus of attention;
- acknowledging, labelling and tolerating (difficult) thoughts and feelings;
- teasing out the mental states (cognitions and emotions) underlying the behaviour of self and others;
- understanding personal triggers and their historical origins; autobiographical awareness;
- being open to multiple perspectives; embracing paradox and ambiguity;
- shifting attention to different levels of meaning-making (eg events, patterns, structure);
- fostering the reflective stance in others/groups/teams.

Lee says, 'We all learn by adapting, we're shaped by our environment, then we have to step away and consider what we know and develop our sense of identity. The more we can flow between differentiation and adaptation, the more in harmony we will be with our internal states and the wider context and with others. Mindfulness is a key part.'

In addition to mindfulness, elements may include the use of narratives. This is about helping leaders become aware of their own stories and connect to values, dreams and purpose, so they are better placed to evoke authenticity in others.

Lee suggests we think in terms of the interior and exterior worlds of the leader. On the inside, we seek:

- mindfulness;
- stability;
- clarity;
- agility;
- self-regulation;
- awareness;
- complexity;
- integration.

The elements above underpin the exterior (cultivating positive leadership):

- traits (what he calls character strengths);
- behaviours;
- situational flexibility;
- leader–follower engagement.

Adaptive leadership

Heifetz (1994) talks about leaders facing two kinds of challenges: technical and adaptive. And in these times of so much complexity and change, leaders are more often required to come up with new ways of approaching problems, using different ways of thinking, doing and being. Climatic change and the meltdown of the current economic system, for example, are adaptive challenges and we need leaders to approach them as such. Trying to apply old patterns and technical solutions to new problems such as these is not going to get us anywhere. With its ability to help in the areas of stress management, self-management, improving relationships with others, developing creativity and improving meta-cognition, mindfulness is ideal for supporting leaders to be adaptive. We can see this from the list of requisites for adaptive leaders who need to:

- stay calm, focused and clear-headed, not operating on automatic pilot;
- manage themselves so they can interact with others;
- collaborate with others – traditional command-and-control organizational cultures do not lend themselves to tackling adaptive challenges;
- approach problems creatively.

In Chapter 18 we look at how mindfulness can help clients be more creative.

CASE STUDY Coaching leaders

Leadership coach Graham Lee has been coaching since the late 1990s, and has had a mindfulness practice throughout but only began incorporating mindfulness into his work in 2009. He now uses it within one-to-one coaching, group work on leadership development programmes and 'mindful coaching supervision'.

Sometimes he calls it mindfulness, other times he calls it 'reflective practice'. Sometimes he refers to Heifetz's image of viewing from the balcony rather than the dance floor (meta-cognition). He says that when talking to leaders, he wouldn't talk about his interior versus exterior model but about cultivating positive leadership.

As always, it helps to link with the desired business outcome. 'It's very much about the quality and capacity for people to think strategically or to handle adaptive challenges. So often, people approach challenges from a technical perspective and they need a more spacious way of being to approach problems. Most leaders will say that's familiar to them but won't have made the connection to mindfulness.

'There is a body of work from a whole bunch of areas (including Bateson and Argyris) showing the value of certain kinds of practices for quality of breadth and spaciousness that leaders can bring to their role. Presented in that way, I find leaders are intrigued and open. Most are unaware of mindfulness until I mention it... For me, some of the science and evidence base gives us such helpful tools for introducing it to clients... There is a raft of things I link it to that might be a problem for the leader I am coaching – mental clarity, spaciousness, complexity, emotional regulation, being overweight and so on. I'm really quite flexible – whatever hooks them. I might link it to playing golf.'

Setting the scene. 'I start coaching sessions with mindfulness to create a space for interrogating, exploring and acknowledging, being aware of the focus of attention and labelling feelings, teasing out mental states of self and others.'

Lee then introduces practices into the coaching session or as homework. He invites the leader to read certain books from a wide range. However, he finds compliance the biggest issue of all: 'Will they really do it?'

His aim is to encourage leaders to have a regular practice, one which they can apply at work, to deciding strategic issues or leading the team, for example.

He shares the story of one client: 'One particular relationship was very stuck. It was about finding ways of not being so triggered, getting into an enquiring place and expanding the ways the relationship can develop.'

With another, a senior strategic project team, mindfulness has been 'very powerful, helping [team members] restrain themselves from leaping for the first solution they came across, exploring different angles and coming up with creative solutions, taking time to check with more stakeholders. And because they'd done that, they got better buy-in.'

He says: 'I think mindfulness promotes all the benefits of emotional intelligence. What does it take to get people into more senior roles? They need their horizon to be broader and to let go of some of their achievements and methodologies which helped them be successful. It's a counter-intuitive thing to do, you may be really successful but need to put some of that aside to expand your repertoire. It's like Tiger Woods (world-class golfing champion) – you're successful, then you change your style. It's so powerful if they do.'

He says mindfulness is a way of setting one's perceptual frame and says that self-compassion comes up, in particular.

'People are so tough on themselves. If they loosen up with themselves, they loosen up with others. The Loving-kindness meditation can be seen as "flaky" but we do it if people are harsh on themselves, I [usually] bring it in later on but sometimes bring it forward if a really harsh inner critic is getting in the way.'

Other examples of how coaches are using mindfulness with leaders and managers

I helped a young CEO who wanted to build a culture of connectivity within his organization but was unable to 'see' that his deep-rooted belief in hierarchy was coming in the way. As I initiated him into meditative and 'presencing' practices, he realized how his strong belief in 'respect' for elders and seniors dictated his expectations from those who reported to him. He realized that the social structure he believed in and the attendant behaviour were what he practised in his workplace though his stated belief was something else.

Sanjeev Roy, executive coach based in India

I worked with a young, high-achieving client promoted to the current limit of his capacity who described himself as 'a rabbit in the headlights' when preparing for and presenting in board-level/CEO presentations. We developed a centring/breathing/mantra-based practice that he used before starting such pieces of work.

Sally Dellow, executive coach based in Hong Kong

When I was working with a fast-track manager whose career had stalled due to an inability to control anger, we used mindfulness and centring/visualization as techniques for self-coaching and calming down.

Angela Hill, life/executive/wellbeing coach and coaching academic based in the United Kingdom

Allowing a leader in the NHS to create a sense of calm for herself, from which position she was able to provide greater resilience in her leadership to others during a time of great uncertainty and stress.

Diane Newell, executive/business/leadership coach/coaching consultant based in the United Kingdom

I worked with project leaders who have worked in projects in which the stress level has been very unhealthy. Having an opportunity to meet me and train [in] mindfulness has given them a breathing space, a kind of oasis in their working

day. It has been an opportunity for them to become more aware of how they are feeling and from that make decisions as to what they need in order to increase their wellbeing and cope with daily stress.

Ingrid Bengtson, life/executive/business/wellbeing/internal coach and coaching consultant based in Sweden

I am working with a senior churchman as a coach, using silence and prayer.

David Megginson, executive coach and coaching academic based in the United Kingdom

Emotional intelligence

According to research by Boyatzis and colleagues, emotional intelligence accounts for 85 to 90 per cent of the difference between outstanding leaders and their more average peers, Chaskalson (2011) has pointed out that emotional intelligence competencies are actually to some extent mindfulness skills.

Self-awareness is particularly important in leaders as there can be so much at stake if they get things wrong. Many leaders recognize this, as the success of programmes such as that run by Professor Hunter testify. Much of the success of executive coaching in general is down to leaders' recognition that they need to be more self-aware.

Self-awareness is also central to approaches shared with executives at IMD Business School in Lausanne, Switzerland, where leadership professor Ben Bryant encourages students to use mindfulness of breath, sounds and sensations to help them centre themselves. And at Harvard Business School, leadership professor William George apparently focuses on helping business people understand their emotions as a way to become more self-aware and thus better leaders. The idea here is that it's a lack of awareness of feelings driving reactions that leads to poor management and leadership.

So too it is particularly important that leaders self-manage, that they are able to control their emotions. All too often we encounter leaders who are unable to or don't want to control their feelings or the direct reports of clients suffering the consequences of a leader's outbursts. Not being able to control one's emotions is one of the main obstacles to success as an executive (McCall *et al* 1988). Mindfulness offers a safe and accessible tool to help leaders work in this arena.

Females

It's often assumed that females tend to be more emotionally intelligent but when it comes to leadership, females are often in a lose–lose situation. Despite widespread recognition of the role emotional intelligence plays in good leadership, managerial and leadership posts are still often seen as requiring so-called masculine attributes (competitive, authoritarian and the like). Yet when women behave in ways that aren't considered feminine, they're seen as less effective and if they act in 'feminine ways', they will be liked but not respected. It seems they can't win. However, research by Kawakami *et al* (2000) suggests one way they might be able to. Apparently, women adopting a more male leadership style but who were more mindful were seen as more genuine, were better liked and were perceived to be more effective leaders than those who were less mindful.

In Chapter 17 we look at how mindfulness can help us work with clients in the emotional intelligence arena. But first we touch on an area perhaps particularly relevant to leadership coaching: ethics.

Ethics

16

> *Our deepest fear is not that we are inadequate. Our deepest fear is that we are powerful beyond measure. It is our light, not our darkness, that most frightens us. We ask ourselves, who am I to be brilliant, gorgeous, talented, fabulous? Actually, who are you NOT to be? You are a child of God. Your playing small does not serve the world.*
>
> **MARIANNE WILLIAMSON, AUTHOR**

The high cost and ubiquity of ethical failure have been only too apparent in recent years: environmental disasters such as the BP oil spill; the widespread economic meltdown which first manifested in the collapse of Lehman Brothers, followed by the exposure of corruption in some of the world's banks – the list goes on. It's easy to become cynical and wonder if things can ever change. Certainly, many of us are less easily shocked by the extent and depth of failure to act ethically or systemically in the light of recent events. We're also perhaps more aware of the potentially vast repercussions of any single event, let alone multiple events. We explored this line of thinking in the chapter on dealing with complexity, change and uncertainty.

In this chapter, I invite you to join me in widening our own perspective to think about mindfulness in the broad sense of being mindful of repercussions and consequences, and also to explore how mindfulness can help us be more ethical ourselves in our coaching and our work with clients around ethics and values, particularly clients in positions of leadership.

Accountability

It has seemed at times that the increased accountability many of us thought would ensue from the economic crisis has failed to materialize, prompting uprisings such as the Occupy movements.

Fewer than two in five CEOs place ethics at the heart of business decisions, according to the Institute of Leadership and *Management Today* magazine's Index of Leadership Trust (October 2011). Half of the respondents to the survey of more than 2,500 workers believed their employer puts financial goals above ethical considerations, with 48 per cent and 44 per cent saying the same of their chief executive and line manager. Only 36 per cent of employees in organizations with more than 1,000 employees believed their CEO has high ethical standards.

There have been moves in some quarters to increase liability and accountability. The United Kingdom's Bribery Act 2010, for example, came into force on 1 July 2011, amending and reforming UK criminal law and providing a legal framework to combat bribery in the United Kingdom and beyond, and making companies more liable if they fail to put in place an effective ethics programme. And certainly, there seems to be more coverage in the press on issues such as sustainable business, and interest among coaches, including *Coaching at Work* readers, in making a difference, including to the sustainability agenda. They also report that more and more of their clients want to make a difference too.

Making a difference

Coach and coach supervisor Marianne Craig, based in the United Kingdom, says:

[Clients] are disillusioned with the corporate world. It's clear to me that they haven't necessarily thought in the past about politics, the way the world works. My sense is that the world has changed, for some people it's since 9/11, for others it's the banking crisis, global warming, Arab Spring. There is a definite shift – perceived greed is a big one: 'I don't know why I am working so hard just to make profits'; asking big questions; they do come to coaching to talk about meaning and purpose. If they're a disaffected lawyer, they find they don't know where to have these conversations, like they've been sold the dream of more, the big car, the holidays, the changed life. Often they've made it and there is a big vacuum and a big gap. So on Sunday night, they're surfing the net, find my website and want to have big conversations about meaning and purpose. They say they don't know what to do, but they want to do something worthwhile. Some might say they want to help people, or make a difference, or put something back. Sometimes they've been embarrassed because they don't want to sound worthy. I say I think we should reclaim 'worthy'.

Mindfulness and ethics

If it is indeed the case that many of us feel moved to make more of a difference, how can mindfulness help here?

One of the problems that we see time and time again is that minor discrepancies and indiscretions are ignored until they escalate into major ethical problems, as leadership coach and strategy consultant Justine Lutterodt has highlighted (2011). 'At this point, "doing the right thing" requires incredible courage, and it is nearly impossible for companies to save face,' she says. She identifies three seeds of ethical failure: top-down management style which means employees are less inclined to feel personally responsible for their actions; suppression of authentic dialogue which we see in organizational cultures which emphasize conformity and 'moral silence'; and unwillingness to experiment and risk making mistakes.

Lutterodt recommends a number of steps to help employees become united by a shared vision. They include alignment of vision; channelling energy; building resilience; and 'tuning in'. We have already explored how mindfulness can build resilience and tuning in is basically about mindfulness. Lutterodt defines tuning in as helping the client:

> gain a deep and intuitive awareness of themselves, their surroundings and the situation at hand... the challenge here lies in exploring natural tendencies without judgement (including less desirable traits), and assuming the legitimacy of other people's perspectives. Curiosity, empathy, openness and honesty are key attributes to be leveraged here.

Thinking systemically

We looked earlier at how mindfulness can support a more systemic approach to coaching and in our clients. An appreciation of interconnectedness is a fundamental underpinning of a more mindful, ethical approach to life.

Sir John Whitmore, executive chairman of Performance Consultants International, has coached hundreds of executives and advised many large organizations across the world. He believes the ability to 'stand outside the box' and to see beyond what's right in front of us is vital to progress on moral issues such as sustainability. More and more are thinking in big-picture terms, he finds, but still far too few.

The world's greatest leaders have understood that none of us operates in isolation. The Dalai Lama talks of 'enlightened self-interest' – if we help others, we help ourselves. The late US leader Martin Luther King appreciated that we are interconnected, saying that we are 'all caught in an inescapable network of mutuality, tied in a single garment of destiny. Whatever affects one directly, affects all indirectly' (McLeod 2006). Unlike Luther King and the Dalai Lama, many leaders do not have an appreciation of the wider picture, causing them to act 'mindlessly'. This was one of the themes that emerged during conversations I held with executive coaches for a series of articles for the *Guardian* Sustainable Business hub on why leaders are failing to drive the sustainability agenda or to bring about change to the current economic model (Hall 2012). Other themes included fear of failure, embarrassment or rejection as a result of 'doing the right thing' or that the latter would adversely affect business competitiveness. There was also a sense of being clueless about how to grasp and manage complexity, bewilderment about what to do next and overwhelm – both in the sense of literally having too much to do to even begin to think about adding in anything else and in the sense of finding the sheer complexity of everything that is going on very daunting.

The coaches I interviewed also highlighted the pressures of organizational culture where distrust and focus on short-term profit are commonplace, collaboration and affiliation often a low priority, and whole-systems thinking a rarity. Mindfulness was mentioned by a number of the coaches I talked to as a way to make sense of and come to terms with complexity, as we've seen, and to step back and see the bigger picture, as we've also seen.

Leadership characteristics

In an article entitled 'Characterising Leadership for Sustainable Development' published on the *Guardian* Sustainable Business hub online, 19 December 2011, Nicolas Ceasar says that we need a different kind of thinking, one underpinned by mindfulness, if we are going to address current challenges such as sustainability, and that even the green growth strategies of the most progressive organizations do not seem proportional to the task at hand. Ceasar, head of sustainability practice at Ashridge Business School, writes: 'Part of the reason for this is that our habits of thought and experience cloud our ability to really engage with the present and its future portent. Mindfulness techniques can help us avoid this. They enable us to fully question the status quo and our internal dialogue with it and to achieve better contact with others. In effect we make ourselves open to being changed.'

Ceasar outlines four characteristics which he sees as important in leadership for sustainability. They are:

- advocacy (arguing in favour of sustainability);
- holding discomfort ('staying with the difficult stuff for long enough');
- femininity ('displaying and using characteristically feminine attributes' such as 'cooperation, understanding, pluralistic knowing and seeking union');
- mindfulness.

Values

Mindfulness also supports our clients to act more mindfully and ethically. Of course, there is plenty of greed in our world, and undoubtedly much of the corruption we're seen in recent years, the poor decisions and the lethargy are rooted in greed and anger, for example. However, when clients (including wealthy CEOs and bankers) talk to their coaches about what they truly care about, it's not usually short-term profit at the expense of others or abusing the planet; it's 'community', 'family', 'making a difference', 'leaving a legacy', 'being happy'. If you suggested what was important to them was building their fortunes while members of their family or local community go hungry, or using up resources so there's nothing left for future generations, for example, the chances are they'd vehemently disagree. Likewise if you asked them if they'd prefer a workplace where nobody truly trusted and respected one another. Yet when they walk through the door on a Monday morning, they so often feel they have to leave their true selves at the reception desk, if they're aware of their real selves at all.

Often in coaching we talk about connecting with our true purpose, with our values. Mindfulness helps us become more self-aware, one of the pillars of emotional intelligence, thus helping us get in touch with our real values.

Challenging

One of the hot potatoes when we talk about ethics in coaching is whether or not it is the place of the coach to challenge their client around ethical considerations. Coaches are divided about the role they have in challenging clients on these issues but most I've talked to think it is important to give it some thought. And the former chairman of the United Kingdom's Institute of Leadership & Management, Peter Cheese, believes it is most definitely the role of the coach to challenge and act 'as a mirror to the individual so they have a better understanding of the context they are operating in and of what is good practice'. He says, 'Historically if they had been doing that really well, maybe we wouldn't have had the problems we had.'

As Cheese says, the dynamic in coaching is an interesting one as although it's confidential, the coach might come across information that might be of wider interest. When it comes to specifics, if coaches become aware of particular decisions, they then need to make a judgement call about what is legitimate and what they need to keep quiet to preserve confidentiality. The coach has a duty not just to the individual but to the collective:

> Coaches can be a valid part of the check and balance of an organization, as a reflection of leaders and to provide wider guidance about what good looks like and to help individuals internalize it... My view is that yes, coaches can challenge leaders. A good coach is in a relationship of trust and I do think in a trusting relationship, they should be able to objectively describe back to the individual where they see issues in decisions, where they are compromising ethics. If they are not doing that, I question the basis of the relationship... If the mirror is partly obscured, it's not an objective mirror.

There are many ways in which mindfulness can support us as coaches to act more ethically. Mindfulness helps us be a clear mirror for our clients – we become more adept at seeing what's there, at gathering data and using and trusting our intuition. It helps us see the bigger picture and make better decisions. It supports us in getting our egos out of our own and others' ways, and in being less attached to outcome so we can trust our motivation more deeply.

Desire

When some people think of Buddhism or even meditation per se, they think of a monk sitting quietly in a cave for months on end, or wafting about at peace, with scarcely any trappings, just their robes and their alms bowl. And they wonder how on earth anyone can live like that. Buddhist teachings talk about extinction of desire, of non-attachment and many of us balk at these concepts. Wanting things and people is part of our nature. However, we live in a culture where overconsumption has got us into all sorts of trouble. And if we think about it, getting what we want doesn't tend to deliver what it promises. I think using mindfulness/meditation to explore our relationship with desire/wanting can loosen its grip and help us be a bit more choiceful. Our desires come and go, we can watch them rise and fall, and it's helpful not to be slaves to them. I admit I personally have a long way to go on this and I'm not advocating we charge in to challenge clients over how much they amass and possess. However, the question Julie Starr asked one of her clients (Chapter 8) is highly pertinent here: 'When is enough, enough?' If we see our clients tying themselves in knots and running themselves into the ground because they want to maintain a certain lifestyle which doesn't seem to be making them or those around them happy, or if we see our clients treading all over others, or making selfish, ill-considered, non-systemically aware decisions, or worse, we're privy to information that our client is behaving highly unethically, we have a call to make. Mindfulness can help us make the right call.

Mini practice: Meditation on desire/wanting

Sit comfortably, relax and gently close your eyes or look at the floor with your eyes half-closed. Focus on your breath coming in and going out, without forcing the breath. Continue to do this for a few minutes or until you notice your breathing deepen and slow down.

Set your intention to explore your relationship with desire/wanting, without judgement, with curiosity and compassion.

Think of a time recently when you really wanted something badly, which you subsequently 'got'. Ask yourself:

Where did you feel the wanting?

What thoughts, images and feelings did you notice?

Were there any recurring themes?

How long had you been experiencing the wanting before you took action? How had the intensity of the wanting evolved?

When you want something and 'get' it, do you still want it as much once it's 'yours'?

How do you feel when you don't get something you want?

Gently come out of the meditation, and capture any reflections.

Tips on using mindfulness to promote ethics

Mindfulness supports us and our clients to behave more ethically by helping us:

- be less stressed and more resourceful so we can be more courageous;
- think more systemically – seeing the bigger picture and how everything and everyone is interconnected ('enlightened self-interest');
- get ourselves out of the way and be less self-serving (more 'wider self'-serving);
- develop more compassion towards ourselves and others;
- be more aware of likely consequences (not burying our head in the sand);
- loosen our grip on dualistic thinking and on making judgements: us versus them, wrong versus right, good versus bad, work life versus home life;
- be more curious and enquiring about what is really going on for us and around us, exploring the nature of ambition, greed, suffering, for example;
- be less risk-averse;
- be more choiceful in how we respond to desire and wanting – we don't have to be a slave to them;
- get more in touch with our emotions and drivers, realizing when we are angry, scared, hurt and so on so we can create a distance allowing us to be more choiceful about how we behave;
- get and stay in touch with our values.

In the next chapter, we explore how mindfulness can help us work with emotions.

Working with emotions

17

> *He aha te mea nui o te ao? Maku e ki atu, he tangata, he tangata, he tangata.*
> *What is the most important thing in this world? I say to you, it is people, it is people, it is people.*
>
> **MAORI *WHAKATAUIKI* (PROVERB)**

Most people now assume it's possible to develop emotional intelligence (EQ), thanks to the likes of Daniel Goleman and Richard Boyatzis. 'If anyone now says you either have EQ or not, I say that's dinosaur thinking,' says Boyatzis. And EQ is frequently on the coaching agenda in one form or another. An individual may ask us to help them improve their relationships with colleagues, or to be more influential in the boardroom, for example. Or a coaching sponsor may contract with us to help an otherwise talented and promising leader to stop flying off the handle at their direct reports, or a brilliant but emotionally illiterate technician gain a greater grasp of how to interact with others. Or perhaps the objective is to deliver a coaching programme for a group of leaders specifically focusing on enhancing their EQ. This chapter looks at how mindfulness can contribute in cases such as these.

My 10-year-old son has a leopard gecko called Rex. Dylan loves Rex and feels very attached to him – although not as much as he did when he first got him as a surprise Christmas present, such is the fickleness of human desire. Sadly, Rex does not return his sentiments. It's just not in his non-mammalian nature to do emotions and attachment. Our dog Ziggy, on the other hand, has a mammalian limbic region like us. Our attachment is different in nature, but mutual nevertheless. As a fellow mammal, Ziggy is hard-wired to connect with us.

The limbic area of our brain – our old mammalian brain, which evolved some 200 million years ago – works closely with the brainstem lower down in our brain and with our body to create our emotions. The limbic regions evaluate whether something is good or bad; we approach the good and avoid bad, as we've seen. So as Siegel says (2010), the limbic regions help create the 'e-motions' which 'evoke motion', motivating us to take action in response to the meaning we give to what is happening in any moment. The limbic area also plays a critical role in how we form relationships and become emotionally attached to each other.

This limbic area helps us to create memories of facts, particular experiences, and of the emotions around these. Two specific neuron clusters, the almond-shaped amygdala and the seahorse-shaped hippocampus, have been the subject of numerous studies. Some researchers attribute all emotions to the amygdala but more recently, there have been suggestions that our feelings come from more broadly distributed areas of the limbic region, the brainstem and the body and are woven into our cortical functioning (Siegel 2010b).

The hippocampus is described by Siegel as a 'master puzzle-piece-assembler' which, as we mature, weaves the basic forms of emotional and perceptual memory into factual and autobiographical recollections. Humans' unique storytelling ability also depends on the development of the highest part of the brain, the cortex, 'the bark' of the brain. The cortex, our new mammalian brain, allows us to have concepts and ideas, to imagine. It allows us to think about thinking. It allows us to create, to innovate, to have wonderful flights of fancy, but as we saw in Chapter 12 on stress, sometimes it allows us to think too much.

The prefrontal cortex, just behind the forehead, has apparently evolved in humans more than any other creature. Yet however sophisticated we may think we are, we've all had those times when we just lose it. Sometimes there is an inner voice reminding us that the best thing to do is stay calm, sometimes there is even an outer voice urging thus – my husband and I have on many occasions been the voice of reason when the other is building up to losing control with one of the children. Actually, it's usually been me, particularly with our eldest daughter, Molly. We're very close but she has developed a well-honed ability to press my buttons over the years. She first started flexing her kick-back muscle when she was two-and-a-half years old. I remember carrying her screaming all the way to the toddlers' group around the corner. She hadn't wanted to put her coat on: 'It's my body!!!' she cried. And she pretty much kept it up on and off until she was about 16 or 17. I remember one time when she didn't want to come along to a family event and I was getting more and more agitated – I have a thing about family loyalty. On the sidelines, my husband was trying to get me to step away. I could hear his voice in the dim distance but couldn't, didn't want to, help myself. So Molly and I screamed at each other (child to child!) and she locked herself in the bathroom, I pounded on the door. She was crying, so was I. And off we went to the event, without Molly. I felt sick to the stomach and spent the next hour texting and phoning furiously until Molly deigned to come to the event, puffy-eyed, by bus. So what happened?

Basically, I lost control of eight prefrontal functions: bodily regulation; attuned communication; emotional balance; response flexibility; fear modulation; empathy; insight; and moral awareness (Siegel 2010b). My heart was beating fast and my stomach was churning (bodily regulation). I couldn't communicate properly with my daughter – my internal state wasn't resonating harmoniously with Molly's internal state (attuned communication). We became unaligned. I was out of balance emotionally (emotional balance). I'd lost the ability to pause before responding (response flexibility). Response flexibility is a big part of emotional and social intelligence. I'd lost the ability to override my cortex to calm down the limbic agitation (fear modulation). I could no longer see things easily from my daughter's point of view (empathy). I'd lost insight and moral awareness – I had a fixed idea that it was important we all showed up to the event as a happy family and wasn't thinking about the wider good. My other two children were getting distressed hearing the argument, my husband was getting frustrated, and it didn't have the desired effect anyway. Yes, Molly did come along but anyone who has had exposure to adolescents will know that the face they pull when they don't want to be somewhere can be the kiss of death to harmony, enjoyment and pleasure.

And my access to intuition – which Siegel describes as how the middle prefrontal cortex gives us access to the wisdom of the body – had been denied because I was too worked up.

How do we regain control of the mind? We need to be able to reflect, to be mindful. In my case, I needed to once again become receptive and open to whatever emerged, rather than being stuck with a fixed idea of how things should be. I needed to be more able to witness what was going on, to self-observe in action so I could choose not to act, or to act differently. I needed to have what Siegel calls 'meta-awareness'.

I didn't do it on this occasion but have done it many other times – tuning into my body, coming to my senses, so I have better control of my emotions.

What Siegel (2010b) calls 'mindsight' (focused attention that allows us to see the internal workings of our own mind) helps us recruit the higher areas of the brain to create a 'cortical override' of limbic activities.

Many deem mindfulness to be a key component of EQ, including Michael Chaskalson, EQ expert Margaret Chapman, and Boyatzis and fellow *Resonant Leadership* author Annie McKee.

'Mindfulness is the practical application of self-awareness, self-management, and social awareness; in short, developing mindfulness means developing emotional intelligence,' say Boyatzis and McKee (2005).

Goleman, who popularized the term 'emotional intelligence' in his 1996 bestselling book of the same name, sets out four main EQ (or EI, as Goleman refers to it) constructs: self-awareness, self-management, social awareness, and relationship management, all of which he says can be developed. From this list alone, we can begin to see how mindfulness might be helpful, particularly in relation to becoming more self-aware and aware of others, managing emotions and managing and improving relationships. Perhaps we should remind ourselves what these constructs are about:

Self-awareness is the ability to read your own emotions and recognize their impact while using gut feelings to guide decisions.

Self-management involves controlling your emotions and impulses and adapting to changing circumstances.

Social awareness is the ability to sense, understand and react to others' emotions while comprehending social networks.

Relationship management is the ability to inspire, influence and develop others while managing conflict.

Although there is plenty in the literature about the importance of EQ, there is less on how to actually develop this, and mindfulness practice can really make a difference here.

'We've come to accept that emotional intelligence is a highly desirable characteristic for leaders but nobody really says how to develop it. But we know mindfulness improves self-regulation, emotional regulation, congruence and self-awareness. So people should be thinking of mindfulness training for coaches and their clients,' says Chaskalson.

Self-awareness

One of the things that apparently differentiates humans from many other animals is our awareness of self. We are able to form an identity for ourselves. However, just as many people have overinflated senses of their self-importance, many don't really know or like who they are.

Becoming more self-aware – one of the core components of coaching – is at the heart of EQ. As Chapman, a coaching psychologist and mindfulness practitioner, says, 'self-awareness is the bedrock of emotional intelligence'.

Mindfulness increases the level of emotional self-awareness, according to one study (Creswell *et al* 2007). Being able to know and articulate what you're feeling correlates strongly with being able to manage the effects of negative feelings.

My client had a behaviour they could not understand and did not like. It highly frustrated them. By stilling, centring and scanning the body they identified, in a felt sense, where the behaviour (and fears and positive intents associated with it) originated from, made fully aware contact with it and developed a whole new relationship with it as a valued part of themselves.

The change in subsequent behaviour was immediate, effortless and sustained.

Neil Scotton, executive coach/coach for leaders
and catalysts, based in the United Kingdom

As homework, for them to practise listening to their thoughts and going through a process of hearing, acknowledging and then ignoring or removing the thought. During the session when I see shifts in a client's emotions I ask them to reflect and be mindful of what is happening for them; the use of silence and patience is needed here and this is extremely powerful in providing opportunity for a client to share and learn more about themselves.

Annalise Roache, life/executive/workplace
coach/mentor based in New Zealand

Self-management

Those of us who meditate know only too well how mindfulness helps us manage our emotions and ourselves in general – when we have had less time to practise, it really shows, as my children are often quick to point out.

One way in which mindfulness helps us to develop EQ is by reducing stress levels. Research in Taiwan (Chu 2010) evaluated the benefits of meditation in regard to EQ, perceived stress and mental ill health. The study looked at 351 full-time working adults with different amounts of experience in meditation and found that those participants with greater meditation experience exhibited higher EQ, and less perceived stress and negative mental health than those with less or none. It then randomly divided 20 graduate students with no previous experience of meditation into a mindfulness meditation group and a control group and measured them before and after. It found that those who completed the mindfulness meditation training demonstrated significant improvements compared to the control group.

Working memory capacity, which is used in managing cognitive demands and regulating emotions, could well be one of the important elements here. Researchers such as Schmeichel *et al* (2008) point out that people with higher working memory capacity are more able to suppress positive and negative emotions, have less emotionally intrusive thoughts and perform better at emotion reappraisal tasks, and that highly demanding tasks take their toll on our working memory capacity. We know that practising mindfulness helps reduce stress and improves performance in attention tasks so it seems likely that it helps enhance working memory capacity, and consequently EQ. One study at least indicates this to be the case (see case study).

Another study (Teper *et al* 2012) suggests that self-control is tied to meditators' acceptance of emotions. Co-author of the study Rimma Teper says previous research has demonstrated that individuals who meditate have better facility with tasks and self-control but that until now it's never been clear why that is. Self-control is defined as the ability to pay attention to appropriate stimuli and initiate the appropriate behaviour, while inhibiting inappropriate behaviour. The research suggests that of the two meditation approaches tested, 'acceptance of emotional states' has more impact on building self-control than 'awareness of the present moment'. Mindful awareness, described as the 'more cognitive' aspect of mindfulness, had little to do with success on the test.

CASE STUDY   Mindful marines

United States marines were found to be better able to manage their emotions and stress after training in mindfulness, according to research by cognitive neuroscientist Amishi Jha and colleagues from the University of Pennsylvania (Jha *et al* 2010) . Some 48 marines took part in the study, with 31 of them practising regular mindfulness meditation for eight weeks before deployment, while the rest received no mindfulness training. The aim of the study was to establish whether mindfulness would improve soldiers' ability to control emotion by improving working memory capacity. The hypothesis was that as well as helping us manage information in reasoning and problem solving, working memory capacity may also help us manage emotion and help the brain function well under stress. As expected, the considerable stress of deployment did decrease the marines' working memory capacity – apart from in those who practised mindfulness for longer periods, who enjoyed a significant increase in this capacity. The 'mindful marines' also experienced more positive moods and fewer negative moods, compared with those in the control group. The study also suggests that sufficient mindfulness practice may protect against functional impairments associated with high-stress challenges that require a tremendous amount of cognitive control, self-awareness, situational awareness and emotional regulation. The programme, Mindfulness-Based Mind Fitness Training, was delivered by co-researcher Elizabeth Stanley of Georgetown University, a former US army officer. It integrated exercises such as focused attention on the breath and mindful movement into pre-deployment training. The Operation Span Task was used to assess the programme's impact on working memory while its impact on positive and negative affect (emotions) was evaluated using the Positive and Negative Affect Schedule. Benefits were only seen in those with high practice time over the eight weeks.

Its findings align with those of research on MBSR programmes suggesting such training can offer those in high-stress situations 'psychological prophylaxis' – protection from cognitive and emotional disturbances.

A US Department of Defense report, 'Mindfulness Helps Soldiers Cope in Iraq', published August 2010, quoted Army Major Victor Won, deputy assistant chief of staff for intelligence in 1st Armored Division's general staff section: 'It would be more effective for soldiers to learn and train mindfulness prior to deployment since the practice will offer soldiers [a means] to cope with their mental stress before getting into a high-stress environment. However, practising the meditation on a regular basis will help anyone, no matter where they are.'

Won said that the army is moving toward developing stress-coping methods, likening mental fitness to physical fitness. Just as running or lifting weights can improve physical fitness, a daily routine of mindfulness will help to strengthen coping mechanisms, making it easier to recognize and react to negative emotions so they don't grow stronger, he said.

Michael Chaskalson says mindfulness is 'like the RAM (random access memory) of the mind'. He says, 'When things are in working memory, you can choose not to react and the more complex the task you can engage in. Working memory is degraded through stress.'

He gives the example of a lone soldier managing a checkpoint in Iraq and someone driving towards him with women and children, without warning. In that moment, the soldier has to make a snap decision about what to do. 'I'd rather the soldier was more, rather than less, mindful. And if the same guy is going into an Afghan village, if he's more mindful, things will go better for all of us. We should ideally offer MBSR for everyone in conflict. In fact, the more mindfulness there is, the better for us all.'

CASE STUDY   Enhancing emotional intelligence

Here's how one respondent to the *Mindfulness in Coaching* survey, a coaching consultant and registered psychologist, uses mindfulness to enhance EQ.

I taught a team leader to use 'mindful breathing' to manage temporarily disturbed emotional reactivity. She had recently had a very nasty experience (really very nasty) and was frequently, with little provocation, completely overcome by tears at work. Her manager had directed her to have a short break from work to recover and I saw her just prior to her return. On her first morning back, she was informed that the section for which she was responsible was about to have an external quality audit, a stimulus which, prior to her nasty experience, she would have happily 'taken in her stride' and afterwards (I think) would have rendered her sufficiently hysterical that she would have been sent home. After learning mindful breathing, her response was dramatically different: she told me that she could feel 'it' coming; immediately excused herself and went to a storeroom and closed the door. She did her breathing and in a few minutes was calm. She returned to her (nonplussed) team and informed them of the impending audit and divided up the last-minute checks that needed to be done. Later, the team member who had been acting team leader told her, 'What's happened to you? We didn't think you would be coming back today at all. We thought you'd gone in there to cry and then you would go home.' When she later asked her manager why he had not told her about the impending audit before she went on leave, he said, 'I knew your section would be fine anyway and there was no point telling you before, it would just have made you worse; if you got better during the break, then you could lead the team with the audit and if it did not, then we'd be no worse off.' She was, by no means, 'better', but she found the mindful breathing a powerful tool.

Social awareness and relationship management

We explored mindfulness in relation to presence and attunement in Chapters 4 and 6. Attunement was about taking our presence into the social sphere, focusing on others and taking their essence into our world. It includes relationship management and part of that is about how we deal with difficult emotions – in ourselves and others.

Difficult emotions

Rumi's poem below, 'The guest house', which is included in MBCT programme material in the United Kingdom, and the Cherokee story also outlined below, say something about how we all experience difficult emotions and how we should turn towards, rather than reject, them.

The guest house

This being human is a guest house.
Every morning a new arrival

A joy, a depression, a meanness,
some momentary awareness comes
as an unexpected visitor.

Welcome and entertain them all!
Even if they're a crowd of sorrows,
who violently sweep your house
empty of its furniture.

Still, treat each guest honourably.
He may be clearing you out
for some new delight.

The dark thought, the shame, the malice,
Meet them at the door laughing,
And invite them in.

Be grateful for whoever comes,
Because each has been sent
As a guide from beyond.

                              Rumi

The Two Wolves

Some of you may have heard the Cherokee story of the Two Wolves. An old Cherokee is teaching his grandson about life, and says, 'A terrible fight is going on inside me between two wolves.

'One is evil – he is anger, envy, sorrow, regret, greed, arrogance, self-pity, guilt, resentment, inferiority, lies, false pride, superiority and ego. The other is good – he is joy, peace, love, hope, serenity, humility, kindness, benevolence, empathy, generosity, truth, compassion and faith.

'The same fight is going on within you too, and everyone else.'

The elder's grandson thought about this for a while, then asked: 'Which wolf will win?'

His grandfather replied: 'The one you feed.'

I love this story and the poem because they recognize that it's normal for us to have 'negative' feelings (although of course the word negative is an evaluation here). Thich Nhah Hanh says we all have seeds for all the emotions in our 'store consciousness', which we can see as another name for the subconscious. The seeds we water are the ones that will grow. The wolf we feed will get stronger. But it's no good just pretending the seeds or the wolf aren't there. As Jung said (1967), 'One does not become enlightened by imagining figures of light, but by making the darkness conscious. The latter procedure, however, is disagreeable and therefore not popular.'

Transpersonal coach Hetty Einzig (2011) says, 'We are living at a time when fear is very near the surface – in organizations and in ourselves. To deny or dismiss the wolf or terror will only encourage it to burrow deeper... Now is the time to address the dark wolf and to cultivate compassion, care and kindness – for oneself and for others – that helps loosen its grip. This process, of looking fear in the face, of mindfulness and compassion, generates the clear thinking and creativity so needed in challenging times.'

As with any non-superficial approach, mindfulness can stir up all sorts of feelings. I ran a session at a conference recently where we discussed this and one of the participants expressed concern that clients may start questioning their mortality, for example. I guess my stance is very much that that is a good thing, that coaching which helps clients address the big questions, to get messy in the name of growth and development, is to be encouraged, if the clients wish to go there.

We can use mindfulness as a spotlight on our emotions – bringing them into our awareness (focusing), being curious about what is there (exploring), once again with compassion and non-judgement. Instead of turning away, we turn towards. 'Turn towards everything,' urged the late Trungpa Rinpoche.

Lots of clients will come to us, not always willingly, because they're struggling with difficult emotions. Mindfulness can help them be compassionate towards themselves so they're not adding that second dart, allowing space and calmness so they can be more choiceful about how they respond. With practice, they can learn to stop feeding the 'big bad wolf'.

In neutral

There's a big difference between thinking positively and being mindful. When we're mindful, we're neither positive or negative. We just are in the moment. We're at peace with ourselves, not striving to be positive, to push away the negative.

Langer (1975) researched a mindful approach to major surgery. Rather than encouraging people to think positively – it *will* be fine and so on – they were encouraged to be mindful, to be neutral. They reported that they felt happier and experienced less stress. And they needed less medication. The key seems to lie in suspending judgement and stopping seeing evaluations as independent of us. Langer points out that although it's likely that there is a higher correlation between positive evaluations and wellbeing, seeing ourselves as fortunate when we have positive experiences means we deny the insight that outcomes and evaluations are products of our own minds. Positive evaluations implicitly rob us of control, says Langer, while mindfulness helps us recognize that every outcome – and all its components – is positive and negative at the same time. And that we can choose to be positive and experience not only the benefits of positivity, but also the advantages of perceived control. Such a stance puts us in a much better position to try new experiences.

When we meditate, we can find ourselves feeling blissful or bored. We can also come face to face with some very difficult emotions, thoughts and memories. Sometimes these may be deeply buried memories that are shocking and painful. Regular meditation can throw all sorts to the surface, some of it meaningful, lots of it apparently not at all. There may be times when we feel overwhelmed by what comes up, or when our clients struggle to cope. Just as we would always do in coaching, we need to be careful not to overstep our own boundaries of competence and refer on where necessary.

Working with mindfulness and 'difficult emotions'

I like to advise clients to check in with their mind as they move through their days. By evaluating the state that our own mind is in before we interact with others, we can prevent conflict, arguments, hurt feelings, etc. For example, how much frustration or anger are we holding? Are we operating from that place of frustration? What will it take to shift ourselves to a place of concern and caring before we have that conversation? Our mind is our lens of the world. It colours our perceptions and affects everything that we think, say and do. Mindfulness helps us to understand the state of that lens.

Holly McKinley, life coach based in the United States

Mindful minute to help a client manage angry reactions in meetings.

Emma Donaldson-Feilder, executive/business/wellbeing coach based in the United Kingdom

I work with a few government defense contractor companies who have referred me clients with high levels of reactivity, anger issues, and a lack of boundaries when it comes to managing others and their expression of emotion. Teaching brief meditation techniques, practising awareness in the moment makes a world of difference when coupled with more traditional anger management and communication skills training. Mindfulness really creates the space to learn.

Frank Del Fiugo, executive coach and coach trainer based in the United States

CASE STUDY   Helping to improve relationships

Beth was a human resources leader who was finding her new boss difficult to work with, so much so that she was considering leaving her job. She wanted to explore whether there was anything she could do to improve the situation with her boss as she would prefer to stay where she was but if not, to explore alternative work options.

She experienced her boss as very controlling, frequently 'checking up' to ensure she had done her work, and seeming not to trust her abilities. She was beginning to stop sharing ideas and to stop willingly offering updates as he 'always seems to pick holes in everything'. She could feel her 'energy draining' each morning as she approached work and her stomach would 'flip over' and her 'heart sink' if she knew she had a meeting with him or whenever she received an e-mail or a text from him.

'I feel like I am shrinking. When I see a text or an e-mail from him, I just think "Oh no, what have I done now?"'

We discussed some of Beth's other relationships. She described her previous boss as very trusting, motivating and encouraging. He had given her lots of projects to get her teeth into and had been very positive about her work. She described most of her other relationships at work as positive and healthy. She felt she was liked – this was important to her – and respected generally, and that she had a reputation for being 'competent, quick and innovative' on the whole.

We discussed the relationship with her boss in more detail, too. She felt there was nothing she could 'do right', that she 'could never please him'. This was important to her, she felt she needed approval. She talked about her relationship with her parents. Her late mother had been loving but also demanding and controlling, hard to please. Beth used to 'feel like my world was falling apart' when her mother was angry with her and desperately craved her approval. She would wind up feeling very hurt and sometimes very angry. Thinking about it, this relationship had had an impact on her relationship with others 'in authority', reflected Beth. In some way, she felt she was trying – and failing – to win her new boss's approval, she realized. She felt angry with him for 'not appreciating' what she had to offer. We looked at how she responded to her boss. Did she ever tell him how she felt? No. Did she think it was obvious to him how she felt? Yes, she thought it was – she was curt sometimes, a little snappy. And she would sometimes catch herself jumping to justify why she had done something the way she had, why she hadn't yet done something and so on.

I asked her how her boss was with other people at work. Actually, he was like that, she said – controlling, checking up, demanding – with lots of other people too, she reflected, although not everyone.

We explored transactional analysis a little as a lens through which to view her relationships. She had a strong 'please others' driver and she was indeed acting from an adapted child ego state in response to critical parent. She realized she was playing a strong part in how the situation played out and vowed to attempt to deal with her boss adult to adult. We did some role play with her trying out different ways of dealing with her boss.

We explored the stories she was telling herself about the situation and how and whether they served her.

Mindfulness came into play in the following ways.

Working with Beth was a real trigger for me as there were many parallels with my own relationship with my mother and how I felt moved to react to those in authority I deemed to be being critical. I made sure to allow enough time before each coaching session to get grounded, to do some meditation so I could be present for her without my own baggage getting in the way. At times, when something she said triggered a strong response in my own body/mind, I shared what was going on for me – this could be valuable information for her or it could be something of my own but this helped build the trust.

We explored where Beth felt different emotions in her body on a number of occasions. We talked about what went on for her when she 'dreaded' a meeting, or when she saw an e-mail or text from her boss. Bringing awareness to these bodily sensations helped her feel more in control. She was able to 'get on top of them' by breathing into them. One big breakthrough for Beth was when she realized how judgemental and angry she was with herself. She had thought her anger and hurt were all about her boss's behaviour. But she saw that she was cross with herself for not being able to 'sort things out', for not 'facing up to' her boss.

We practised various short mindfulness practices she could easily incorporate into her working day – the Three-minute breathing space (Chapter 9) and Awareness of breath (Chapter 5). These she began to use before meetings with her boss, and even during phone calls and meetings with him. She reported 'feeling much calmer and more able to respond from a more adult stance'. She reported that she was less likely to 'get stuck in this self-justifying space I kept getting stuck in, where he would ask about something I was working on and I would get all defensive'. Instead, she found herself volunteering where she was with projects. She realized she hadn't been just keeping him in the dark to protect herself but 'out of spite'. Volunteering information on a regular basis seemed to be helping – her boss was 'checking up' on her less and had begun to give her positive feedback sometimes. However, a real turning point came when Beth starting practising the Loving-kindness meditation (Chapter 7). In this meditation practice, as we've seen, the idea is to send loving-kindness to ourselves, someone we care about, someone we feel neutral about and someone we feel aversion towards – in that order.

Beth chose her boss as the person she felt aversion towards, practising whenever she could but committing to doing so at least twice a week. She said she felt scared about sending him loving-kindness and was convinced it would not be possible. She reported that it was difficult at first but after the first three or so times, she began to find it much easier. To begin with, she imagined her boss when he was a young child or when he was at home with his family, which helped her to de-demonize him. Soon, she was able to imagine him being verbally abusive towards her at work. She reported noticing her heart softening. She noticed that she felt much more compassionate towards him and started to think about all the pressures he was under to prove himself in his new job and how badly it would reflect on him if she underperformed. She started to appreciate the difference between her 'hard heart' which she felt as a contraction in her stomach and heart area and a 'tightening around the eyes and jaw' and her 'soft open heart' when she was practising loving-kindness towards him. She found she could sometimes soften her heart at will when she was at work.

What she also noticed very early on – from around the third time she practised – was that her boss was acting differently towards her. He was smiling at her more often. He cracked the odd joke at his own expense. He even broached the subject of how they were working together, which allowed her the chance to voice how she felt criticized at times and that he didn't trust her. He had sounded surprised, she said, explaining that in his view it was part of his job to check up on how people were doing as the 'buck stopped' with him.

Of course, this more open and warm attitude from Beth's boss could have been purely down to him having been in situ for longer and experiencing less performance anxiety. It could have been just down to her having proved her worth. However, strange things often happen in coaching – I've found that attending to an issue in a relationship within a coaching session often precedes a real shift in the relationship without the client even doing or saying anything. And the Loving-kindness meditation is a lovely way of attending to a relationship.

Self-esteem, self-compassion and self-acceptance

Many of our clients present with issues around low self-esteem. Our ability to judge can be incredibly useful but it can cripple us when we apply judgements to ourselves with harshness and a lack of compassion. Judging and rejecting themselves are very painful for people and can lead them to avoiding anything that might aggravate this pain. McKay and Fanning (2000) identify two types of self-esteem: situational and 'characterological'. Situational here means that we may feel we are bad parents but great at our job, for example. Our level of esteem depends on the situation we find ourselves in. Characterological low self-esteem usually stems from early abandonment and/or abuse and it's harder to tackle, they say. Just trying to change negative thoughts is unlikely to be enough for such a client, and of course it may be time to refer on. McKay and Fanning say what's needed here (although they are talking about therapy) is an emphasis on the negative identity, on self-compassion and a commitment to non-judgement.

Clients often come to us because they want things to change, because they are fed up with feeling this way. Perhaps they are held back from taking risks and opportunities, from opening up to people. Perhaps they are fed up with reacting to others in unhelpful ways as a form of protection or with misusing drugs, alcohol, food and the like. Low self-esteem is surprisingly common and not always as obvious as we would think.

We will all have our different ways of helping our clients raise their self-esteem. Cognitive behavioural coaching (CBC) can be useful in helping the client identify cognitive distortions and all those shoulds, musts and oughts. It can help them identify all the automatic thoughts that they are often unaware of but which lead them to feel all those unpleasant painful emotions and behave in certain ways nevertheless. It can help identify experiments they can try out. And mindfulness works beautifully here too, alongside CBC or other approaches such as narrative coaching.

Mindfulness can build clients' self-esteem by helping them:

- become more aware of their negative automatic thoughts (self-awareness);

- develop self-compassion and self-forgiveness;

- put in place self-nourishing strategies to bring about calmness and relaxation, better sleep patterns and so on, building their resourcefulness;

- accept themselves for who they are, without judgement.

I have found that helping a client develop a mindfulness practice enabled him to be more in the moment, and less prone to being self-critical and less caught up in catastrophic thoughts. Over time he became more self-accepting and self-confident.

Carolyn Mumby, life/executive coach and
coach trainer based in the United Kingdom

Self-esteem is seen as a problematic term by some – what we don't want, of course, is high self-esteem at the expense of holding others in high esteem, manifesting as narcissism at the extreme end of the scale. Self-compassion is different in meaning from self-esteem but it is perhaps a more helpful way of framing this. The key thing is to be kind to ourselves, to afford ourselves the same kindness and compassion we afford others.

Kristan Neff, who studies self-compassion at the University of Texas, suggests there are three components: self-kindness, common humanity and mindfulness. Helping our clients practise compassion towards themselves helps them stop being overly self-critical when they fail. It can help normal-ize their experiences, viewing what they're going through as part of the larger human experience, and through mindfulness, they can learn to hold painful, unpleasant thoughts and feelings in equanimity – balanced aware-ness – rather than identifying overly with them (Neff 2003).

Developing self-compassion and helping our clients to do the same help counter self-judgement, isolation, depression and anxiety. They help us care for others and be less judgemental of them too. We stop relying on putting others down to make ourselves feel good.

Professor Jeremy Hunter says, 'I find there is a softening that happens when you encounter your own suffering and you realize you're not the only person doing this.' He gives an example of 'a white, conservative, Orange County person' who, five weeks into one of Hunter's mindfulness-based programmes, had a direct experience of self-compassion in relation to others. 'I asked him what was happening. His face was soft. Tears welled up in his eyes and he said he'd realized "I'm not the only person suffering. It sounds so banal." '

He says coaches really have to practise this.

The physiological changes fostering compassion brings about in our bodies help to boost our immune system and other systems relating to health while 'negative emotions' have the opposite effect, according to a number of studies, including Rein *et al* (1995). The latter found that anger images and fantasies had a detrimental effect on the functioning of the immune system of those with such images, whereas compassion-focused fantasies and im-ages were found to have a very positive effect.

Growth in self-criticism

Gilbert says self-criticism and self-dislike seem to be growing at an 'alarming rate'. A colleague of his who was researching self-compassion as an antidote to self-criticism attracted a high number of participants for the study and was surprised at how many admitted to having problems with self-criticism, making them anxious and undermining their confidence. And when the Dalai Lama first came to the West, he was struck by how much self-dissatisfaction, self-disappointment, self-criticism and self-dislike he came across.

Having this as our backdrop when working with clients is helpful – normalizing these feelings. Self-criticism is a common theme for those with mental health problems. Gilbert says that the one core element the many people he has seen over the years have lacked is 'the ability to be kind, gentle, warm and compassionate with themselves'.

Gilbert teaches clients these skills, using an approach influenced by Buddhist-informed psychology and based on how our brains work. He developed compassion-focused therapy (CFT) with and for people with chronic and complex mental health problems linked to shame and self-criticism but there is much we can learn from his approach that we can apply to our coaching practice, interlinked with mindfulness. CFT adds a compassion focus to traditional CBT approaches, and includes mindfulness amongst the things it uses.

We can rest on our laurels and think that coaching is different from therapy and that as coaches we only deal with the well, even if they are the 'worried well'. Or we can be realistic and recognize that many of those we coach, and ourselves, will risk tipping into mental ill-health at some point and may actually become mentally unwell. The World Health Organization has estimated that by 2020, depression will be the second most common disorder in the world, with other mental health problems in the top ten. Developing self-compassion – and compassion for others – is one of the ways to stave off problems of this ilk.

Not easy

As Gilbert points out (2010), 'helping people develop compassion to others, and especially themselves, is not always easy. Indeed, some people are positively frightened of it and resistant to the idea. They see self-compassion and self-kindness as a weakness or an indulgence; to them, it means you're going soft or letting your guard down. If they started to feel self-kindness or compassion, it could ignite feelings of grief because they would recognize how alone they'd been feeling for so long.'

John Bowlby suggested that if a therapist shows kindness to a client, they can activate the client's 'attachment memories'. If those memories are of neglect or unkindness, the associated feelings can re-emerge. So it's possible that we might encounter clients who feel awkward, anxious and resistant to compassion. We should be on the lookout for this and, as always, be gentle in how we proceed, mindful of boundaries and referring on where appropriate.

Some of us may be involved in coaching those from disadvantaged backgrounds. They may well have experienced a lack of love and affection when they were growing up, and may experience difficulties in feeling safe.

Gilbert says when we are kind to ourselves, it is not just our thoughts but our feelings that our key. He says the challenge is to 'create nurturing and nourishing relationships with the many parts of our selves, so that no part is split off, forgotten, ignored, hated or avoided'. Combining mindfulness with work around sub-personalities (see Chapter 19) can be helpful in recognizing that we are all made up of lots of different 'selves', which are sometimes in conflict with one another.

We've seen how cultivating more nurturing and compassionate relationships with ourselves and others helps move us into an approach state. Operating from this state has been linked to increased creativity. In the next chapter, we look in depth at the relationship between mindfulness and creativity.

Recommended mindfulness practices

The Body scan to help clients be more able to pick up on signals from others, and read others' and their own body language.

The Loving-kindness meditation.

Building in lots of short practices to help with self-management.

Creativity

18

> *When you ask creative people how they did something, they feel a little guilty because they didn't really do it, they just saw something... Creativity is just connecting things.*
>
> **STEVE JOBS, FOUNDER OF APPLE**

> *True intelligence operates silently. Stillness is where creativity and solutions to problems are found.*
>
> **ECKHART TOLLE, AUTHOR**

Today's culture is highly geared towards judgement and evaluation. And as Ellen Langer (2005), a professor in Harvard University's psychology department, explores in her book, *On Becoming an Artist: Reinventing Yourself through Mindful Creativity*, evaluation all too often gets in the way of us being creative. Langer surprised herself one day when she told an artist friend that she planned to take up painting. She subsequently did and discovered for herself just how helpful mindfulness can be in fostering creativity. Understanding how to think mindfully is the best way to break through the roadblocks that keep us from developing our creative selves, she believes.

Many of us write ourselves off as uncreative while others believe we are all creative. Julia Cameron, author of *The Artist's Way*, believes that creativity is the natural order of life and is our true nature. She says that 'blocks are an unnatural thwarting of a process at once as normal and as miraculous as the blossoming of a flower at the end of a slender green stem'. Cameron was forced to uncover a new way of being creative after her alcohol problem got the better of her. She says she learnt to get out of the way and let the creative force work through her, to 'just show up at the page' and write down what she heard.

Langer says when we are mindfully creative, we are authentic; we're not being reactive but acting according to our own scripts. We can be original and we are liberated from having to do things 'the right way'.

Getting out of our own way

It is very hard to get out of our own way, which we are often urged to do as coaches, in particular. We tend to be so bogged down and blocked by long-held stories and by concerns about what others will think of us, and of anything we might create. We tend to accept others' negative evaluations as truth, and of course, we can be our own worst critic. As Langer points out, almost all our thoughts are concerned with whether what we or others are doing or thinking is 'good' or 'bad'.

I remember one balmy night in Marrakesh when I was in my twenties. We'd just arrived in the city and I was gazing out from our open bedroom window in our new lodgings. I inhaled the exotic-smelling night air, feeling a warm gentle breeze on my face. I smiled at how free and exhilarated I felt being somewhere so different from England. I could see the silhouette of a palm tree against the navy midnight sky. All looked beautiful and full of possibility. When we awoke, I looked out from the same window. Now, everything looked dirty and dusty, there were piles of rubbish on the rooftop terrace opposite, broken bits of furniture, and the exotic tree of the previous evening was actually a large twisted aerial. I felt cheated, I felt silly, a stupid tourist. Later on, however, I reflected that all *had* been beautiful for me in those moments that night, and how our perception is all.

I am reminded also of something one of my Buddhist teachers used to say to us: that as well as trying not to get caught up in any sounds going on around us when we were meditating, we could try 'transforming' them. So a bleating car horn can become a mindfulness bell of sorts, or that instrument Tibetan monks play to accompany chanting – the latter being equally discordant to my ear yet somehow acceptable for being 'exotic'. Or the rushing sound of traffic can become the sound of a river.

'Mistakes' and mindfulness

When we're very young, we tend to just create without worrying about what others think of our creations. As time goes on, we begin to seek approval from our parents, our caregivers. At first, it's enough to hear, 'That's beautiful, darling' from our parent. But gradually we become more and more critical. I used to get really upset with one of my daughters who used to paint these fabulous colourful paintings which I would start eyeing up with a view to displaying on the kitchen wall, only to see her tear them up in yet another fit of pique, because they weren't perfect, or because the final creation didn't match up with the idea in her head. Sometimes it was because she was concerned about what her friends would think – always a big preoccupation for her. The interference in her mind meant she could no longer enjoy creating for creating's sake, she could no longer lose herself in mindful painting.

That said, if you ask a young child to paint a landscape, they will typically depict the sky with a blue line at the top of the page, and a tree in the shape of a lollipop, and everything will be in block colours, with no shading, no different tones. I remember my artistic late mother encouraging me to really look at what I saw – the sky was all around, there were shadows, the trees were all sorts of different shapes, with branches and leaves, and there were many different shades of green. I remember being surprised! So in a way, even as a child, we do not always see all the finer details and nuances. To really unleash our creativity and our ability to be innovative, we need not only to learn how to undo the blocks consisting of judgements and fears so we can express ourselves in all our original and authentic glory, we need to increase our openness to possibility – to operate from Siegel's plane of possibility (Siegel 2010a). We need to increase our attention to detail, our ability to notice. So it's about rediscovering our ability to be mindful and really letting loose, but also about developing it further, so we can really look deeply, and really see, hear, feel, touch, experience.

I don't do much drawing or painting these days – I look forward to taking it up again in the future and enjoying the watercolour set I asked for one Christmas – but I remember that after my initial disappointment when something had 'gone wrong', I used to enjoy turning the 'mistake' into something else. Sometimes, things continued going 'downhill'; other times, something more interesting or beautiful would emerge. Either way, I would enjoy the process.

Ellen Langer outlines four perspectives we can engage with when we 'make a mistake' while drawing. We can throw the picture away because we can't stand mistakes – like my daughter used to; we can opt to live with the mistake as it is; we can try to fix the mistake so we get back to where we were; or we can reconsider the mistake and decide to make the most of it, which was what I used to enjoy doing. Langer says it is this fourth perspective that brings us most of what we value about art but that our culture teaches us to only consider the first three perspectives.

Trying to reframe situations, thinking that something good will emerge from something bad – the every-cloud-has-a-silver-lining line of thinking – is different from 'developing an awareness that the very thing which is evaluated as negative is also positive', says Langer. All events and experiences can be positive and negative, depending on our perspective, nothing is inherently anything.

Mindfulness is a powerful tool to help stop the self-critique which keeps those creative juices flowing. As we've explored earlier, it encourages us to be curious, notice new things and giving up preconceived mind-sets, help us become more open to possibilities and thus add fuel to the creativity tank.

Langer (2005) says that mindlessness 'freezes our responses and closes us off to the possibility of change'. She says we don't realize the power of uncertainty, that our culture leads us to try to reduce or even eliminate uncertainty, which she sees as the essence of mindlessness. 'We learn to do so in order to know what things are, so we can control them. Instead, we should consider exploiting the power of uncertainty, so that we can learn what things can become and so that we can become more than we previously thought possible. The antidote, then, is to avoid becoming mindless and to learn to be more mindful… Mindfulness makes us sensitive to context and perspective.'

When we're 'mindless', we're trapped in rigid mind-sets whereas when we are mindful, says Langer, 'we are actively drawing on novel distinctions rather than relying on distinctions drawn in the past. And it is just these rules, routines and mind-sets that are the roadblocks to living a more creative life.'

Mindful music

Apparently, the audience can tell the difference between mindful and 'mindless' music playing. Musicians inevitably get bored playing the same piece again and again. Langer, along with composer and conductor Timothy Russell, asked the Arizona State Symphony Orchestra to play a piece of music twice – once trying to recreate their best performance of it, and second by seeking to discover subtle ways of making the music new to them. The idea was that the first would be a more 'mindless' approach compared to the second more mindful approach. Langer comes at mindfulness from a Western, scientific perspective. She defines mindfulness as the process of noticing new things – seeing the similarities in things thought different and the differences in things taken to be similar. The musicians were asked how much they enjoyed playing the piece and how they had tried to make the second performance new. They overwhelmingly reported that they enjoyed the more mindful performance more than the other one. And after tapes of both performances were played to around 150 members of the orchestra's chorus, almost 90 per cent noticed a difference between the two, with more than 80 per cent preferring the mindful performance. The findings were the same in studies with other orchestras, and with novice musicians – judges rated their 'mindful performances' as more competent and creative.

Helping our clients be more creative

How will becoming more mindful help our clients be more creative? Being more relaxed has something to do with it. We know that when we're stressed, our ability to think more strategically and creatively is impaired. There is some evidence suggesting that increased activity in the left prefrontal cortex, which seems to come about when people practise mindfulness, is linked to creativity while increased activity in the right prefrontal cortex is linked to caution.

We explored earlier how we've evolved two different neurological processes: the behavioural inhibition system (avoidance) and the behavioural activation system (approach). These systems have an impact on how creative we are, according to research at the University of Maryland (Friedman and Forster 2001). Researchers gave two groups of students a paper-based puzzle to solve, with the same goal of 'freeing' a cartoon mouse trapped in a maze by drawing a line from the mouse to the exit. One group was given a positive 'approach-orientated' version of the puzzle, with a piece of cheese depicted at the exit. The other group was given a negative 'avoidance-orientated' version – no cheese but an owl hovering over the maze. Both groups completed the task in around two minutes but there were noticeable differences in their performance in a creativity test afterwards: the students who helped the mouse avoid the owl performed 50 per cent worse than the students who helped the mouse find the cheese. The suggestion is that their state of mind was one of caution, avoidance and vigilance, with increased activation in the right prefrontal cortex. Not a state conducive to creativity or flexibility.

If we don't want our clients to be like mice with owl complexes and want them to feel more like mice with cheese prospects, then we need to be open hearted, welcoming and positive. This ties in with the 'compassionate coaching' approach proposed by Richard Boyatzis and colleagues which we explored in Chapter 7, which encourages us to actively seek to arouse positive emotions in our clients.

Creative thinking

Of course, it's not just about being more creative in an artistic sense. Mindfulness can also help us and our clients be more creative in our thinking, and problem solving. Meditation promotes the divergent creative style of thinking, according to research by Colzato *et al* (2012). Colzato and colleagues at Leiden University looked at two meditation techniques: Open Monitoring (OM), in which the individual is receptive to all the thoughts and sensations experienced without focusing attention on any particular concept or object, and Focused Attention (FA), where they focus on a particular thought or object. They found that OM meditation induces a control state that promotes divergent thinking, a style of thinking that helps in the generation of many new ideas while FA meditation does not support convergent thinking, the process of generating one possible solution to a particular problem.

Mindfulness appears to improve insight problem solving (but not non-insight problem solving), according to another study from the Netherlands (Ostafin and Kassman 2012). Insight problems are those which typically generate a eureka moment, usually requiring the person to think out of the box. The researchers from the University of Groningen claimed to be presenting the first findings documenting a direct relation between mindfulness and creativity.

Using mindfulness with the client

There are a number of ways in which mindfulness can help our clients be more creative – in the strictest sense of the word, but also in the sense of creative problem solving.

For **Professor David Clutterbuck**, co-founder of the European Mentoring & Coaching Council, creativity is one of the main benefits of bringing mindfulness into a coaching session:

> At the beginning of a coaching or mentoring session, the client often arrives anything but mindful – high on adrenaline, still in the grip of 'business stress'. I use a combination of relaxation and mindfulness techniques to bring them to a mental state where they are truly receptive to coaching. I help them become more aware of their physical presence and state, their emotional state, the sounds and the visual environment around them. All of which helps them be more open and creative in their thinking and the conversation they have with themselves.
>
> We might reconnect to this state during the session, if the conversation loses its creative underpinning; or at the end, to add depth to the client's summary of their learning.

Mindfulness enhances our own and our clients' creativity by helping us:

- suspend our judgements and evaluations, and not pay too much attention to those of others;
- be more choiceful about *what* and *whom* we listen to;
- not see things as mistakes, and just enjoy the process in the present moment;
- embrace authenticity and originality;
- get ourselves out of the way;
- be more curious and open to possibility;
- improve divergent thinking;
- be more relaxed and approach-oriented;
- create spaciousness in our lives for creativity.

CASE STUDY   Unblocking creativity

Georgia is a journalist, writer and mother of two. She says:

I have far too much to do, and a default position of blaming myself/repeating negative and energy-sapping thought patterns rather than maximizing what time I do have. So my reasons for wanting some coaching were around feeling I am not reaching my full potential, feeling blocked, wanting to shift these unhelpful ways of thinking, and also to try and re-energize my self-belief so I could be more creative.

A severe professional setback in my work as a novelist – a publisher which had not only dropped me, but failed to properly promote my second book – had left me feeling very dispirited, and as if I might never find the energy or will to write a novel again. And my attempt to 're-engineer' my career meant taking on not only a time-consuming and underpaid job teaching creative writing, but also embarking on an equally time-consuming and expensive MA in the same subject. Then I lost the regular freelance work which I had hoped would keep the whole show on the road.

Through the coaching, I realized that the new endeavours, both teaching creative writing for the first time and becoming a student, were getting to me because I was entering the unknown. I had the sense that I was doing something stupid, or foolishly overreaching myself. (Part of my habitual, negative way of viewing my own efforts!)

After the first session, the mist had lifted to the extent that a few days afterwards I realized I had been avoiding/evading a much more deep-seated issue, which is the fear that I can't write another book, a horrible feeling, fear mixed with impotence. In the next session, we explored some CBT techniques, which I found really interesting, and once again a very helpful way of analysing and understanding what had seemed like an amorphous and intractable set of problems. It was also good to see that I have thinking patterns which other people share – mind reading, catastrophizing amongst others.

We also explored the stories I tell myself and how I could rewrite these and change the way I think.

I was also introduced to mindfulness. We did the Mindful minute which I now do immediately after writing my Morning pages (one of Julia Cameron's suggestions) if I am feeling really time-pressured, which helps me approach my work more calmly. If I feel I have more time, I now meditate before I go for a run. I try to keep in mind that I am not my thoughts – which is just as well as they are pretty damning! And I try to observe what is going on in my body. I was finding that my stomach was contracting with nerves whereas now, I think at least in part due to the mindfulness, my irritable bowel syndrome is much improved. I was also getting a lot of neck pain – the more stressed I felt, the more I hunched over the computer. Now when I check in with my body and realize I have hunched my shoulders, I make a conscious effort to relax them, which is really helping to ease the pain.

But most of all, I have got rid of the fear of embarking upon a new novel. Somehow, creating a gap between me – whatever me is – and my thoughts, getting some peace and quiet from all the judgement I overlaid over everything, have helped me be more creative. When my writing is going well, I get thoroughly absorbed in the process – it feels very mindful. But I can now induce a mindful state on purpose (sometimes!), which helps me relax and let the creative juices flow. I also sometimes find that when I am meditating, supposedly focusing on my breath, I suddenly have a brainwave – perhaps a novel solution to a problem with the plot or an innovative way to tell the story.

I am learning not only more about my own problems, but about how we all think, about the common inner experience of being an imperfect person in an imperfect world, and about ways to live and deal with that.

Exercise (10–20 minutes)

Creativity: before-mindfulness and post-mindfulness

In this exercise, you're exploring whether mindfulness makes a difference to how creative you can be. I've chosen drawing here, but you could try it instead with something else such as playing the piano.

Make sure you won't be disturbed for the duration of the exercise. Prepare the creative exercise material you will need. For example, get some pieces of blank paper and some pens/pencils ready to use. And choose something or someone to draw.

Before you start, think about all the e-mails piling up, about that work you still have to complete, those problems you need to solve. Then move straight away into drawing whatever or whoever it is, attempting to copy as best you can what you see in front of you. Don't bother to try to bat away any remaining thoughts about work. After about 5 or 10 minutes, put the drawn-on piece of paper to one side.

Now, choose a mindfulness practice, one you've done before. For example, the Three-minute breathing space or the Witness meditation. And give yourself permission to give yourself over to the practice.

When you've finished the practice above and when you're ready, pick up another piece of paper and once again, draw the object or person you've chosen. Again, try to copy what's in front of you. When you've completed the drawing (or whatever creativity exercise), reflect on any differences in how you felt in both cases. What, if any, were the differences? You might like to compare the two drawings. You may find you prefer the second, or not. You may find you enjoyed the second experience more than the first, or not. Just noticing what you notice! Without judgement and curiosity.

You may like to try this out with something you're trying to problem solve too. In my own experience, as I've said, I often find mindfulness – meditation in particular – helps me come up with an alternative that hadn't crossed my mind. And I do find that my ability to write is hugely helped by me being mindful, and hindered by me feeling stressed, harassed and 'unmindful'.

The role of mindfulness in helping to foster a creative thinking environment is highlighted in the work of Nancy Kline, for example, which we look at in the next chapter, along with where mindfulness is found or can be woven into a range of other approaches.

Tips for using mindfulness for creativity in clients

- Help to move clients to an 'approach' state by being open hearted, welcoming, positive and appreciative, and actively seeking out positive emotions in them.
- Invite clients to play around with being creative when they are mindful, and when they are 'mindless', comparing their 'performance', experience and levels of enjoyment.
- Start sessions with a short mindfulness practice to move clients into approach state, helping them be resourceful and creative in their thinking within the session itself.
- Encourage clients to 'do' mindfulness practices at home to help them switch off and move more frequently into 'approach state'.
- Encourage clients to incorporate mindfulness practices into their daily working lives, and particularly when they're required to be creative at work (including thinking strategically).

The Witness meditation (a variation)

Let your attention be drawn by one sensation in particular, really focusing on this sensation then moving to the next which draws your attention.

Just going with the flow, noticing what comes up, just observing it without seeking to interpret.

Noticing how these sensations always change, how they're always in motion and flux.

Noticing how even though there is flux, there is something in you that is constant and can watch these changes. Ask yourself:

Am I my sensations or am I more than my sensations?

Who am I in the midst of this continuous stream of sensations?

Let the questions land and just be.

Now allow your attention to be drawn to your emotions. Allowing yourself to be drawn to any single emotion in particular. Allowing just to be with this emotion, just observing and witnessing it. Not trying to change anything.

And noticing how your emotions change, how their quality and intensity change, grow, or fade away. Noticing how like your bodily sensations, your emotions are always in flux. However, as these emotions come and go and shift, noticing that there is something else within that is there all the time, able to watch your emotions as they come and go. Ask yourself:

Am I my emotions or am I more than my emotions?

Who am I in the midst of this endless stream of emotions?

Let the questions land and just be.

Now turning your attention to your thoughts (mental events).

Noticing which thoughts are coming up. Allowing your attention to be drawn to a particular thought, without identifying with it, without having to interpret it, just noticing, just observing, just witnessing.

And noticing that other thoughts pop up, and another and another. A stream of thoughts popping up, passing by like bubbles on a fast-moving stream as the Buddha allegedly said.

And noticing that as they come and go, there is something constant, an Observer or Witness, that can watch the thoughts come and go. And ask yourself:

Am I my thoughts or am I more than my thoughts?

Who am I within this endless stream of thoughts?

Let the questions land and just be.

Noticing now your overall experience, made up of your bodily sensations, your emotions and your thoughts. Noticing its overall tone and quality and noticing that if you turn your attention to your experience, it too is always changing from moment to moment. Yet something within you remains constant, allowing you to watch your experience come and go. And ask yourself:

Am I my experiences or am I more than my experiences?

Who am I within this constant stream of experiences?

And let the questions land and just be.

When you're ready, gently and slowly come back into the room (and carry on witnessing and observing).

And capturing any reflections.

Recommended mindfulness practices

Short regular practices to maintain the client in more resourceful approach state including: Three-minute breathing space and the Mindful minute.

The Witness meditation (to encourage clients to be more open to possibility and to what's there).

In the next chapter, we look at mindfulness and other approaches.

Mindfulness and other approaches

19

We've already seen where we can find mindfulness in some of the more popular leadership frameworks. We can also find mindfulness to a greater or lesser degree within a number of existing coaching approaches. It may not always go by the name of mindfulness and in some cases, practitioners of those approaches may not even have made the connection that what they're doing is mindfulness or closely related to it. In this chapter, we explore where we can find mindfulness in some of these approaches. My intention here is in part to honour and acknowledge where the cultivation of mindfulness is already taking place. It's also to continue to foster debate about what it is and where and how it can be cultivated. It doesn't have to be something Out There or Over There, an additional add-on tool or technique. Just as we can weave mindfulness into our daily lives, so too can we make space for it within existing coaching frameworks and processes.

After a brief exploration of mindfulness in movement, we will look at three approaches which intentionally work with the body – somatics, in particular, before moving on to look at some others. I realize that there are many approaches we could look at, including existential coaching, NLP and so on. However, in this chapter, we will look at:

- gestalt;
- somatics;
- ontological coaching;
- transactional analysis;
- psychosynthesis and transpersonal coaching;
- cognitive behavioural coaching (and acceptance commitment therapy);
- inner game;
- thinking environment.

Mindfulness in movement

> Mr Duffy... lived at a little distance from his body.
>
> James Joyce, *Dubliners*

I sometimes attend a workshop called Danceitation, billed as 'ancient Buddhism meets intelligent clubbing' and led by Jayagita, a coach and long-standing meditator. We dance free-form to an inspired selection of music as we're guided through variations on meditations such as the Loving-kindness meditation. At times, I just enjoy having a good old dance in a meditative sort of way, letting my hair down without dreading a hangover the following day. At other times, transformation occurs. There's something about actually moving about that can enable shifts to occur that may not otherwise. In one session, in which we worked with the breath, letting in and letting go, I embodied a transformative insight which was immensely healing. It embedded something deeply which I'd known conceptually for some time but which had seemed superficial, out of my reach and lacking in ability to heal or comfort. It was to do with accepting that my late parents and sister were no longer suffering in this world, that whatever they'd been, they no longer were now (whatever they may be now). I understood, albeit briefly – these things are evasive – the nature of impermanence and death. Since then, I no longer experience with such intensity the sorrow and grief which had been weighing me down to do with not having been able to 'save' my father, who attempted suicide a few years after losing my mother, and who died lonely and broken-hearted on a psychiatric ward. I no longer experience flashes of childish petulance or anger about how he was prepared to 'abandon' me and the rest of our family. I realize there was much work I had done leading up to this healing, which contributed to this shift, but I maintain that it was the combination of mindfulness, movement and music that created the momentum for something to unlock and for the insight to take hold.

The tradition of 'mindful movement' is very much alive and kicking and seemingly growing in popularity, with multiple expressions, from Gabrielle Roth's 5Rhythms dance to Tai Chi, yoga and Mindful walking. Mindful movement is incorporated into many mindfulness programmes – Tai Chi is included in MBSR and MBCT programmes all over the world, for example. We're finally accepting or remembering in the West what the East never forgot, it seems: that the mind and body are inextricably linked. Thanks in part to the science that formerly fuelled the belief that mind and body are separate, this view is increasingly rejected. As we explored to some degree in Chapter 3, research now shows a direct link between our brain and body, through neural pathways, through neurotransmitters in our heart, gut and connective tissue. Our brain extends throughout our body, with our enteric nervous system consisting of some 100 million neurons. Pharmacologist and author of *Molecules of Emotion: the science behind mind–body medicine*, Dr Candace B Pert has said: 'I can no longer make a strong distinction between the brain and the body.' A great believer in meditation as the 'single quickest, easiest, shortest and cheapest route to feeling good', Dr Pert also believes 'molecules of emotion run every system in our body' and that 'this communication system is, in effect, a demonstration of the bodymind's intelligence, an intelligence wise enough to seek wellness'.

Practices such as walking mindfully can be done anywhere and are very easy to incorporate into our daily lives. We can walk mindfully to a coaching session, for example. However, it's particularly beneficial to set aside time to practise Mindful walking, without any destination in mind. I invite you to set aside some time now for some meaningful meandering.

Practice: Mindful walking (10–30 minutes)

Set your intention to dedicate at least 10 minutes (working up to 30) to cultivating mindfulness through this Mindful walking practice. You are not aiming to get anywhere but solely to walk for walking's sake. Choose a place where you are going to walk, perhaps circling a large room or outside. Or you may choose to go back and forth between two points 30 or so feet apart. Deciding where you are going to walk beforehand is helpful – otherwise, you may find you get caught up in mental chatter about whether this area is good enough and wondering whether somewhere else would be quieter, more beautiful, warmer and so on. You can set your own pace. Personally, I find it easier to walk mindfully if I walk slowly.

Thich Nhat Hanh recommends combining walking mindfully with the breath. So you might breathe in as you lift your leg/foot, and breathe out as you place it down.

Bringing your attention to your feet, noticing the sensations as the balls of your feet, then your heels meet the ground. Noticing the sensations in your ankles, your calves, the rest of your legs.

Noticing how it feels as you lift your foot then place it back on the ground. Noticing you are lifting as you lift your foot, and noticing that you are placing your foot on the ground as you place it on the ground.

Noticing too how it feels as you shift your weight.

Noticing all the little details of this experience of walking. You may like to keep yourself focused by saying certain words to yourself as you move, such as 'lifting', 'shifting', 'stepping'. Or you may like to count as you take steps, up to 10 then back to the beginning.

Your mind will wander; gently bring it back when it does so. You may find that in addition to getting caught up in thoughts, you get caught up in seeing what's around you. Or you may be caught up in hearing. That's fine, and often you may find you notice all sorts of hitherto unnoticed details – the world can suddenly look more colourful, for example, However, what you're really trying to do is focus on walking. You may like to note 'seeing' or 'hearing', for example.

> When you're ready, bring the practice to a close. And notice any differences in yourself and/or your experiences after the practice.
>
> You may like to experiment with other types of mindful movement, such as mindful yoga, mindful jogging or mindful swimming.
>
> This is another wonderful practice to share with clients. And you can even incorporate some Mindful walking together into a coaching session.

Recognition by people including psychoanalyst Wilhelm Reich of the role the body plays in healing has led to the development of a range of coaching approaches which work with the body, including gestalt and somatics. We'll first look at gestalt.

Gestalt

Awareness is curative.

Fritz Perls (1969), co-developer of gestalt therapy

Gestalt therapy and subsequently gestalt coaching have enjoyed many influences, including those of Sigmund Freud, Wilhem Reich, Kurt Lewin and of Zen Buddhism. So it's not surprising that its foundations include awareness and acceptance; attending to the present; using the body as a tool (Reich was a pioneer in working through the body to bring about self-understanding and personality change); and working with the fact that none of us operates in isolation (Lewin emphasized the interrelationship of the person with the environment).

Already, we can see how gestalt and mindfulness speak the same language or can at least understand one another easily. The aim in gestalt is to 'live fully', a similar concept to 'living mindfully'.

As in mindfulness, gestalt is not concerned with the past or future. Life happens in the present; it's only here in the present that we can live fully. According to gestalt, we develop defences which prevent us from experiencing the present in a full and authentic way. Working in the present, with awareness, helps us undo these resistances or blocks to good 'contact' with others and our environment. These blocks include 'introjection' (unquestioning acceptance of others' ideas and attitudes) and 'projection' (making others responsible for feelings and attitudes which are part of ourselves). John Leary-Joyce, founder of the Academy of Executive Coaching and gestalt therapist/coach, goes as far as to say that in gestalt, 'the only goal is awareness'.

Awareness in gestalt

Gestalt seeks to bring into awareness, in the moment, the gaps between someone's presentation and how they respond to others.

'Gestalt doesn't give you any objectives… It's all about being aware in the moment. In terms of a gestalt intervention, I look at how we interrupt our natural flow. When we look at two- or three-year-olds, they're perfect gestalt practitioners, totally focused and engaged in the moment. It makes them beautiful. Then we learn how to think, we learn codes and systems and our minds come in to interrupt that natural flow. We lose that level of spontaneity and the challenge is how to get back. Mindfulness is like being a child, but being able to witness it, be aware of it,' says Leary-Joyce.

'When I work with a client, I identify what the client is wanting to work on and then we put that on the shelf and work with what's (actually) going on… there are two approaches to change: doing something different, and becoming aware of who you are.'

Awareness – or mindfulness – can be brought to the following aspects of human experience: sensations and actions; feelings; wants; and values and assessments. The gestalt-informed coach works with in-the-moment data that their client brings into the room, without seeking to interpret ('phenomenological exploration'). Gestalt is about process, not content, just noticing what's going on rather than seeking to understand or make sense of it, paying attention to 'opening', another important concept in gestalt.

Leary-Joyce talks of one client who 'opened out into her anxiety about being too forceful with a direct report'. He says, 'The last time she'd been too forceful and the person left so now she was pulling herself into being tentative. So the work was about how she held the authenticity. Gestalt is about the quality of the impact on the relationship. If I can be open and aware of my judgements, I can be responding to you as another human being. I am taking what you say and processing it through my own system.'

He says that with this client it was about: 'sitting with the anxiety and allowing the anxiety space to breathe'. Mindfulness pays attention to that sensation, and identifies the thinking that goes along with it.

Integration

Gestalt doesn't seek to reject undesirable symptoms or behaviours but sees them as desirable elements in the change process. As well as acceptance of what is, gestalt seeks integration, both of which are seen to lead to change. Like mindfulness, gestalt doesn't attempt to push away the unacceptable or to polarize.

Gestalt requires coaches to be highly self-aware and to be able to use that self-awareness in service of the client. So, as Leary-Joyce explains, as a gestalt coach, he continually asks himself: 'What am I thinking/feeling now and what of this do I need to share with my client in order to enhance the relationship?' So a gestalt coach or someone drawing on the gestalt approach will pay close attention to their response to the client and share this with the client (boredom, agitation, excitement, nervousness, fearfulness). They will then invite the client to notice how they're showing up in the moment, including their posture and their tone of voice.

Also important in gestalt is the concept of ebb and flow, explains Leary-Joyce. 'Ebb and flow are critical… You can't breathe in unless you're breathing out… You're aware of the present, then of the future and awareness is like a torchlight.'

This too has resonance with mindfulness, certainly with some of the teachings underpinning mindfulness which are about going with the flow, surrendering and accepting what is. Meditations such as those involving us becoming aware of our in and out breaths put us in touch with this natural flow.

CASE STUDY   Gestalt meets mindfulness

Edwina Love-Lawrence, a coach based in the United Kingdom, is informed by gestalt, mindfulness and transpersonal coaching. She says:

The basis of gestalt is that we're aware of the lever for change; if you're aware of something, it will shift. So we work with what emerges and what the client becomes aware of. Outcomes are important but goals held lightly so clients who work with me don't get action plans in between sessions, although we might discuss how they could experiment with a particular feeling or how they experience themselves in a particular situation. My meditation and yoga practice help me to tune in to my experience of my client in my body and emotions, and I work with this to support the client in their own self-awareness. My work is emergent and exploratory, so sometimes I'm not sure where we're going and I make that explicit to the client which is usually really exciting for both of us, although if I have a client who is STJ (Myers–Briggs: sensing, thinking, judging), they think it's a bit weird. When I was working as an internal coach, I worked with people who were very like that and my practice was much more structured, but since I've been working for myself I've let it loosen up.

I had one client who had a big issue about making decisions and prioritizing in her professional life so I asked her to talk me through how she had decided what to wear that day. I asked her to describe this in a very granular way, so she was aware of her decision-making process almost in slow motion, in a mindful way. The insight that came up as a result was that she was making decisions on the basis of what other people wanted, not on the basis of what worked best for her. She came up with a lot more nos after that! Many years ago I used to teach assertiveness with CBT-style activities for saying no but it only went so far in enabling change. I'm finding with the way I coach now, it's about deeper and higher choices, in the same way that Assaglioli [talked about how] the deep and higher selves play off each other, and that the change that comes from this is more fundamental.

Mindful coaching and gestalt coaching work with the whole person, not just bits of the person. Sometimes that means the client works with the shadowy aspects of themselves they may not like very much, and they don't always like me very much during that part of the process. Again this is where my mindfulness practice is helpful because I can tune into the connection and we can sit with the awareness about how they are feeling about me and about themselves. It's about awareness of what we're holding onto and what would be good to let go of... breathing in, breathing out, letting come, letting go, is it the client, is it the coach? You don't know until you explore it. This gets quite close to therapy at times, which is why I receive supervision from someone who is therapeutically qualified and has a gestalt background. Clients are attracted to working with me because they want to work on a transpersonal agenda, sometimes without realizing it. They might start off thinking they want to sort out e-mails but almost invariably we get onto the other stuff. Being a reiki master also informs my coaching, my levels of mindfulness, stillness and ability to connect. Mindfulness meets gestalt in the granularity, the detail, being present, attuned awareness moment by moment. When I'm working with clients who are up for it, it's [about] just catching something as it happens. I pick up what they're feeling, using somatic resonance which I call 'whole body listening'. For example, if I feel unusually nervous, I'll name the nervousness and ask the client how nervous they're feeling. The attunement comes up emotionally, physically and spiritually and sometimes I'll not have a clue where it's from. The granularity is the door to it. When you get to the little stuff, you get to the bigger stuff. It doesn't matter where it is, whether it's emotional or physical subtlety (not intellectual), that's where the shift happens, that's the door to Narnia.

Somatics

Somatic coaching also owes a debt to Reich and in turn, gestalt has contributed to the development of somatic-based coaching. Dr Richard Strozzi-Heckler, one of the thought leaders in the field of somatics, has spent more than 40 years researching and developing the methodology of embodiment, developing a somatic coaching approach which integrates practices of embodiment, gestalt and linguistics, with the martial art of aikido and teachings of meditative practices. Somatic-based coaching works through the body explicitly – the word 'soma' means 'body'.

The Strozzi Institute describes a somatic perspective as including 'our thinking, feeling, emotions, and acting; this also accounts for our narratives and stories, our moods, and our energetic body... While some systems may simply add the body as an element in their coaching curriculum, we treat the body as a fundamental place of change, learning, and transformation.' It holds that the self and the body are indistinguishable.

Somatic coaching involves an inquiry into our 'lived body' by observing and exploring ourselves through sensing and moving, and awareness, which includes attending to our external senses (sight, hearing, tasting, smelling and touching) as well as to sensing of our movements (proprioception).

Eunice Aquilina, a certified somatic coach, says, 'Working somatically, the coach helps the client notice the sensations that are disconnected from what they are saying. For example, if someone says "I'm fine" when in fact they are feeling nervous, it sends an inconsistent message and raises a warning flag of distrust. Our inner self is revealed through our bodies. When we learn to observe our actions, sensations and automatic reactions we begin to give ourselves more choices.'

For Aquilina, mindfulness sits within somatics: 'Somatics recognizes how our experiences and our way of being become lodged in our living tissues. It works with the body–mind connection to unlodge from our muscle memory that which no longer serves us. Mindfulness sits within that... In somatic coaching, for example, mindful practice is incorporated. This might mean a sitting practice, which can be a way of quietening the mind, of letting go of stuff and being in the present moment. It allows you to hear what's going on in your soma (body), to notice what's happening such as where you are contracting in your body and how your emotions show up.'

CASE STUDY   Mindfulness meets somatics

Neela Bettridge used to 'shy away' from somatic coaching until she realized how 'powerful' it can be. And for her, mindfulness is key. 'It has to be from a basis of mindfulness, those who don't have that basis find it difficult to deal with somatics.' Bettridge has trained with the Strozzi Institute as well as Newfield, which offers ontological coach training.

She finds mindfulness combined with somatics particularly helpful with 'clients grappling with presence' issues. Here's how she worked with a senior partner in a headhunting firm using the two: 'Despite being the best fee earner, she was very timid and never got the accolades. She was totally unaware of herself. Her somatic presence was very small. Working in mindfulness and judging her presence in terms of width, breadth and length, we were able to increase her presence. The mindfulness is much more linked to emotional space and mood, and somatics is the process by which you get there.' Although she doesn't always call what she does 'mindfulness', she tends to be explicit about what clients need to do. 'At its very simplest, it's around centring, breath sitting practice, mindful raisin eating. The aim is for them to take their attention to something completely and fully, with all of their senses.'

CASE STUDY   Embodying wisdom

I remember being on the receiving end of some powerful coaching early on in my coaching career. I was stuck in an unwelcome yet familiar storyline, something about Professional Liz having to be a certain way, in tension with The Real Me, whom I felt obliged at times to hide. I started to gabble on about how I knew what I needed to do – align the two, be more authentic, how could I expect to work on authenticity with clients if I hadn't cracked it for myself? And so on. I could hear myself speaking more quickly, trying to make sense of it all, yet feeling more and more disengaged, which made it harder to follow what I was thinking. 'OK, let's stop a minute,' my coach said gently. 'Take a few deep breaths.' I did, realizing that I had been getting out of breath. 'What's going on for you in your body?' I tuned in. I could feel my heart beating fast. I could feel a massive knot in my stomach. I breathed into it. Then as my coach asked me questions, she encouraged me to stay in my body. I can remember – gazing out over London's River Thames – a fight going on between my head which wanted to take over, and a feeling, bodily, knowing place. Every time I lost the battle and was pulled back into my head, there was cloudiness and lack of clarity. When I stayed in my body, I really *knew* all the stuff I thought I knew already, that I had just been articulating. I embodied it deeply and although it remains a work-in-progress, it has stayed with me since. We did other work too, informed by gestalt – Professional Liz speaking to Real Liz, each in different chairs, and some more stuff shifted. But the most powerful work was when I was mindfully tuning in to what was happening to my body, subsequently speaking from this place of quietness and feelings, with the chatter stilled for a while.

One of the core practices within somatic coaching and one which has been adopted by some Ontological Coaching practitioners too, is Centring, which we tried out in Chapter 4.

Ontological coaching

Ontological coaching, co-founded by Julio Olalla, has been informed by the work of people including Chilean philosopher and politician Fernando Flores, Rafael Echeverria, author of *The Ontology of Language*, and biologist Humberto Maturana with his exploration of humans as linguistic beings and observers. Ontology means the study of being, and ontological coaching works with the client's way of being through three domains: language, emotions and the body. There is arguably less emphasis on the last than there is in somatics although ontological coaching does encourage us to notice what's going on in ourselves and to make any appropriate shifts in body posture, for example, to better enable us to expand our range of movements and emotions. This requires us to build awareness of what we do and don't do already.

The observer

Key in ontological coaching is exploring ourselves as observers, which has resonance with mindfulness and its meta-cognitive aspect. Aboodi Shabi, head of training and coaching for Newfield Europe, one of the ontological coach training bodies, explains that ontological coaching seeks to help clients observe the observer they are, inviting them to look at what that gives them and what it costs them, so they can build and expand their range accordingly.

For Olalla, how we observe what we observe and our ability to make distinctions between what we and others observe are key to our growth and self-development. He offers the following example: 'I was in North Chile, in the most deserted place on the planet where it rains once every 10 years. I went with a group of friends and we lay down on the floor looking up at the extraordinary world of the stars. The next day our friend came with us and started telling us about the planets, galaxies, satellites and stars. So the sky was completely different because she was providing so many distinctions.'

On the third night, 'by beautiful synchronicity', they met an astrologer with another perspective: 'Where were all these things before we met this person? Nowhere for me. I lacked the distinctions... when you enlarge the distinctions, something becomes available' (Hall 2010).

CASE STUDY   Mindfulness meets ontological coaching

For Aboodi Shabi, there are a number of threads that connect ontological coaching and mindfulness, including curiosity, seeking different perspectives and thus challenging assumptions, accessing what's meaningful, acceptance and slowing down. 'There is something about the idea that we get caught up in tinkering with details of our lives and [we need to] learn to observe life differently. This is probably where peace and contentment lie instead of [thinking] "I'll be happy when . . ." I feel we're all part of a paradigm of "more" and it creates dis-ease. It's hard for us to declare satisfaction and be comfortable with what is. Some coaching has fallen into that paradigm of helping people to have more and to forget to ask questions about why. I think we have a crisis of meaning – the financial crisis, issues of trust in the government, the Occupy movement. These all point to something not being right, people are beginning to shift. People are becoming more mindful about how we live. Is life about acquiring more or appreciating what we have?

'Having an outside view helps us not get caught up in the world view of the coachee or the world view that is dominant… What is this time we have really about? I think we might be looking in the wrong places. [In many regions] we have better healthcare and education, all the external measures have increased exponentially since World War II [in the West] yet human happiness has diminished. Mindfulness seems to be about savouring life in the moment. There is nothing wrong with having aspirations but we see so many coaches caught in this idea that "over there" is better than "over here". Julio [Olalla] says, "What wants to manifest?" A new way of thinking is beginning to percolate… I think when we do slow down and take a look, whether somatically or otherwise, we can say, "What have we been running for?" We keep running and we don't know why any more. We're efficient because we have to be efficient. It connects to this thing of meaning. When we get mindful, we start to savour things again. Mindfulness is one of the critical parts of coaching. And sometimes the mindfulness becomes the aim of coaching. [We may realize] the other stuff might not matter as much, that maybe it's OK to be overlooked for promotion but to spend time with the wife and kids. When things drop away and we stop striving, we can realize we have a pretty good life. It connects with the Jewish tradition of Shabat, slowing down on the seventh day, taking moments to sit and to be with what is. It doesn't mean we don't have to go back and have things to do but we build the capacity to reflect and find ways to do both.

'One of the things we talk about a lot in ontological coaching is looking at who we are. Ontology is the study of being and the first person we study is ourselves. How come we do what we do and believe what we believe?'

He believes mindfulness is very helpful in building self-awareness and in helping us pay attention to how we see the world, and how we show up are in our relationships.

'We encourage students to continually sit back and be present, with breathing, for example… If I'm not present to myself, I can get caught up by needing to come up with great questions, and (in) not being comfortable with not knowing… if we don't meditate, we can walk in nature, for example… It's not enough for the coach to not take care of themselves, to arrive screeching to a halt, take a deep breath and say, "I'm ready."

'It's important to do [mindfulness/reflecting] before there is a crisis so the body already knows what to do rather than trying to reflect suddenly. We can learn something quickly but this practice is a lifetime's work.'

Transactional analysis

Transactional analysis (TA) was founded by Eric Berne, author of *Games People Play*. Even those coaches who say they aren't informed by TA are likely to be familiar with TA concepts such as 'I'm OK, you're OK,' 'drivers' (hurry up, be perfect), and 'parent, adult, child (PAC)', for example. Talking of the last and referring back to the importance of making distinctions in ontological coaching, one of TA's leading figures, Julie Hay, shares the follow-ing 'TA folk story' about another encounter with an astrologer. This time it's

Berne meeting an astrologer on a plane. 'On learning that Berne was involved with TA, the astrologer commented that he knew all about TA because it was PAC. Berne is said to have responded that he knew all about astrology, because it was Twinkle, Twinkle, Little Star.'

TA concepts may have entered common parlance but its system is comprehensive and far from unsophisticated. And it has many links with mindfulness, says Hay, who created developmental transactional analysis (DTA) as a counterbalance to the psychotherapeutic TA which focuses on pathology. One of the five original founders of the European Mentoring and Coaching Council, Hay runs an MSc in DTA that offers a specialization for coaches, under the auspices of Middlesex University where she is a visiting professor.

A core TA concept is autonomy, explains Hay, and within this is awareness. Berne (1972) defined autonomy as 'awareness, spontaneity and intimacy'. Hay has added in authenticity to help clarify the somewhat misleading term of spontaneity, actually meant by Berne to indicate that we have options about how to behave.

'Awareness relates directly to mindfulness as it refers to being fully aware of the moment – who we are, who others are, what we are feeling, whether our currently experienced emotion belongs to the here-and-now or is a replay of a childhood experience – in TA jargon, are we being authentic? Or is it a racket, or substitute feeling that we learned was acceptable in childhood? For example, the stereotypical but nevertheless common "Big boys don't cry but they can get angry" and "Little girls don't get angry but daddy cuddles them if they are sad,"' says Hay.

Within the TA framework, awareness is seen as the antithesis to 'script', which is the unconscious life plan we adopt as a child and which reflects our version of the themes of Greek myths and worldwide fairy stories (Campbell 1972). These include Tantalus never getting what s/he wants, or Arachne forever condemned to re-spin a web of earlier mistakes.

A key TA construct for helping clients increase awareness is the notion of discounting (Mellor and Schiff 1975). This is a process whereby we minimize or ignore some aspect of reality, whether of ourselves, of others or within the situation. It keeps us sane, helping us to tune out stimuli to avoid overload but unfortunately we often discount factors that do need our attention but which clash with our frame of reference about ourselves and/or others. Thus, for example, if we have adopted the existentialist life position of 'I'm OK, you're not OK,' we may well discount any indications of our own shortcomings and notice only the weaknesses of others.

Hay suggests that her Steps to Success model can become a structured approach to increasing client, coach and supervisor awareness of what is really going on, of the bigger picture (mindfulness/meta-cognition). As she says, 'we are often aware of discounting by others but "We don't know what we don't know" – hence the value of a coach who can bring our unconscious discounting to our conscious attention.'

The steps to success – identifying and overcoming discounting:

- *Situation* – this first step refers to what we might be discounting, or overlooking, in the situation. For example, Lionel had been 'sent' for coaching because 360-degree feedback indicated that he had poor relationships with colleagues – but was protesting that this was just because the colleagues didn't like him, didn't really know him, and were so unskilled themselves, so there wasn't really a problem. He needed prompting to 'notice' what was happening such as how he had often miscommunicated to his colleagues and how colleagues reacted with irritation or confusion when he talked to them. Until Lionel noticed what was happening, he could not move up to the step of recognizing he had a significant problem to solve. But because he was discounting those aspects within the situation, he needed someone else to 'push' him to pay attention to the evidence.

- *Significance* – this step is about becoming aware that what is happening in the situation has significance – in other words, we have a problem that needs attention.

- *Solutions* – this is about being aware of possible solutions. People who discount at this step will accept they have a significant problem but seem unable or unwilling to believe anything can be done. Mindfulness can be helpful in bringing their attention to options available to them.

- *Skills* – this step is about being aware of skills in place or required, and what can be done to acquire them.

- *Strategies* – this is about becoming aware of potential strategies.

- *Success* – having been helped by the coach to identify the significance of the problem, to generate solutions for which Chandak had the requisite skills, and design a strategy in the form of an action plan for implementation, it became evident that Chandak had an irrational belief that doing nothing would mean no one would notice the problem. The coach had to 'remind' Chandak to adopt a meta-cognitive approach, considering the likely consequences of failing to resolve the problem. The fear of management criticism (or worse) was finally enough to prompt Chandak into action in spite of misgivings, especially when it became clear that the misgivings were misguided fantasies.

Adapted from Hay's *Transactional Analysis for Coaches & Mentors*, due out in 2013, reproduced with permission

Hay points out that the well-known TA concept of ego states – PAC in its most simplistic and oft-quoted form – is similar to the transpersonal concept of sub-personalities, which we explore next. 'Rather than synthesis, however, TA suggests that we need to integrate into our adult, or here-and-now, ego state the useful content from parent, which comprises "copies" of parent figures from our past, and from child, which comprises "recordings" of our experiences during childhood,' she says.

Transpersonal coaching and psychosynthesis

> The transpersonal recognizes and works with our yearning, ingrained in the human psyche, for something beyond the personal, beyond the material and the everyday.
>
> Sir John Whitmore (2008)

Transpersonal means 'beyond the person'. Transpersonal psychology and later transpersonal coaching concern the way in which we connect with a realm beyond our personal ego, or 'I'. For many, this means a spiritual realm, but not for all. It could be about a connection with nature, for example, or the wider community.

Transpersonal coaching draws together numerous threads and influences, including:

- Roberto Assaglioli, founder of psychosynthesis;
- Abraham Maslow (who explored the relationship between self-realization and motivation);
- Carl Jung (who studied how individuals can feel fulfilled);
- Victor Frankl (a prisoner of Second World War concentration camps who found that those who could invest their lives with meaning had a greater chance of survival);
- Carl Rogers, whose client-centred approach is built on unconditional positive regard for the client.

Self-actualization

Rogers's approach sought to help the client develop a healthier stronger sense of self – 'self-actualization'. Rogers, along with Perls and Maslow, founded the humanistic psychology movement. Maslow is known for contributions such as his hierarchy of needs model which saw self-actualization as a need which can be met after more basic needs have been met. Maslow suggested that we self-actualize intermittently when we have what he calls 'peak experiences', usually once we reach adulthood, and that such experiences take us into momentary transcendence beyond our usual perceptions. These experiences are quasi-mystical moments which may involve feelings of intense joy and wellbeing, wonder and awe. Qualities that a self-actualized individual would demonstrate, according to Maslow, included being excited and interested in everything, and the capacity to be creative and inventive.

Whitmore (2008) describes transpersonal coaching as 'the inevitable evolution of the psychological basis of coaching, moving beyond humanistic and positive psychology. It does not reject them; indeed, it regards them as its platform.'

Both self-actualization (awareness) and self-realization (self-responsibility) are important in transpersonal coaching, and arguably more important in these highly uncertain times than ever. Whitmore says, 'We are all going to need our higher qualities, creativity, aspirations and inspiration, in the uncertain world that is emerging.'

Self-actualization is obvious common ground to me between transpersonal coaching and mindfulness. And for many who come to mindfulness, connecting with something wider than our limited 'I' is an explicit aim, just as it is in transpersonal coaching. With self-actualization, and with transpersonal connections, comes self-responsibility too. Obviously, as we've seen, people come to mindfulness and meditation for a number of reasons – stress management, developing presence and so on. But certainly for many, it is a vehicle to self-actualization and to connecting beyond ourselves. We explored the aspect of interconnectedness in Chapter 15.

Multiplicity/sub-personalities

There are times when I look over the various parts of my character with perplexity. I recognize that I am made up of several persons and that the person that at the moment has the upper hand will inevitably give place to another.

W Somerset Maugham, author

Another aspect of transpersonal coaching is multiplicity, the idea that we are made up of lots of different sub-personalities. This underpinning has been informed by Carl Jung's work, which in turn was informed by archetypes and mythology. As we embrace mindfulness, practising meditations including the Witness meditation (Chapter 6), we can find ourselves wondering who we are and we may become aware that the self is rather hard to pin down. We can use mindfulness practice to explore whether we have a single, solid self. If we think we do, we might like to ask ourselves where this single, solid self lives in our body. Is it in our head? Our heart? Our feet? And so on. Personally, I haven't yet been able to find a solid constant self! Many mindfulness teachings guide us to explore what the self is, and this is common territory in Buddhist teachings. And although many coaches will shrink back from an explicit what-is-the-self exploration, certainly exploring meaning and purpose is common stomping ground. Meaning and purpose are integral to coaching, according to a survey carried out jointly between the Association for Coaching and *Coaching at Work* (2008). Four out of five (82 per cent) of the 1,046 respondents said they addressed meaning and purpose in their coaching.

One way of exploring who we are in transpersonal coaching and with mindfulness is to look at sub-personalities. A sub-personality is a synthesis of habit patterns, traits, complexes and other psychological elements.

Psychosynthesis argues that for there to be synthesis, there has to be a centre around which the synthesis occurs.

The aim in transpersonal coaching/psychosynthesis work with sub-personalities is to recognize that the latter are not who we really are, and for us to dis-identify from them, accessing a clearer sense of 'self', our core. And for there to be harmony and integration between the different sub-personalities.

But if we are not just each of those sub-personalities we adopt on different occasions, then who are we?

We all have a large number of sub-personalities and as we recognize and harmonize them, they 'become organized and synthesized around a "higher order centre"… what we have called the "I", the personal centre of identity of "I-ness"… this higher order synthesis becomes the integrated personality – the harmonious and effective means of expression of the self-actualized human being' (Vargiu 1974).

We become able to choose at will which sub-personality we want to express. 'An increasing number of people have discovered that recognizing the diversity of subpersonalities in us, learning to direct them, and to deal with them operationally, *in the moment*, enhances rather than diminishes the sense of "I" – of personal identity and unity' (Vargiu 1974).

Assagioli used the metaphor of a conductor of an orchestra to represent the 'I, which he said is comprised of pure consciousness and pure will. Our sub-personalities are like the members of an orchestra and we can become like the conductor, able to call forth each member's talents and qualities at will.

The idea of the conductor is similar to the Observer or Witness, or the Big Mind described by Zen monk Dennis Gempo Merzel.

Exercise: Awareness of inner voices

Set aside 10 minutes when you won't be disturbed. Get some paper/your journal and a pen. Make yourself comfortable, with your back straight and in a 'dignified posture'. Relax your jaw, relax your shoulders, close your eyes. Take three deep breaths then breathe naturally. Focus on your breath. Count 10 in breaths and 10 out breaths. Stay with the breath for as long as you feel is helpful to shift into 'mindful mode'.

Now open your eyes and recall a time when you felt in conflict about how to spend your time. For example, you may have awoken on a sunny day and contemplated going for a walk. However, almost immediately a contradictory voice suggested it's easier to stay home, rationalizing that you deserve the rest. Or perhaps a second, or even a third, voice urged you to stay at home and catch up with some work. Ask yourself:

How long did it take until one particular voice got its way?

Which voice got its way?

How come that particular voice got its way?

How did 'you feel' as these different voices 'chattered amongst themselves'?

What can you remember about the 'you' that wasn't these voices?

Write down a list of at least five of your most common voices. Give them a suitable name, such as the victim, the controller, the hero, and then add what each one wants and what strengths it has. Now ask yourself:

When and under what circumstances do you adopt each one?

What does doing so give you?

How does it limit you?

What might be some other ways to get that need met?

Any other reflections?

Remember not to judge, and to be compassionate towards all your sub-personalities as they are part of you.

Take some time to capture any reflections.

Adapted from Whitmore (2008b) *Coaching at Work*

Cognitive behavioural coaching

Many coaches will be familiar with the cognitive behavioural coaching (CBC) approach, informed by cognitive behavioural therapy (CBT), developed by Aaron Beck and originally known as cognitive therapy. Other influencers on its development have included Albert Ellis and David Burns. CBC techniques and thinking have been widely adopted by coaches to help clients identify and challenge the self-defeating beliefs they hold. Ellis identified three core beliefs: 'I must be perfect', 'Life must be easy' and 'Others must like me'. Common thinking errors, according to CBC (Cooper and Palmer 2000), include all-or-nothing thinking (viewing things in absolute terms), emotional reasoning, mind reading and discounting the positive.

CBT has been combined already very successfully with mindfulness in work such as that of Professor Mark Williams, who identified that whilst CBT was helpful in treating depression – it is the United Kingdom's government-sponsored therapy of choice – it wasn't always helpful in preventing recurrence. Mindfulness-Based Cognitive Therapy (MBCT), as we've seen, is now widely recommended for those suffering a recurrence of depression, or as a way to prevent it in the first place. It was only a matter of time before we saw the development of Mindfulness-Based Cognitive Coaching (MBCC) which interweaves skills associated with CBC with mindfulness-based aware-ness training, providing 'skills and strategies to devise new and healthier beliefs about self, others and the world, with the ability to connect to the present' (Collard and McMahon 2009).

CBC meets mindfulness

Concepts that CBC shares with mindfulness include:

- *We are not our thoughts* (thoughts are not facts, they are psychological events, according to CBC).

- *It's all about perception* ('We don't see things as they are, we see things as we are' – author Anais Nin).

- *Self-awareness and self-evaluation* are key.

- *Examining our thoughts* helps us increase meta-cognitive awareness, and develop alternative perspectives.

- *We can train our mind* to think differently (reframing/reappraisal). The focus is on the *here and now*.

CBC thinking skills (Cooper and Palmer 2000) with common ground with mindfulness include:

- *De-labelling* (mindfulness encourages us to shift beyond labels and just experience what comes up. This is different from CBC's de-labelling, which is about avoiding universal or global labels and just focusing on specifics; for example, just because we have failed an exam doesn't mean we are totally stupid. However, both CBC and mindfulness urge us to just work with what is actually there.)

- *Befriending yourself* (mindfulness encourages us to be compassionate and non-judgemental towards ourselves; CBC encourages us to think what a colleague or friend would say, usually something less critical and harsh than we say about ourselves.)

- *Looking for evidence* (mindfulness encourages us to notice what's there, rather than making assumptions.)

- *Broadening the picture* (mindfulness encourages us to step back and take a wider view.)

- *Demagnification/deawfulizing* (mindfulness encourages us to get things in perspective and step away from problem-solving, ruminative mode.)

- *Thinking more coolly or flexibly* (mindfulness encourages us to be flexible in our thinking and responses.)

Combining mindfulness with CBC can broaden the appeal of the latter. CBC tends to suit logical left-brain thinkers in particular, and can seem formulaic and somewhat lacking in 'heart' to some. It has a compelling evidence base, however, and can deliver rapid results. Bringing in mindfulness practices, with an emphasis on compassion, can be enormously powerful. Although CBC has a focus on the present, with limited reference to the past, it is highly goal-oriented and incorporating mindfulness can help clients stay with what they need to stay with, not moving into goals prematurely.

Acceptance and commitment therapy

Acceptance and commitment therapy (ACT) is a type of CBT but it has a very different focus, one which is very aligned with mindfulness. Mindfulness is more deeply woven into the approach than it is in MBCC, it seems to me. Unlike CBT, it doesn't advocate the disputing of troublesome thoughts, suggesting instead that the person quietly observes these in a mindful way. ACT has been designed for application within a clinical setting. However, its core ideas are increasingly being applied in coaching, particularly in Australia and New Zealand. In a non-therapy setting, it is usually called acceptance and commitment training. Its explicit goals are to effectively handle painful emotions, thoughts, feelings and images, and to create a rich and fulfilling life.

Russ Harris (2009), a well-known writer and teacher in the field, suggests that ACT has six core elements, the first four of which are about mindfulness:

- *Contact with the present moment.*
- *Active acceptance* – dynamically allowing the thoughts and feelings that arise to be there, making space for unpleasant feelings and urges instead of trying to suppress or escape from them.
- *De-fusion* – connecting with your thoughts and feelings in a new way, learning to quietly observe and notice these thoughts and feelings without trying to do anything with them, thus resulting in them having less influence over you.
- *Observing self* – this is the Witness mind we've discussed already. This requires an awareness of present, of thoughts, feelings and sensations, and includes noticing and staying with unpleasantness without trying to do anything about it.
- *Knowing your values* – this is central to ACT.
- *Committed action* – this is about what you decide to do in order to live a rich and fulfilling life.

Thinking environment

Everything we do depends for its quality on the thinking we do first. Our thinking depends on the quality of our attention for each other.

Nancy Kline

Nancy Kline outlines 10 components for creating a 'thinking environment' and 'attention' is number one (listening with respect, interest and fascination). The other components are: incisive questions; equality; appreciation; ease; encouragement; feelings; information; place; and diversity.

Alister Scott, leadership coach and co-founder of the One Leadership Project, often uses the thinking environment in his work, particularly to help build appreciation amongst clients. He believes passionately that people thrive on encouragement, recognition and appreciation.

'I used it with one group where there was a very senior woman paired with someone who had been consistently difficult and rude in boardroom meetings. He was given the opportunity to appreciate her and this cascade came out. It turns out the rudeness is driven by desire to make the organization better and he really appreciated that she had taken all of that (rudeness). It was transformative for her understanding of him and for their relationship.

'Mindfulness is not, to my knowledge, an explicit part of Nancy's approach, but combines very well with it. The willingness to "listen profoundly", as Nancy asks us to do, is a challenge to any person's mindfulness – of their own "stuff" whilst listening, as well as the simple yet surprisingly difficult ability to pay full attention for a sustained period to another person or to a group's dynamics,' he says.

Inner Game

There is always an inner game being played in your mind no matter what outer game you are playing. How aware you are of this game can make the difference between success and failure.

Tim Gallwey

Developing self-awareness ('attunement with self') and the ability to get ourselves out of our own way so we can be more choiceful are at the core of the Inner Game methodology first shared by long-standing meditator Tim Gallwey in the 1970s in his book, *The Inner Game of Tennis*. Gallwey went on to further develop the approach with Whitmore for use in the business world. The Inner Game has roots in Eastern philosophies and meditation, drawing on visualizations and non-judgemental observation of what is happening right now. The aim is to help the client operate more easily from a relaxed, aware state, with a centred, focused mind, so they can perform at their peak.

The Inner Game philosophy rests on two foundations: that we all have more potential within than we recognize, and that we all interfere with the discovery and expression of that potential more than we like to admit. The latter is expressed in the following formula: P (performance) = p (potential) − I (self-interference).

The methodology for evoking potential and reducing self-interference is based on three principles: increased awareness of current reality is in itself curative; choice − which is essential to achievement; and trust in one's own potential − which can overcome the roots of self-interference. Gallwey says that the 'coach's role is to facilitate the mobility of the client (their capacity to learn and achieve outcomes in a fulfilling way), whether individual or in a team, by increasing awareness, choice and trust. In short, this enables the client to be more conscious in thought and action while being hampered less by unconscious habits that interfere' (Whitmore and Gallwey 2010).

PART FOUR
The future

We've looked at core underpinnings, how mindfulness can support the coach and client, and now we look at next steps. How is mindfulness being woven into coaching out there and what is its future? First I'd like to share the results from an online survey I carried out.

The *Mindfulness in Coaching* survey

20

When I began researching this book in earnest, I searched high and low for data on how coaches were using mindfulness in coaching. There didn't seem to be anything out there. As far as I know, this survey is the first to look at mindfulness in coaching, including which mindfulness practices coaches have in place, what benefits they get from mindfulness and how they use it with clients.

Coaches' experience of mindfulness

The majority of respondents to my *Mindfulness in Coaching 2012* survey have at least some experience of mindfulness, ranging from having come across it through activities such as yoga and martial arts or reading a book on it to a daily practice and attending lengthy meditation retreats. Some 59 per cent of respondents said they have a regular (more than three times a week) mindfulness practice in place. One-third said they had a daily/almost daily mindfulness/meditation practice. Table 20.1 shows what experiences coaches have of mindfulness while Table 20.2 shows what practices they have adopted.

Only 5.8 per cent had no experience at all. Obviously my sample is a self-selecting group so this low percentage is not surprising. However, the survey shows a large showing of hands from the growing body of coaches exploring how to incorporate mindfulness into their lives and into their coaching practice in one way or another.

TABLE 20.1   Coaches' experiences of mindfulness

	%
None	6
Have read a book or two on mindfulness	60
Encountered meditation/mindfulness through yoga or martial arts	40
Have attended a meditation course	37
Have dabbled/dabble with mindfulness and meditation at home through own reading/studies	35
Meditate/practise mindfulness daily or almost daily	33
Have attended at least one retreat	31
Have attended an MBCT or MBSR programme	19
Sometimes attend drop-in meditation classes	14
Have attended a Mindfulness for Coaches programme	11
Other encounters with mindfulness	'weekly labyrinth walk with a church'

Meditation appears to be the most common mindfulness practice amongst coaches: 69 per cent of coaches responding to my survey meditate. The Body scan, Centring and Mindful walking are also popular – 51 per cent, 48 per cent and 35 per cent respectively. Some respondents pointed out that they attempt to lead their lives mindfully, rather than just doing isolated practices. Others said they did mindfulness as part of yoga or martial arts. In my survey, I deliberately asked about practices included in programmes such as MBSR because these seem to be the best known rather than because I believe they are necessarily the best or only practices. There are lots of other practices I have encountered and personally find enormously helpful,

TABLE 20.2   Mindfulness practices among coaches

	%
Meditation	69
Body scan	51
Centring	48
Mindful walking	35
Three-minute breathing space	32
Mindful eating	28
Retreat	19
Mindfulness classes	13
Other practices: Mindful being Mindful minute Focusing Loving-kindness/Compassion meditation Chanting Yoga Tai Chi Jin Shin Jyutsu Prayer	

including the Tibetan Buddhist practice of *Tonglen*, where you seek to 'take on' others' suffering and transform it. I also accept that for some coaches, their mindfulness practices will form part of an approach such as somatic, ontological or gestalt coaching as we've explored.

Direct benefits for coaches

So why do coaches practise mindfulness? One of the main reasons is to help them live more in the moment (74 per cent). Also important is becoming more self-aware (73 per cent), managing/preventing stress (67 per cent) and as a way to be more present for their client (65 per cent). Table 20.3 shows some of the reasons coaches are mindful.

TABLE 20.3   Why do you practise mindfulness?

	%
To help me live more in the moment	74
To help me be more self aware	73
To manage/prevent stress	67
To help me be more present for my client	65
To help me focus	64
To help me relax	63
To help me not get too caught up in thoughts	57
To help me be more aware of others	54
To help me be more resilient	53
To help me manage my reactions/responses	49
To help me prepare for coaching sessions	47
To help me be more intuitive	44
To help me be happier	40
To help me manage work–life balance	36
To help me be more productive	35
To manage depression	13

Other responses:
To help me live in a state of grace
To be kinder and to see things more clearly

Table 20.4 shows how many are using mindfulness explicitly with clients; Table 20.5 how coaches are using mindfulness in their coaching. Table 20.6 shows the types of practices coaches share with clients, and Table 20.7 why they are using mindfulness with clients.

TABLE 20.4   Do you use mindfulness with your clients?

	%
No	17
Yes, but rarely	20
Yes, sometimes	34
Yes, often	20
Yes, always	9

TABLE 20.5   How coaches use mindfulness within coaching

	%
Sharing mindfulness practices with clients to do at home	74
I use mindfulness for myself within the session	67
Inviting clients to do mindfulness practices within the session itself	64
If you use mindfulness for yourself within the session, which practices do you use?	
Mindfully checking in with what's going on in my body/mind	86
Mindful breathing	51
Centring	50

TABLE 20.6   Types of practices coaches typically share with clients

	%
Mindful breathing	71
Centring	50
Body scan	40
Meditation	39
Three-minute breathing space	33
Mindful walking	23

Other practices included:
Mindful minute meditation
Loving-kindness meditation
Recommending a book then discussing it
'Focusing'
Guided acceptance meditation
Acceptance and commitment therapy/training

TABLE 20.7 Coaches use mindfulness to help their clients...

	%
become more self-aware	70
be calmer/less anxious	59
manage stress	55
be more centred	55
manage reactions/responses	51
focus	49
gain clarity	47
improve their wellbeing	45
live more in the moment	43
become more aligned with their values	40
become more emotionally intelligent	39
see the bigger picture	36
become more aware of others	34
embed behavioural changes	34
improve their decision making	33
improve relationships with others	32
manage work–life balance	31
achieve their goals	30
manage/tackle depression	18
be more ethical	12

More than half of coaches (56 per cent) responding to my survey agreed that mindfulness helps us and our clients be more reflective, while 61 per cent agreed that 'In being more reflective, our clients are better able to identify what they really want.' I also asked about any concerns coaches have about using mindfulness explicitly. Table 20.8 shows the responses.

TABLE 20.8   Concerns about using mindfulness with clients

	%
No concerns	76
'Client will think coach is "woolly/fluffy/unprofessional".'	18
'Encouraging clients to practise mindfulness might expose them to unpleasant feelings, buried experiences that will be difficult to deal with in the coaching.'	7

Comments included:

I sometimes worry about its 'face validity'. For some of my clients an eyes-closed, short meditation session is too big a step.

It's not the use I have concerns about. It's the reaction if I introduce it and they take it as a criticism. Reflecting on when sharing mindfulness would have been really useful, the clients were typically in a heightened emotional state or had come from an environment where they had been very defensive in order to protect themselves. Paradoxically, the very need for mindfulness I had perceived was creating a wall to mentioning it. I recognize the learning edge for me there both in my own practice and embodiment (I know some very mindful people and their way of being simply invites mindfulness), and perhaps some personal stuff about upsetting people.

The following Table 20.9, shows responses about the potentially conflicting foci we talked about earlier.

TABLE 20.9   What are your thoughts about the present moment/being/acceptance focus in mindfulness versus the future/doing/action/goals focus of much coaching?

	%
'In being more reflective, our clients are better able to identify what they really want.'	61
'Mindfulness helps us and our clients be more reflective.'	56
'Mindfulness helps us achieve goals anyway.'	52
'Mindfulness acts as a welcome antidote to an overemphasis on doing in our present culture.'	47
'I haven't given this any thought.'	6
'There is a potential tension between the two foci.'	5
'Mindfulness is incompatible with the future/doing focus of coaching.'	3

General comments

Coaching without mindfulness is only temporary in its benefits...
it doesn't get to the core of the situation and my goal is to launch
productive clients who no longer need my services because they are able
to do things independently and only need occasional follow-up sessions.

[It's a] useful tool but careful thought is required as to [for] whom and
when it is used. It's not for everyone.

I was in a workshop the other day as a participant and, for one
exercise, as a 'client'. We started with a Centring exercise and what
then came out of my mouth as my intention for the subsequent
coaching session was completely different from what I had been
thinking about before the centring. Much more meaningful and took
me to a deeper place much more quickly. Also uncovered a major
insight for me, which I don't think I would have had if we'd not
centred and gone straight in.

It is an area that will grow within coaching, not just because of the
promotion of mindfulness as a practice but as a reaction to what is
going on in the world and the fear instilled by the media. People need
to be more present and less in fear of the future. The only certainty in
life is the present moment and we need to be able to enjoy being in that
moment.

I think it could be part of a growing trend in coaching from 'pull' to
'push' or 'Coach knows best' if not applied carefully, with permission
and very relevant to context and the individual concerned. The path
to mindfulness is there when we are ready to seek it.

I passionately believe in the value of mindfulness in the workplace and
intend to incorporate this much more into my coaching practice in
2012. I am a scientist as well as a business coach and I find the wealth
of neuroscientific data is invaluable to draw on when articulating the
business case for mindfulness – especially to the more sceptical clients –
as it gives tangible evidence that this is real and not 'dippy hippy'.

Since being more involved in executive coaching I realize how little I use
mindfulness in these sessions especially when coaching long distance by
telephone. A recent experience as a coachee using mindfulness reminded
me of how powerful this is in coaching.

I tend to refer to a qualified practitioner for a short course, or to
recommend books/tapes, which we can then discuss at the next session.
I do not practise mindfulness with my client as such but my philosophy
very often returns to the principles, so it pervades my coaching practice
and is very much part of who I am/what I say!

As with so many other things, it risks being a bandwagon. Potentially then a little knowledge can be a dangerous thing, with a few points from mindfulness books and so on being taken out of context into coaching. I don't know how much of a problem that is, or what the evidence is (ie does it matter, or are a few 'random' mindfulness practices out of context better than doing nothing?).

It's a great tool and it would be great to see organizations use it more, but it is not a panacea, and it doesn't fit all coaching clients/needs. I do have some concerns about the ethics of its use in some circumstances.

Under whatever label, this state of awareness and balance in the moment is a foundation capability that should be mastered by all who work in people-related professions which use conversations and dialogues.

It's critical – part of the foundation of coaching is self-awareness and self-knowledge – and we all have moments where we are present and moments where we are not... to be present for a coaching conversation is absolutely critical – it's a duty to our client!

All coaches should learn mindfulness – from a properly qualified teacher.

My main use for mindfulness is because it heightens any experience, helps me get more from it and feel more alive, more positive, more capable and more joyful.

Mindfulness is hard. I read Jon Kabat-Zinn's book and tried the tapes, but didn't have the patience or persistence.

I think mindfulness builds awareness. Awareness increases choices. And isn't that what coaching is all about?

About the survey

I sent out response invitations to *Coaching at Work* readers via the printed/online magazine and *Coaching at Work*'s monthly newsletter as well as a number of social media sites including LinkedIn groups for *Coaching at Work*, the European Mentoring & Coaching Council, the Association for Coaching and Kogan Page.

Some 156 people responded, from the following countries: UK, Spain, Denmark, Sweden, Germany, Canada, Peru, New Zealand, US and India.

Here's how respondents identified themselves:

executive coach: 51 per cent;

business coach: 40 per cent;

life coach: 25 per cent;

coaching consultant: 24 per cent;

coach trainer: 21 per cent;

wellbeing coach: 14 per cent;

coaching academic: 8 per cent;

internal coach: 7 per cent.

Other self-selected descriptions included:

career coach;

health coach;

spirituality coach;

ontological coach;

leadership coach;

team coach;

psychologist;

mentor;

facilitator;

coaching supervisor;

therapist-coach;

relational coach;

cognitive behavioural coach;

retreat coach.

The future is mindful

21

'**A** desperate act to reunite our interior and exterior worlds which have been separated for 500 years.' This is how Julio Olalla, the co-founder of ontological coaching, described coaching at the International Coach Federation's conference in June 2011. He could just as easily have been talking about mindfulness, or about mindful coaching.

It's precisely that reunion that many seek when they turn to mindfulness, and it's one of the reasons why we're seeing a rise in interest. Along with 75 per cent of respondents to the *Mindfulness in Coaching* survey, I am convinced this interest will continue to grow (see Table 21.1). In this chapter, we will look at coaches' thoughts on this growth and at some of the trends for the future, before concluding.

TABLE 21.1 Will the use of mindfulness grow in coaching over the next three years?

	%
Yes	75
No	1
Don't know	24

What coaches think about the rise in mindfulness

Because I think people are desperate for ways to slow down, focus and reflect, and there is a growing acceptance that mindfulness and meditation connect you to something deeper and more meaningful than our busy corporate lives allow. I think it appeals to something within most people about meaning and purpose. More and more research is beginning to prove the psychological and physical benefits.

Kate McGuire, life/executive coach, United Kingdom

It is probably the most powerful way of becoming self-aware and with this begins the learning and transformation process of an individual.

Meena, life/executive coach/coaching consultant/coach trainer, India

Because people are seeking more balance in order to be congruent with their goals.

Elke Vaikla, life/business coach, United Kingdom

I have observed a widespread growth in interest of the subject of mindfulness and the number of coaches I meet who are interested in exploring its use in coaching continues to rise. Awareness of mindfulness has increased significantly; given the amount of literature and courses available on the subject there is a clear desire to engage with the subject and practice. Coaching lends itself to a mindful approach for those of us who embed mindfulness into our own lives. My style of coaching is person-centred with a range of eclectic influences informing my practice. As a dedicated practitioner and keen advocate of personal and professional development, I embrace aspects of mindfulness in coaching. Mindfulness informs my way of being, underpins my presence and the reflective space coaching involves. [There is] growing awareness of mindfulness generally and also it fits beautifully with some approaches to coaching, eg gestalt.

Internal coach, United Kingdom

[There is] growing awareness of the role of deeper realization of self and the need for self-mastery as essential leadership traits.

Sanjeev Roy, executive coach, India

It is an excellent, easy-to-apply way of thinking about some of the issues that all people face. Because it is an essential practice in increasing resilience, and because it allows individuals to be more 'skilfully authentic' in leadership.

Diane Newell, executive/business/leadership coach, coaching consultant, United Kingdom

My sense is that clearly coaching needs to be purposeful, mindfulness is a great means of helping individuals reintroduce themselves to themselves and so helps them become more aligned with their true purpose.

Murray Thomas, executive/business coach, United Kingdom

The benefits of reflection will, I believe, be recognized more in the near future and will inevitably lead to its increased usage in coaching via mindfulness and other such focused techniques.

As more research is done, I believe the benefits will become much clearer and widely known – it's an ideal way to control stress and anxiety, and promote positivity and wellbeing. It works well with a goal-focused approach in that identifying what already exists and focusing on it can help in the achievement of future goals. I also think an important element of coaching is not necessarily striving for specific material goals, but rather a client exploring themselves – their attitudes, beliefs, values and thoughts. Only by becoming more mindfully aware of them can we begin to change ourselves and our way of thinking.

I think that mindfulness is another antidote/supporting factor in helping people to cope with the ever growing pace of change. In my view, time to stop and check in with your feelings will be increasingly important.

It is growing anyway in society and coaching is an obvious place for it to impact.

Many coachees have sought out mindfulness in order to deal with a stressful situation. Clarity and self-confidence usually follow when it works for the coachee. It also creates a bond of trust between coach and coachee when the coachee opens up to other possibilities for themselves.

As a meditation teacher I see a steadily increasing desire for a true solution to our daily sufferings, and this solution is rooted in mindfulness. Mindfulness as a buzzword does not encompass what mindfulness really is. It's not just 'really thinking about what you are doing'. It is full awareness of our authentic selves at all times. It is holding positive, energetic states of mind at all times. It is walking our talk at all times. This aligns with coaching. As people continue to open themselves to the solutions of mindfulness and awareness, there is no doubt that the use of mindfulness in coaching will continue to grow.

Holly McKinley, life coach, United States

More demand for mindful leaders.

Stress is widespread – and people increasingly recognize they don't think well when stressed. And the challenges facing people (and organizations) are complex and often paradoxical. Reactive and linear thinking is not capable of addressing these well. There is also a shift from having and doing to being. Increasing numbers of people are recognizing the value of wellbeing and happiness, and how mindfulness can help bring these.

Neil Scotton, executive coach, coach for leaders/catalysts, UK

People have worked themselves into the ground (myself included) with the belief that harder is better. Building in a practice of breathing, stepping back and observing, decreasing stress, etc will be a welcome addition to goal setting for more evolved companies.

Frank Del Fiugo, executive coach, coach trainer, US

If not, why not?

May be seen as too fluffy, especially in corporate culture so may need to be reframed for business.

In some models of coaching, self-management and developing skills perceived as 'softer' are not even considered. A great loss, in my opinion. Once coaches gain the trust of their clients, the opportunity to invite clients to share this knowledge is a gift we can all share.

Mindfulness in Coaching 2012 survey

Trends

Neuroscience

The increasing focus on mindfulness within neuroscience is likely to continue to help to fuel further interest in mindfulness in general. Along with neuroplasticity, one of the most exciting developments in modern science is that of epigenesis, the idea that our genes can be influenced. Yes, we are born with certain DNA but the extent to which our genes are activated or not depends on all sorts of factors, including, it seems, our mental state.

Practising mindfulness may actually impact us at a genetic level. Speaking at the Creating a Mindful Society conference in New York on 30 September–1 October 2011, Professor Richard Davidson said, 'The extent to which those genes are turned on and turned off and are expressed to do their business very much depends upon our environment, it depends upon our training, it depends upon our experiences and it depends, we think, on one's quality of mental state.'

Davidson continues: 'If these ideas have some merit, again they provide a framework for understanding how contemplative practices may actually not just change the brain, but change the brain down to the level of gene expression.' He said that although there is as yet no evidence for this idea, 'certainly everything would lead us to believe that this may indeed be true'.

Evaluation

Those of us working with mindfulness are fortunate to have a wealth of research at our fingertips, from a range of fields including neuroscience. However, we need more research on mindfulness in business coaching, in leadership and the like. And we need to think about whether and how we evaluate our work with clients, with regard to mindfulness. Obviously, the degree to which we consider return on investment (ROI) and evaluation will vary widely, depending on our own bent, on our own and our clients' culture (organizational, regional and so on) and on individual clients and the like. And just as we would do with any coaching intervention, we'll need to decide which metrics we'll use, in consultation with clients where appropriate.

In addition to metrics such as those for measuring stress and resilience amongst others, there are a number of mindfulness measures available such as those listed by the Mindfulness Research Guide, an electronic resource and publication database that provides information to researchers, practitioners and the general public on the scientific study of mindfulness (see box). As time goes on, we're likely to see more scales being developed and existing scales being fine-tuned.

> ### Mindfulness assessment scales
>
> These include:
>
> - The Mindful Attention Awareness Scale (MAAS);
> - Five Facet Mindfulness Questionnaire (FFMQ);
> - Kentucky Inventory of Mindfulness Skills (KIMS);
> - Cognitive and Affective Mindfulness Scale (CAMS);
> - Freiburg Mindfulness Inventory (FMI);
> - Philadelphia Mindfulness Scale (PHLMS);
> - Mindfulness-Based Relapse Prevention Adherence and Competence Scale (MBRP-AC);
> - Self–Other Four Immeasurables (SOFI);
> - Self-Compassion Scale;
> - Solloway Mindfulness Measure.
>
> **www.mindfulexperience.org**

Compassion

Another area in which I predict we will see growth in relation to coaching and mindfulness is that of compassion-focused work. We've already seen important tranches of work in the field of therapy, notably Professor Paul Gilbert's compassion-focused therapy. And as we know, historically coaching has very often followed in the footsteps of its sister helping professions. There is also a growing raft of work in the arena of compassionate leadership.

Integrity

As I said at the beginning, I have some concerns about mindfulness as a 'brand' because I worry that people without any real understanding or training in mindfulness will do it a disservice. I've seen a few people out there doing the rounds speaking about mindfulness who really don't appear to have a regular practice in place, nor to even truly understand what mindfulness is. I hope I've shown in this book that it's possible to gain benefits from just a little bit of mindfulness. However, I think it's important not to dilute mindfulness in a bid to widen its reach. Mindfulness can be adapted for all sorts of settings; it's very flexible. But let's not throw out its core essences. As Margaret Chapman (February 2012, Mindfulness at Work conference, Cambridge) has said, 'We want adaptation, not dilution.'

Conclusion

In the course of writing this book, I have become increasingly convinced that mindfulness and coaching are the perfect bedfellows. I have immersed myself in piles and piles of books about coaching, mindfulness, meditation, spirituality, leadership, psychology, counselling and psychotherapy, Buddhism and so on and I have enjoyed following numerous threads. As I came across something else, some approach or other I hadn't yet considered or recalled, I would then question whether there was a connection or relevance to mindfulness. Some connections were obvious and right from the outset I was keen to honour them – gestalt and somatics are examples. And vice versa – in my deepening exploration of meditation and mindfulness, I would ask whether there were implications for coaching I hadn't yet considered. Very often, the answer would come back as yes. At one point I felt overwhelmed because it seemed that to do the field of mindfulness-meets-coaching justice, there was just way too much to include. And I worried that this book would morph into a lengthy sales pitch for mindfulness as a cure-all for every human ill and travail and something to be ignored at your peril if you're a coach.

In the course of researching this book, the journalist, the coach and the emerging researcher in me all kept asking questions and I like to think that especially when going back to the text after the first draft, I was tough (albeit still biased). However, I have to say I remain convinced that mindfulness and coaching make for a beautiful partnership. I think all coach education programmes should include mindfulness. We are expected as coaches to attend to so many different elements of our practice – developing presence, rapport, empathy, deep listening and so on, and sometimes I feel we aren't given enough help in *how* to do all this. I think mindfulness should be included in all leadership and other employee development programmes, all school education programmes, all... I could go on. I'm with Michael Chaskalson (Mindfulness at Work conference in 2012), who said: 'I believe that mindfulness can be a panacea for what bothers you. I truly believe if you're better at working with your mental state, things will go better for you. Mindfulness is fundamental mental hygiene. It's a fundamental human skill we should have all learnt at school... I believe that those organizations who offer mindfulness, all other things being equal, will do better than those who don't. Of all the managerial skills, it's the most effective.'

I realize mindfulness is by no means the only practice, tool, set of techniques, way of being, whatever we want to call it, and as I said earlier, I have endeavoured to highlight some of the arenas and approaches which share similar territory. I also appreciate that mindfulness isn't the whole story, it's only part of it. But do I think mindfulness is everything it's cracked up to be? Absolutely. Mindfulness is the perfect underpinning for this work-in-progress that is being a human doing, and doing a human being.

REFERENCES

Baer, R A, Smith, G T, Hopkins, J *et al* (2006) Using self-report assessment methods to explore facets of mindfulness, *Assessment*, **13**(1), pp 27–45

Berne, E (1972) *What Do You Say After You Say Hello?* Grove Press, New York

Blakey, J and Day, I (2012) *Challenging Coaching*, Nicholas Brealey, London

Boyatzis, R and McKee, A (2005) *Resonant Leadership: Renewing yourself and connecting with others through mindfulness, hope, and compassion*, Harvard Business School Publishing, Boston

Boyatzis, R, Jack, A *et al* (2010) Coaching with Compassion: An fMRI study of coaching to the positive or negative Emotional Attractor, presented at the Academy of Management Annual conference, Montreal

Bryant, B and Wildi, J (2008) Perspectives for managers – Mindfulness, IMD, **162**

Cade, M and Coxead, N (1979) *The Awakened Mind: biofeedback and the development of higher states of awareness*, Wildwood House, London,

Cameron, J (1992) *The Artist's Way: A Spiritual Path to Higher Creativity*, Tarcher, New York

Campbell, Jenny (2009) Personal Resilience and its links to Organisational Resilience, lifetimeswork

Campbell, Joseph (2008) (3rd edn) *Hero with a Thousand Faces*, New World Library, Novato

Carmody, J, Vangel, M (2011) Mindfulness practice leads to increases in regional brain gray matter density, *Psychiatry Research: Neuroimaging*, **11**(1) (January), pp 36–43

Carter, O L *et al* (2005) Meditation alters perceptual rivalry in Tibetan Buddhist monks, *Current Biology*, **15**, pp 412–13

Ceasar, 2011, *The Guardian* Sustainable Business hub, http://www.guardian.co.uk/sustainable-business/leadership-sustainable-development-characteristics?INTCMP=SRCH

Chartered Institute for Personnel and Development (CIPD) and Simplyhealth (2011), *the Absence Management Survey*, London

Chaskalson, M (2011) *The Mindful Workplace: developing resilient individuals and resonant organisations with MBSR*, Wiley-Blackwell, Chichester

Chu, L C (2010) The benefits of meditation vis-à-vis emotional intelligence, perceived stress and negative mental health, *Stress and Health*, **26**, pp 169–80

Clough, P and Strycharczyk, D (2012) *Developing Mental Toughness: improving performance, wellbeing and positive behaviour in others*, Kogan Page, London

Collard, P and McMahon, G (2009) Being here, *Coaching at Work*, **5**(2)

Collins, J (2001) *Good to Great: Why some companies make the leap and others don't*, HarperCollins, New York

Colzato, L S *et al* (2012) Meditate to create: the impact of focused-attention and open-monitoring training on convergent and divergent thinking. *Frontiers in Psychology*, **3**, p 116

Cooper, C and Palmer, S (2000) *Conquer Your Stress*, Chartered Institute of Personnel and Development, London

Creswell, J D *et al* (2007) Neural correlates of dispositional mindfulness during affect labelling, *Psychosomatic Medicine*, **69**(6), pp 560–5

Dale, S and Lancaster, H (2012) How to coach for wellbeing, *Coaching at Work*, 7(3)

Davidson, R J (2000) Affective style, psychopathology and resilience: Brain mechanisms and plasticity, *American Psychologist*, 55, pp 1196–214

Davidson, R J (2004) Well-being and affective style: Neural substrates and biobehavioural correlates. *Philosophical Transactions of the Royal Society*, 359, pp 1395–411

Davidson, R J, Kabat-Zinn, J *et al* (2003) Alterations in brain and immune function produced by mindfulness meditation, *Psychosomatic Medicine*, 65, pp 564–70

De Haan, E (2008) *Relational Coaching; journeys towards mastering one-to-one learning*, John Wiley & Sons, Chichester

Depue, R and Morone-Strupinsky, J (2005) Modeling human behavioural traits and clarifying the construct of affiliation and its disorders, *Behavioural and Brain Sciences*, **28**(3), pp 371–78

Dobkin, P L (2008) *Complementary Therapies in Clinical Practice*, **14**, pp 8–16

Dolman, E and Bond, D (2011) Mindful leadership: Exploring the value of a meditation practice, *The Ashridge Journal* (spring)

Einzig, H (2011) The beast within, *Coaching at Work*, 6(6)

Ekman, P (2007) *Emotions Revealed: Recognising faces and feelings to improve communication and emotional life*, Henry Holt & Company, New York

Fazio, R, Effrein, E and Falender, V (1981) Self-perceptions Following Social Interaction, *Journal of Personality and Social Psychology*, **41**(2), pp 232–42

Fossell, T (2011) Human nature, Buddha nature: On Spiritual Bypassing, Relationship, and the Dharma, interview with John Welwood, *Tricycle* (spring)

Frankl, V E (1959) *Man's Search for Meaning*, Beacon Press, Boston

Frederickson, B L (1998) What good are positive emotions? *Review of General Psychology*, 2, pp 300–319

Freeman, R (2011) *Coaching at Work*, 6(6)

Friedman, R S and Forster, J (2001) The effects of promotion and prevention cues on creativity, *Journal of Personality and Social Psychology*, **81**(6), pp 1001–13

Garland, E L, Frederickson, B, Kring, A M *et al* (2010) Upward Spirals of Positive Emotions Counter Downward Spirals of Negativity: Insights from the Broaden-and-Build Theory and Affective Neuroscience on The Treatment of Emotion Dysfunctions and Deficits in Psychopathology, *Clinical Psychology Review*, **30**(7), pp 849–64

Garland, E L, Gaylord, S and Park, J (2009) The Role of Mindfulness in Positive Reappraisal, *The Journal of Science and Healing*, **5**(1), pp 37–44

Gershon, M (1999) *The Second Brain: A groundbreaking new understanding of nervous disorders of the stomach and intestine*, HarperCollins, London

Gilbert, P (2009) *The Compassionate Mind*, Constable, London

Gilbert, P (2010) *Compassion-Focused Therapy*, Routledge, Hove

Gilbert, P and Irons, C (2005) Focused therapies and compassionate mind training for shame and self-attacking, *Compassion: Conceptualisations, research and use in psychotherapy*, Routledge, Hove

Gilbert, P, McEwab, K, Mitra, R *et al* (2008) Feeling safe and content: A specific affect regulation system? Relationship to depression, anxiety, stress and self-criticism, *Journal of Positive Psychology*, 3, pp 182–91

Goleman, D (1995) *Emotional Intelligence: Why it can matter more than IQ*, Bantam, New York

Gray, J A (1981) A critique of Eysenck's theory of personality, *A Model for Personality* (ed H J Eysenck), Springer-Verlag, Berlin, pp 246–76

Grepmair, L, Mirrerlehner, F, Loew, T *et al* (2007) Promoting mindfulness in psychotherapists in training influences the treatment results of their patients: A randomised, double-blind, controlled study, *Psychotherapy and Psychosomatics*, **76**(6), pp 332–8

Hall, L (2009) The Dharma School comes home, *Mandala*, http://bit.ly/nX1lW4

Hall, L (2012) Why is sustainability seen as a rollercoaster for business leaders?, The *Guardian* Sustainable Business hub (May)

Hall, L (2010) Mystery man (interview with Julio Olalla) *Coaching at Work*, **5**(4)

Hall, L (2011) Palmer: Health 'next big thing', *Coaching at Work*, **6**(5), p 65

Harris, R (2008) *The Happiness Trap: How to stop struggling and start living*, Shambala Publications, Boston

Harris, R (2009) *ACT Made Simple*, New Harbinger, CA

Hay, J (2007) *Reflective Practice and Supervision for Coaches*, Open University Press, Maidenhead

Heifetz, R (1994) *Leadership without easy Answers*, Harvard University Press, Cambridge, MA

Helminski, K E (1992) *Living Presence: a Sufi way to mindfulness & the essential self*, Penguin Putnam, New York

Hölzel, B K *et al* (2008) Investigation of mindfulness meditation practitioners with voxel-based morphometry. *Social Cognitive and Affective Neuroscience*, **3**, pp 55–61

Hölzel, B K, Carmody, J, Vangel, M *et al* (2011) Mindfulness practice leads to increases in regional brain gray matter density, *Psychiatry Research: Neuroimaging*, **11**(1) (January), pp 36–43

Hyun-nie, A and Wampold, B E (2001) Where oh where are the specific ingredients? A meta-analysis of component studies in counseling and psychotherapy, *Journal of Counseling Psychology*, **48**(3), pp 251–7

Iacoboni, M (2008) Mirroring People: *The New Science of How We Connect to Others*, Picador, New York

International Coach Federation (2010) Coaching Core Competencies, www.coachfederation.org/research-education/icf-credentials/core-competencies

International Labour Organization, Mata-Greenwood, A (2001) The Hours that we work: the data we need, the data we get

Jha, A P *et al* (2010) Examining the protective effects of mindfulness training on working memory capacity and affective experience, *Emotion*, **10**(1), pp 54–64

Jung, C G (1967) *Alchemical Studies: The Collected Works of CG Jung Volume 13*, Princeton University Press, New York

Kabat-Zinn, J (1994) *Wherever You Go, There You Are: Mindfulness meditation for everyday life*, Piatkus, London

Kabat-Zinn, J (1991) *Full Catastrophe Living : How to cope with stress, pain and illness using mindfulness meditation*, Piatkus, London

Karpman, S (1968) Fairy tales and script drama analysis, *Transactional Analysis Bulletin*, **7**(26), pp 39–43

Kawakami, C, White, J and Langer, E J (2000) Mindful and Masculine: Freeing Female Leaders from Gender Role Constraints, *Journal of Social Issues*, **56**, pp 49–64

Kenexa High Performance Institute, January 2012, *Stress: What's the impact for organizations?*

Killingsworth, M A and Gilbert, D T (2010) A wandering mind is an unhappy mind, *Science*, **330**, p 932

Kimsey-House, H, Kimsey-House, K and Sandahl, P (2011) (3rd edn) *Co-Active Coaching: changing business, transforming lives*, Nicolas Brealey, Boston

Kirk, U, Downar, J and Montague, P R (2011) Interoception drives increased rational decision-making in meditators playing the ultimatum game, *Frontiers in Decision Neuroscience*, **18**(5), p 49

Kline, N (2006) Catalytic converter, *Coaching at Work*, **2**(3)

Kobase, S C (1979) Stressful life events, personality and health, *Journal of Personality and Social Psychology*, **37**(1), pp 1–11

Kornfield, J (2000) *After The Ecstasy, The Laundry: How the heart grows wise on the spiritual path*, Bantam Books, London

Kowalski, R (2011) *Mindfulness & Mindbalancing Handbook*, Speechmark Publishing, Milton Keynes

Langer, E (2005) *On Becoming an Artist: Reinventing yourself through mindful creativity*, Ballantine Books, New York

Langer, E *et al* (2000) unpublished to date, Harvard University, cited in *On becoming an artist*

Langer, E, Janis, I and Wolfer, J A (1975) Reduction of Psychological Stress in Surgical Patients, *Journal of Experimental Social Psychology*, **11**, pp 155–65

Lazar, S *et al* (2005) Meditation experience is associated with increased cortical thickness, *Neuroreport*, **16**:1893–7

Lee, G, and Roberts, I (2010) Coaching for Authentic Leadership. In Passmore, J (2010) *Leadership Coaching*, Kogan Page, London

Lee, G (2003) *Leadership Coaching: from personal insight to organisational performance*, Chartered Institute of Personnel and Development, London

Love, A and Maloney, J (2009) Mindfulness as capacity: at the threshold of leadership's next wave?, *NeuroLeadership Journal*, **2**

Luders *et al* (2009) The underlying anatomical correlates of long-term meditation: larger hippocampal and frontal volumes of gray matter, *Neuroimage*, **45**, pp 672–8

Luther King, M in McLeod, M (ed) (2006) *Mindful politics*, Wisdom Publications, MA

Lutterodt, J (2011) Moral support, *Coaching at Work*, **6**(2)

Lutz, A, Brefczynski-Lewis *et al* (2008) Regulation of the neural circuitry of emotion by compassion meditation: Effects of meditative expertise, *PLoS ONE*, **3**(3):e1897

Lutz, A, Greischar, L L, Rawlings, N B, Ricard, M and Davidson, R J (2004) Long-term meditators self-induce high-amplitude gamma synchrony during mental practice, in *Proceedings of the National Academy of Sciences of the United States of America*, **101**(46), pp 16369–73

Macy, J and Johnstone, C (2012) *Active Hope: How to face the mess we're in without going crazy*, New World Library, Novato

Maguire, E *et al* (2000) Navigation-related structural change in the hippocampi of taxi drivers, *Proceedings of the National Academy of Sciences*, **97**, pp 398–403

Marmot, M *et al* (1997) Contribution of job control and other risk factors to social variations in coronary heart disease incidence, *The Lancet*, **350**, pp 235–9

McCall, M W, Lombardo, M M and Morison, A M (1988) *The Lessons of Experience: How successful executives develop on the job*, Free Press, New York

McCraty, R, Atkinson, M, Tomasino, D *et al* (1998) The electricity of touch: Detection and measurement of cardiac energy exchange between people. In Pribram, K H (ed) *Brain and values: Is a biological science of values possible*, Lawrence Erlbaum, New Jersey, pp 359–79

McCraty, R (2002) The Energetic Heart: Bioelectromagnetic Interactions within and between People, Publication 02-035, HeartMath Research Center, Institute of HeartMath, Boulder Creek

McCraty, R, Atkinson, M and Bradley, R T (2004a) Electrophysiological evidence of intuition: Part 1. The surprising role of the heart, *Journal of Alternative and Complementary Medicine*, **10**(1), pp 133–43

McCraty, R, Atkinson, M and Bradley, R T (2004b) Electrophysiological evidence of intuition: Part 2. A system-wide process?, *Journal of Alternative and Complementary Medicine*, **10**(2), pp 325–36

McKay, M and Fanning, P (2000) *Self-Esteem: A proven program of cognitive techniques for assessing, improving, and maintaining your self-esteem*, New Harbinger Books, Oakland (CA)

Meaning and Purpose survey by the Association for Coaching and *Coaching at Work* (2008) Generation why?, *Coaching at Work*, **3**(6)

Megginson, D *et al* (2007) How useful is it? *Coaching at Work*, **2**(3), p 17

Mellor, K and Schiff, E (1975) Discounting, *Transactional Analysis Journal*, **5**(3), pp 295–302

Mental Health Foundation (2010) *Be Mindful*

Nataraja, S (2008) *The Blissful Brain: Neuroscience and Proof of the Power of Meditation*, London, Gaia House

Neenan, M (2009) *Developing Resilience: A cognitive-behavioural approach*, Routledge, Hove

Neff, K (2003) Self-compassion: An alternative conceptualisation of a healthy attitude toward oneself, *Self and Identity*, **2**, pp 85–101

Nelson T O *et al* (1999) Metacognition and clinical psychology: A preliminary framework for research and practice, *Clinical Psychology and Psychotherapy*, **6**, pp 73–9

Norenzayan, A and Shariff, A F (2008) The origin and evolution of religious prosociality, *Science*, **332**, pp 58–62

Office for National Statistics Psychiatric Morbidity Report (2001)

Ostafin, B and Kassman, K (2012) Stepping out of history: Mindfulness improves insight problem solving, *Consciousness and Cognition*, **21**(2), pp 1031–6

Palmer, S (2000) Physiology of the stress response, Centre for Stress Management

Palmer, S and Cooper, C (2007) *How to Deal with Stress*, Kogan Page, London

Parashar, F (2009) Positively blooming, *Coaching at Work*, **4**(6)

Passmore and Marianetti (2007) The role of mindfulness in coaching, *The Coaching Psychologist*, **3**(3), pp 131–7

Pert, C (1997) *Molecules of Emotion: The science behind mind–body medicine*, Touchstone, New York

Preston, S D and de Waal, F B M (2002) Empathy: Its ultimate and proximate bases, *Behavioural and Brain Sciences*, **25**, pp 1–72

Prochaska, J O and DiClemente, C C (1983) Stages and processes of self-change of smoking: Toward an integrative model of change, *Journal of Consulting and Clinical Psychology*, **51**(3), pp 390–95

Radin, D J and Schlitz, M R (2005) Gut feelings, intuition, and emotions: An exploratory study, *Journal of Alternative and Complementary Medicine*, **11**(5), pp 85–91

Rein, G, Atkinson, M and McCraty, R (1995) The physiological and psychological effects of compassion and anger, *Journal for the Advancement of Medicine*, **8**, pp 87–105

Reivich, K and Shatte, A (2002) *The resilience factor: 7 keys to finding your inner strength and overcoming life's hurdles*, Broadway Books, New York

Rock, D (2009) *Your Brain at Work: Strategies for overcoming distraction, regaining focus, and working smarter all day long*, HarperCollins, New York

Rosenzweig, S (1936) Some implicit common factors in diverse methods of psychotherapy. *American Journal of Orthopsychiatry*, **6**, pp 412–15

Rowan, J (1983) *The Reality Game: A guide to humanistic counselling and therapy*, Routledge & Kegan Paul, London

Sallatha Sutta: The Dart, translated from the Pali by Nyanaponika Thera http://www.accesstoinsight.org/tipitaka/sn/sn36/sn36.006.nypo.html

Schmeichel, B J et al (2008) Working memory capacity and the self-regulation of emotional expression and experience, *Journal of Personality and Social Psychology*, **95**(6), pp 1526–40

Scouller, J (2011) *The Three Levels of Leadership: how to develop your leadership presence, knowhow and skill*, Management Books 2000, Oxford

Selye, H (1975) Confusion and controversy in the stress field, *Journal of Human Stress*, **1**, pp 37–44

Senge, P (1990) *The Fifth Discipline: The art and practice of the learning organisation*, Doubleday, New York

Scharmer, O (2007) *Theory U: Leading from the Future as it Emerges*, Society for Organisational Learning, Cambridge, MA

Scharmer, O www.ottoscharmer.com; http://www.ottoscharmer.com/publications/summaries.php

Siegel, D J (2007) The Mindful Brain: Reflection and Attunement in the Cultivation of Well-Being, *Infant Mental Health Journal*, **22**, pp 67–94

Siegel, D (2010a) *The Mindful Therapist: A clinician's guide to mindsight and neural integration*, WW Norton & Company, New York

Siegel, D (2010b) *Mindsight: The New Science of Personal Transformation*, Bantam Books, New York

Silsbee, D (2010a) *Presence-based Coaching: Cultivating self-generative leaders through mind, body and heart*, Jossey-Bass, San Francisco

Silsbee, D (2010b) (2nd edn) *The Mindful Coach: Seven roles for facilitating leader development*, Jossey-Bass, San Francisco

Singer, T, Seymour, B, O'Doherty, J et al (2004) Empathy for pain involves the affective but not sensory components of pain, *Science*, **303**, pp 1157–62

Singer, T (2006) The neuronal basis and ontogeny of empathy and mind reading: Review of literature and implications for future research, *Neuroscience and Biobehavioral Reviews*, **30**, pp 855–63

Soma: New Latin sōma, from Greek, www.thefreedictionary.com

Spence, G B, Cavanagh, M J and Grant, A M (2008) The integration of mindfulness training and health coaching: An exploratory study, *Coaching: An international journal of theory, research and practice*, **1**(2), pp 1–19

Starr, J (2003) *The Coaching Manual: The definitive guide to the process and skills and personal coaching*, Pearson Education, Harlow

Strozzi-Heckler, R (2007) *The Leadership Dojo: Build your foundation as an exemplary leader*, Frog Books, CA

Tang, Y *et al* (2007) Short-term meditation training improves attention and self-regulation, *Proceedings of the National Academy of Sciences*, **104**, pp 17152–6

Teper, R and Inzlicht, M (April 2012) Meditation, mindfulness and executive control: the importance of emotional acceptance and brain-based performance monitoring (online), *Social Cognitive Affective Neuroscience*

Thich Nhat Hanh (1975) *The Miracle of Mindfulness*, Beacon Press, Boston

Thich Nhat Hanh (1991) *Peace is Every Step: The path of mindfulness in everyday life*, Bantam Books, New York

Tolle, E (2001) *The Power of Now*, Hodder

Urry, H L, Nitschke, J B, Dolski, I *et al* Making a life worth living: Neural correlates of well-being, *Psychological Science*, **15**, pp 367–72

Vargiu, J (1974) *Synthesis Volume 1: The Realization of the Self*, The Synthesis Press, CA

Walsh, R and Shapiro, S L (2006) The meeting of meditative disciplines and Western psychology: A mutually enriching dialogue, *American Psychologist*, **61**, pp 227–39

Weiss, A, Bates, T and Luciano, M (2008) Happiness is a Personal(ity) Thing, *Psychological Science*

Weissbecker, I *et al* (2002) Mindfulness-Based Stress Reduction and Sense of Coherence Among Women with Fibromyalgia, *Journal of Clinical Psychology in Medical Settings*, **9**, pp 297–307

Whitmore, J and Gallwey, T (2010) Inside out, *Coaching at Work*, **5**(3)

Whitmore, J (2008a) Transpersonal Coaching in Action, Performance Consultants International hand-out at transpersonal coaching masterclass, British Pyschological Society Special Group in Coaching Psychology annual conference, London

Whitmore, J (2008b) Live and learn, *Coaching at Work*, **3**(6)

Whitmore, J (1992) *Coaching for Performance*, Nicholas Brealy, Boston

Williams, M and Penman, D (2011) *Mindfulness: a practical guide to finding peace in a frantic world*, Piatkus, London

Wise, A (1997) *High Performance Mind*, Penguin Putnam, New York

World Health Organization, *World Health Report*, (2001)

FURTHER READING

Beisser, A R (1970) *The paradoxical theory of change*, in Fagan, J and Shepherd, I L (eds) *Gestalt Therapy Now*, pp 77–80, Science and Behaviour Books, Palo Alto

Chodron, P (1994) *Start Where You Are: A guide to compassionate living*, Shambala Publications, Boston

Dalai Lama (1998) *The Art of Happiness: A handbook for living*, Riverhead Books, New York

Doidge, N (2007) *The Brain that Changes Itself: Stories of personal triumph from the frontiers of brain science*, Penguin Books

Hay, J (2006) In the final analysis, *Coaching at Work*, **2**(4)

Kline, N (1999) *Time to Think: Listening to ignite the human mind*, Octopus, London

Leary-Joyce, J (2006) Feeling groovy, *Coaching at Work*, **2**(5)

Ricard, M (2006) *Happiness, A guide to developing life's most important skill*, Brown and Company, New York

Palmer, S and Dryden, W (1995) *Counselling for Stress Problems*, Sage, London

Palmer, W (1994) *The Intuitive Body: Aikido as a clairsentience practice*, North Atlantic Books, Berkeley, CA

Pascale, R, Milleman, M and Gioja, L (2000) *Surfing the Edge of Chaos: The laws of nature*, Three Rivers Press, New York

Ridings, A (2011) *Pause for Breath: Bringing the practices of mindfulness and dialogue to leadership conversations*, Live It Publishing, London

Strozzi-Heckler, R (1993) (2nd edn) *The Anatomy of Change: A way to move through life's transitions*, North Atlantic Books, Berkeley, CA

Wilber, K (2000) *A Theory of Everything: An integral vision for business, politics, science and spirituality*, Shambhala Publications, Boston

INDEX

NB: page numbers in *italic* indicate figures or tables